Terrestrial
TV news
in Britain

MANCHESTER
UNIVERSITY PRESS

Terrestrial TV news in Britain

The culture of production

Jackie Harrison

Manchester University Press
Manchester and New York
distributed exclusively in the USA by St. Martin's Press

The right of Jackie Harrison to be identified as the author of this work has been asserted by her in accordance with the Copyright, Designs and Patents Act 1988.

Published by Manchester University Press
Oxford Road, Manchester M13 9NR, UK
and Room 400, 175 Fifth Avenue, New York, NY 10010, USA
http://www.man.ac.uk/mup

Distributed exclusively in the USA by
St. Martin's Press, Inc., 175 Fifth Avenue, New York, NY 10010, USA

Distributed exclusively in Canada by
UBC Press, University of British Columbia, 6344 Memorial Road,
Vancouver, BC, Canada V6T 1Z2

British Library Cataloguing-in-Publication Data
A catalogue record for this book is available from the British Library

Library of Congress Cataloging-in-Publication Data
Harrison, Jackie, 1961–
    Terrestrial TV news in Britain: the culture of production/Jackie Harrison
        p.   cm
    Includes bibliographical references and index.
    ISBN 0–7190–5589–X – ISBN 0–7190–5590–3 (pbk.)
    1. Television broadcasting of news—Great Britain. 2. Public interest—Great Britain.
    I. Title.
    PN5124.T4 H37 2000
    070.1'95 21—dc21

                                                                          99–042215

ISBN 0 7190 5589 X *hardback*
     0 7190 5590 3 *paperback*

First published 2000

06 05 04 03 02 01 00   10 9 8 7 6 5 4 3 2 1

Typeset in Photina
by Northern Phototypesetting Co. Ltd, Bolton
Printed in Great Britain
by Biddles Ltd, Guildford and King's Lynn

For Neil and Luke

Contents

Figures

Tables

Acknowledgements

My research for this book began in the early 1990s and I should like to thank all those people who have been involved with its development. I owe a debt of gratitude to Maurice Roche, whose insights, help and encouragement have been invaluable. I should also like to thank Philip Schlesinger, Nick Stevenson and Barrie Gunter, whose detailed comments on my work were of enormous help. Special thanks go to those who allowed me to observe them at work in different television newsrooms over a period of time at the BBC in London and Leeds, ITN's Channel 3 and Channel 4 newsrooms, and Yorkshire Television in Leeds. Thanks are due to the many people who patiently answered countless questions, and I am grateful to many national and regional broadcast journalists for their help with this study. With regard to the presentation of my findings, both from interviews and newsroom observation, I am following the repeated requests for anonymity made by the journalists I have interviewed between 1994 and 1997.

My love and thanks also go to Joan and Ron Mason, who have been a constant source of encouragement and support.

Abbreviations

ATF	Alcohol, Tobacco and Firearms Agency
BBC	British Broadcasting Corporation
BSkyB	British Sky Broadcasting
CBI	Confederation of British Industry
CNBC	Consumer News and Business Channel
CNN	Cable News Network
EBU	European Broadcasting Union
EC	European Community
EU	European Union
FBI	Federal Bureau of Investigation
GMT	Greenwich Mean Time
GMTV	Good Morning Television
HTV	(*formerly* Harlech Television)
IBA	Independent Broadcasting Authority
IT	Information Technology
ITA	Independent Television Authority
ITC	Independent Television Commission
ITN	Independent Television News
ITV	Independent Television
LWT	London Weekend Television
NHS	National Health Service
oov	Out of Vision
RTVE	Radio Televisión Española
S4C	Sianel Pedwar Cymru
TASS/ITAR	Information Telegraphy Agency of Russia
TSW	Television South-West
TVS	Television South
ULR	Uniform Resource Locator
WTN	Worldwide Television News
YTV	Yorkshire Television

Introduction: terrestrial TV news and the new media environment

At the start of the twenty-first century, most communication researchers are producing books about satellite, cable and digital broadcasting, the development of on-line services and cyberspace. Consequently the changes occurring in terrestrial television news are in danger of being ignored in relation to the fast-moving events of the wider broadcasting environment. Terrestrial television news has to exist in a new world order of broadcasting, characterised by the coexistence of public and commercial broadcasting, the evolution of multi-media organisations and the constant debate over the meaning of public service broadcasting values. It is clear that terrestrial television news is changing. But there has been little detailed analysis of the nature, form and content of that change in the 1990s.

On the one hand television news producers claim they provide a diverse range of distinctive, high-quality terrestrial television news programmes (necessary to maintain social and cultural plurality). On the other hand academics and other media commentators argue that terrestrial television news is becoming increasingly homogeneous in content (McNair, 1994) and market-driven (McManus, 1994). Both diversity and homogeneity, it is said, result from a need to pander to the lowest common denominator in order to increase audience ratings, simultaneously reducing the 'quality' of news information. Increased choice is driven by the market-oriented rush towards the provision of niche news products, as terrestrial and global news providers try to find ways of acquiring a share of the market for news and information. Diversification of the television news genre is occurring in response to the macro pressures caused by the globalisation of news and information supply and demand and by the new commercialisation of television news and technological developments. At the same time diversity within television news content is being challenged by these same forces, leading to similar types of news content (packaged and branded differently) being provided by different and competing news organisations. These are contradictory forces which affect the television news genre. I shall look at these later.

1

These contradictory forces can also be seen at a micro level in terms of newsroom practice. Terrestrial television newsrooms operate according to similar cultures and values, but in Britain particular terrestrial television newsroom styles and priorities produce a diverse range of information content. In theory a pluralistic television industry can contribute to diversity of news content in three main ways: first, via representative diversity in communication, which corresponds to and reflects the diverse range of groups in society; secondly, via diversity of access, when the media make available access points for a variety of different voices; thirdly, via diversity of choice, which provides consumers with a wide variety of different programmes to choose from (McQuail, 1992). Whilst market-led diversification leads to greater choice for the consumer it does not necessarily lead to a more pluralistic service. Diversity of representation and diversity of access are generally compromised by a market-led service. In Britain diversity of content has traditionally been provided by careful regulation of the Independent Television system (ITV) and via public service broadcasting. I shall subsequently elaborate on the problems of diversity and similarity in news and the issues these developments raise.

Changes in the broadcasting environment are far from over. It is therefore timely to assess where we are now. The focus of this work is the 1990s and terrestrial television news. Unless stated otherwise, the phrase 'television news' used in this work refers to terrestrial television news and not satellite news.

I seek to provide an analysis of a broad range of British terrestrial television news in the context of its resistances and its adaptations to change. I focus on both the content and the production processes of television news, namely the context in which terrestrial television journalism operated in the 1990s and the type of informational content produced. I argue for a reconsideration of traditional approaches to the study of television news and its role in a democracy. Television news needs to be analysed in relation to the informational contribution it can realistically make to the well-being of society, as well as considering whether its role as an important institution of the public sphere has been irrevocably compromised. I will address the problems facing broadcasting policy makers who need to consider the changing relationship between the public and private sector, and to understand the role of terrestrial television news in relation to the local and global networks which now exist.

Although most of the current research paradigms are oriented towards analysing new technological developments, technology has not yet moved the terrestrial television broadcasting environment away from a mass communications broadcast model. The majority of citizens still rely on terrestrial television news for a good deal of information about the world. Although cable and satellite television have introduced over seventy channels already, they account for only a small percentage of viewing – according to Curran

(1998), about 10 per cent. In Britain the mainstream mass audience channels still account for over two-thirds of peak time viewing. The British Broadcasting Corporation (BBC), the ITV system and Sianel Pedwar Cymru (S4C) are still regulated according to public service broadcasting principles, which though weakened are not yet abandoned. The importance of terrestrial television news is still enormous and some analysts, such as Barnett (1998), question the likely success of digital services. In these times of change there is a need to address seriously developments in terrestrial television news provision and the implications this has for the citizen.

There is an assumption that the new media are replacing or will replace the space once occupied by terrestrial television news, or that different new forms will coexist (Katz, 1996). The optimistic analyst will argue that the diversity of news and information services will allow citizens greater choice and access to information, whilst the more pessimistic will be concerned with the creation of ever-widening gaps between the information rich and poor and their opportunity to access high-quality services (Schiller, 1996). The era of a limited supply of free-at-source, universally accessible, high-quality news serving a national mass audience appears to be almost over. It is expected to be replaced by news supplied from many different sources, from a diverse range of channels, to a fragmented and possibly active audience.[1] And yet an informed democracy still relies (and will do so for some time to come) on terrestrial television news to help to create the conditions whereby citizens can become knowledgeable and informed about the society they live in. As the media have grown, television has risen to a prominent position as a media institution of global importance, above the print media and radio institutions (McQuail, 1994). Thus, one of my abiding concerns is whether the changing nature of the television news environment is actually restricting the possibility of the democratic participation of citizens in the political, economic, social and judicial realms of understanding and debate. Indeed the broad tradition of enquiry into the role of the mass media and their potential for public interest leads to one of the key concerns of this book: that terrestrial television news can, and should, make a contribution to the welfare of a democratic society and that it should be accountable as a source of public information. That is, it should be socially responsible.

What follows is an analytical study of terrestrial television news based upon content analyses, newsroom observations, interviews with journalists and the consistent watching of a variety of British television news programmes over a five-year period from 1992 to 1997. The dual methodological approach used in this study was influenced by Semetko *et al.* (1991: 183–4) who found that:

---

[1] See McQuail's (1994:312) 'Old and New Media Assessment Models Compared'.

content analysis can document what news media have covered in what manner but cannot reach to the behind the scenes forces, relationships, judgements and decisions that produce detected patterns. On the spot observation can shed much light on how media personnel interpret their roles and the kinds of reports they should provide, but only content analysis can show whether such orientations and aspirations have real consequences for what actually gets into the news. The pairing of these methods is particularly suited to comparative analysis of (political) communication systems.

A content analysis was made of one week's output of television news programmes (excluding short bulletins) broadcast on British terrestrial television on weekdays only. In relation to output by the fourth channel in Britain, only that on Channel 4 was coded, as S4C output could not be received in Sheffield, where I was based. Consequently, although some references to S4C are made in this book there is no data available from its news programmes. A week's sample was analysed, as 'a one week sample has been demonstrated to be as generalisable to a year's programming as larger randomly drawn samples' (Canino and Huston, 1986:151). The programmes recorded were taken from four terrestrial channels – BBC1, BBC2, ITV and Channel 4 – and totalled fourteen programmes per weekday. The programmes recorded each day were BBC1's *Breakfast News*; BBC1's *News at One O'Clock, Six O'Clock* and *Nine O'Clock*; BBC1's *Children's Newsround*; *GMTV News*; ITN's *12.30 p.m. News, 5.40 p.m. News* and *News at Ten*; Channel 4's *Big Breakfast*, and *Channel 4 News* at seven o'clock; and BBC2's *Newsnight*. Two regional programmes were also included in the sample, BBC1's regional news programme *Look North* and Yorkshire Tyne-Tees Television's regional news magazine programme *Calendar News*, which were the only two I could receive in the Sheffield area.[2] The recording period was 19–23 April 1993 inclusive.

A full news bulletin is constructed from a number of items, all linked together in a way which makes the whole programme flow as a totality. These items include the introductory sequence, headlines, the actual news reports (themselves made up of a variety of items), 'advertisement' of stories to come, commercial breaks, weather, summaries, chatty handovers and sign-offs, and credits. In order to ensure that the content analysis analysed only the news items, the other areas of the programme were 'disaggregated' (see Brunsdon and Morley, 1978:39). Bonney and Wilson (1983) found that a thirty-minute broadcast on a commercial station in Australia would on average contain only about seventeen or eighteen minutes' worth of main news items.

---

[2] Two full pilot days were run to study the output of fourteen different television news programmes. These pilot studies improved and clarified the data collection method, the Coding Frame and the Television News Code Book (see appendices).

One of the major problems of analysing television news is the definition of the actual news story. It is not sufficient to say simply that the BBC news programmes broadcast a story about the end and aftermath of the Waco siege on 20 April 1993. To record it as one story would ignore the complexity of the influences on news content (see Figure 1 in Chapter 1), as it is the finer distinctions which each television news programme makes between the same event which are of concern in this study. Each content category of a news story has been coded as an individual 'story' in order to escape from the rigid format and content categories already imposed on the audience by the presentational style of the news. This has also allowed the examination of the finer distinctions of television news content and format style, which have often been ignored by other researchers.

The indicators for the content analysis fall into two main categories for data collection: content categories (see Appendix I) and format categories. The content categories have been selected after considering several other studies (Glasgow University Media Group, 1976; Ericson *et al.*, 1991; Wallis and Baran, 1990; Hartley, 1989; Stempel, 1989; Bell *et al.*, 1982; Langer, 1987). The format categories measure the structure of news stories via: the proportion of national and international news shown by each news programme and by each channel; the proportion of the news programme that is dominated by the presenter; the proportion of the news programme that is devoted to live two-ways; the proportion of the news programme that is devoted to interviews with spokespersons; the use of film; the use of graphics; and the mean length and frequency of news stories broadcast by each news programme. Information relating to the content and format structure of each news programme and each news story was coded on to the Coding Frame (see Appendix II). The information from the coding schedule was then analysed using a Statistics Package for Social Scientists (SPSS).

Observation of journalistic practice was undertaken in four national and regional newsrooms, where ten different news programmes were closely observed.[3] Interviews were conducted in each television newsroom for each television news programme. In all newsrooms the chief editor or his or her equivalent, the deputy, the programme editor, the editor for the day, the chief sub-editor, the news editors (home and foreign news), producers, specialist and other correspondents, reporters, production assistants, programme directors and presenters were interviewed. The description of the structure and

---

[3] BBC television newsrooms: *One O'Clock News* desk (one week); *Six O'Clock News* desk (one week); news summaries desk (two days); *Nine O'Clock News* desk (one week); newsgathering – home and foreign news and forward planning (one week and two days); and *Newsnight* (three days). ITN television newsrooms: *12.30 p.m. News* desk and news summaries (one week); *5.40 p.m. News* desk (one week); *News at Ten* (one week); intake – home and foreign news and forward planning (intermittent observation over a three-week period); and *Channel Four News* – intake (one week), output (one week). Yorkshire Television newsroom: *Calendar News* (two weeks). BBC North regional newsroom: *Look North News* (two weeks).

practices in national and regional newsrooms, and the attributed and non-attributed quotations, anecdotes and observations provided by journalists throughout this book, are based on notes from my own observation of journalists at work in the different national and regional newsrooms.

Clearly, technological developments have had a strong impact on the changes occurring in the television news environment, but this work does not seek to provide an in-depth description of these developments as such. (For a description of current technological developments see MacGregor, 1997.) Rather I am concerned with the cultural and professional production of terrestrial television news. Where technology impacts upon this I have analysed it. I theorise about some of the wider implications of technological development and other macro influences on the terrestrial television news genre as they affect us all.

The key impetus for this work is the recognition that terrestrial television news has reached a critical juncture in British broadcasting. The rationale of the two systems of broadcasting which have coexisted for forty years is disintegrating in the multi-media age and is affecting the relationship between the public and private sectors of the broadcasting environment (Murroni *et al.*, 1996). Of pressing concern is the way the processes and practices of communication in society are closely linked to concerns about an informed citizenry and to a citizen's ability to reflect critically upon the society he or she inhabits. Directly related to this is the question of how terrestrial television news in particular forms a sphere of public communication and to what extent this is protected from, or affected by, changes occurring in the media environment. Habermas's idea of the public sphere is useful in this context. This represents the notion of a sovereign, rational, deliberative and well-informed public, which is enlightened and further informed through discursive and rational communication.

The power of the communications sector to manage, direct and disperse information has traditionally ensured that the broadcast media industries have had a specific importance in relation to public policy. In Britain, in common with much of Europe, the broadcasting media have to some extent been controlled by the state, usually via direct ownership or, when private ownership has been allowed to develop, via strong regulatory frameworks that have been imposed to protect and contribute to the public interest.

Television news output and the organisations which produce it were, in the 1990s, being strongly affected by politico-economic developments (the new wave of commercialisation of television news in the 1990s and the distinctive organisational relationship to political pressure exemplified by the BBC), technological development (digital formats and the infrastructure for the growth of new information networks) and transnational developments (which facilitate the circulation of information through global networks) (Barker, 1997; Mowlana, 1997). The extent of the changes taking place in the broadcasting environment provides many new problems for policy makers, particularly over the need to redefine the relationship between the public and private sectors, the viability of public service broadcasting in a multi-channel environment and the feasibility of national regulation in a global media environment. As yet policy makers do not appear to have found a solution to these problems (Murroni *et al.*, 1996).

The implications these developments have had for building and maintaining a vibrant public sphere or public spheres, for definitions of public interest via regulatory frameworks and for the role and responsibilities of television news in a democracy need to be analysed. A study of the importance of television news in the 1990s and early twenty-first century must also extend to a consideration of how far the idea of a public sphere can be taken in relation to transnational frameworks of democracy.[4] The importance of maintaining public service broadcasting values in the European context has been recognised.[5] The preamble to the Amsterdam Protocol states 'that the system of public broadcasting in the Member States is directly related to the democratic, social and cultural needs of each society and to the need to preserve media pluralism' (EBU, 1998:1).[6] A further statement made by the European Broadcasting Union (EBU) reinforces this, stating that the absence of public service broadcasting organisation would mean 'quality programming for all sections of society would not be provided, since the market itself cannot and will not produce it' (EBU, 1998:1). There is broad agreement in the European Union (EU) that both a strong public and a prosperous private broadcasting industry are necessary for strengthening European television content.[7]

Schlesinger (1995) argues that there are historical, social and political obstacles to the emergence of a single European public sphere that centres on an understanding of public service broadcasting values. Clearly, difficulties are inherent in getting each nation to agree, in the first instance, on what constitutes public service broadcasting and, secondly, on how broadcasting should be regulated. Problematically, public service broadcasting is defined and organised differently in different member states, and the Amsterdam Protocol does not specify how public service broadcasting should be defined, or require that minimum standards be set. As a result, different member states are at liberty to define their public service broadcasting remit in a general manner, making reference to issues of quality and provision for the social, cultural and political needs of their particular society without having to meet a prescribed set of common European standards. Nevertheless

[4] On average three hundred and forty million Europeans watch television for over two hours a day (Commission of the European Communities 1992:3).
[5] For a resolution on public service broadcasting, see R(96)10 on the guarantee of the independence of public service broadcasting, 11 September 1996. The European Parliament Resolution was adopted 19 September 1996, doc. A4-0243/96.
[6] URL <*http://www.ebu.ch/leg_public-service.html*> accessed 14 August 1998.
[7] Speech by Albert Scharf, 'The Media and the European Model of Society', European Audiovisual Conference, Birmingham, 6–8 April 1998 (Harrison and Woods, 1999).

there remains a pressing need for a European public sphere to be constituted, if only to correct the democratic deficit of European public institutions and the lack of public knowledge relating to the European Parliament. The successful fostering of the ideal of a European citizen requires that a European public sphere must first be established and internalised as an agreed-upon and desired value system, thereby contributing to the construction of a possible European form of identity. At the moment British television news is far from providing a value system that seeks to understand the issue of a European citizen as an object of news interest (Harrison and Woods, 1999).

Institutions such as the BBC are still relatively successful in conveying a particular set of values within the context of a nation state (although the BBC's values are predominantly nostalgic and reflect the south-east of England).[8] It is unclear how terrestrial television news organisations can keep up to date with the flows of information circulating round the globe, given that television accounts for 70 per cent of people's leisure time (*Marketing Focus*, November 1996) and is the most trusted source of news information (Gunter and Winstone, 1993). Consequently we should be concerned about the future value of the contribution terrestrial television news can reasonably be expected to make to the knowledge citizens have about their region, their nation and the world. This is another theme I shall return to.

We must be realistic about the strengths and weaknesses of the medium. Even if television news is generally informative, practices such as bombarding viewers with information about politics, which gives the illusion of political participation, may result in audience passivity (Hart, 1996). The explosion of news information via the television medium indicates to some that we have entered an information society (Webster, 1995) which could result in a better informed citizenry. Baudrillard (1976) in contrast offers a more pessimistic, postmodern analysis. He argues that the increase in images and signs constituting the media does not necessarily add meaning to our lives. The availability of more television news outlets does not necessarily make us more informed. We recognise manufactured signs made by the media simulations and, in Baudrillard's view, do not bother to understand the message but simply enjoy the spectacle. Herbert Schiller (1996) acknowledges this explosion of signs and images, but argues that if used adroitly (in the unlikely event that information inequality is overcome) they can be used to improve democratic social relations and a sense of community.

But again, any sense of terrestrial television contributing to improved democratic social relations or improved community feelings is challenged by a variety of issues and developments. Television news is becoming more and more homogeneous (MacGregor, 1997; McManus, 1994; McNair, 1994).

---

[8] S4C in Wales has greater success in broadcasting the Welsh language and Welsh issues to Welsh people. This success is increased by the joint acquisition by HTV and S4C of Welsh rugby broadcasting rights, which attract viewers who might not otherwise have been likely to watch Welsh programming.

British terrestrial television news is increasingly covering domestic news, entertaining events and cameo politics (via concentration on political personalities and images rather than issues), and using an array of visually interesting format devices and shorter sound-bites (see, for example, Barnett and Gaber, 1993; Channel 4, 1994; Hume, 1996; McManus, 1994). Schiller's (1996) cautious optimism regarding the more positive qualities of image bombardment thus invites the question of whether market-driven news can make any effective contribution to a sense of the public sphere at sub-national, national and European levels.

Concern about the future of television news information diversity is well founded, but it is also true to say that British terrestrial television news organisations are diversifying their programmes in an increasingly sub-national orientation aiming for different niche-markets. The American television news organisation trend towards developing a variety of new news formats has been indicated by Altheide and Snow (1979), for whom the news format refers to the way in which news material is selected, processed and presented, and includes economic concerns, audience ratings and news content.

In Britain the BBC has been buffeted and battered by conflicting forces in the broadcasting environment. In September 1997 BBC staff protested strongly against management-imposed changes to the news production process. The proposal was to introduce super-editors to oversee clusters of BBC news programmes. This was perceived by BBC staff to be a way of centralising and homogenising news production and content in the name of efficiency savings. Although the BBC management was forced to respond to this strong organisational resistance to change, the future of individual BBC news programmes seemed to be uncertain. In the 1998 Programme Strategy Review (BBC On-Line, 1998), the BBC announced what appears to be a complete change of news policy. Over the next two years the BBC planned deliberately to differentiate each of its mass audience news programmes on BBC1. Conflicting organisational policy of this type illustrates the contradictory tensions inherent in public service broadcasting in the late 1990s. The need to reconcile efficiency and maximising ratings with the maintenance of public service values and the transmission of important but potentially boring news is extremely problematic. Analysis of the nature of British terrestrial television news in the 1990s reveals that there was continued diversification and fragmentation of the television news genre into a variety of different programmes, where each programme was constituted by the selection of a number of news sub-genres. I clarify and elaborate the concept of genre in Chapter 1.

As I have already indicated, when considering terrestrial television news we can no longer refer to a single type of television news, but need to address the wide variety of news programmes currently available. A contradictory development appears to be occurring within the television news genre itself.

Although the diversification of the news genre is resulting in a variety of television news sub-genres which have different formats and are niche-marketed (in a similar way to newspapers), the diversity of news informational content may be being compromised through the diminishment of public service broadcasting values, which may further damage the relationship between television news and the public sphere.

The data in this book refers to British television news in the mid-1990s, but it is worth noting in more detail the changes that the BBC indicated it would make to its mass audience news programmes between 1998 and 2000. It is too early, at the time of writing, to make anything other than general comments about these changes, and it is not possible to collect or show any statistical data, but some initial thoughts are in order. The 1998 Programme Strategy Review showed that the BBC intended to target audiences more specifically, possibly moving even further away from its somewhat paternalistic approach to news provision. The result of the audience survey was no great surprise; what was, was that the BBC planned to make changes in direct response to audience views. Viewers indicated that they would like their news to be accurate, trustworthy and easy to understand, with clear language and a broader agenda which included personally useful news. It was the BBC's interpretation of these sentiments which was of concern. The esoteric business news shown in BBC's *Breakfast News* was to be replaced with general news which would be repeated every fifteen minutes until 8.45 a.m., when the news would be replaced by phone-ins and features. The adoption by the BBC of a format and content style that appear to be similar to British Sky Broadcasting's (BSkyB's) morning news programme showed a definite change in news philosophy. The *One O'Clock News* was to be less political, implying that audiences who do not work do not need to be politically well informed. *The Six O'Clock News* was to be presented in a magazine format and would contain little political news and more domestic news. The style of the programme was to be friendly and aimed at women. The implication was that women do not need, or are less interested in, complex news or foreign news. The *Nine O'Clock News* remained as the flagship programme, which was to work to a quota system and ensure that 50 per cent of its programme covered overseas news.

Using a new look, new logo, new music, more 'star' correspondents, familiar presenters and a warmer, more accessible and friendly feel, the BBC was trying to rebrand its product. It appeared that the BBC was trying to be all things to all people as well as reconciling its public service broadcasting remit with a market-based and audience-led philosophy. There were concerns that it was spreading itself rather thinly (*Broadcast*, 30 October 1998). Superficially the BBC appeared to be broadening its appeal, being more responsive to its audience and providing a more diverse (in terms of programme choice) range of programmes. However, those people who only watch the *Six O'Clock News* would be less well informed about political issues and the rest of the world than before. The BBC's programme differentiation meant there was more choice but that each programme covered a narrower range of topics. The BBC seemed to be 'trading down' some of its programmes in the same way as some of the broadsheets have done, to gain a larger audience.

Overall this book focuses on the differences and similarities exhibited by diverse television newsroom cultures in relation to their reaction to macro forces in the media environment. It also focuses on micro level production processes and newsroom processes, which show that a shared journalistic culture produces agreement on newsroom practices and normative assumptions in which the concept of newsworthiness is grounded. It shows too that, notwithstanding the existence of a shared journalistic culture, there are clear differences of opinion within the journalistic profession about what constitutes newsworthiness. Even when a story is recognised by all the news programmes as being newsworthy, such as a major air crash, or the death of a senior politician, or even the death and funeral of a princess, news programmes may adopt different ways of telling the story, with different interpretations of the same event. Sometimes such interpretations may be only superficially different and still adhere to the same set of common-sense assumptions, which result in basically similar informational content. On some occasions a great deal of difference between the rationale and culture of the different television newsrooms is evident. Sometimes the paternalistic and public service broadcasting ethos of BBC journalism, in contrast to the commercial imperative of Independent Television News (ITN), *GMTV News* and *Calendar News*, emerges around contentious stories. Such differences in rationale and culture in different television newsrooms and different organisations are strongly illustrative of differing journalistic views about what serves the public interest, what constitutes television newsworthiness, or what depth and quality of information or degree of entertainment should be provided for their particular audience. Such decisions are also illustrative of the degree of reaction and concession particular broadcasting organisations are making to the general pressures of market-led competition and technological change.

In Chapter 1 I introduce the Habermasian idea of the public sphere. The theme of television news as a democratic forum is developed through an analysis of the politics of representation underlying television's role. The chapter considers whether television news can be a 'true' representation and considers what is meant by information quality. The analysis of the role of television news in a democracy and its relationship to the public sphere lead to a consideration of critiques of Habermas's work and some of the developments which have sprung from it; for example, the work on the fragmentation of the unitary public sphere and the increasing segmentation of the television audience (McGuigan, 1992). Continuing with this theme, I develop a model of television news which is used to indicate how different terrestrial television news programmes have developed, providing a variety of alternatives for the television news consumer. The development of a variety of new news formats or sub-genres clearly produces increased diversity of choice. It seems likely that television news will diversify further, resulting in: different types of news; on-line unedited news; short, heavily edited television news bulletins on the free-to-air channels; longer, more analytical stories on pay-per-view premium channels; twenty-four-hour rolling news bulletins using repetition of news stories made possible due to the lack of appointment viewers (i.e. those who watch at specific times to view a particular programme); live rolling news which is unedited; and so on. Whilst in theory more information will be available, those with the means to do so will be able to pay for well-presented and carefully edited news, whilst those who cannot could find themselves restricted to an unedited blizzard of information or short, uninformative news bulletins on television. Therefore the blanket accusation that television news values are becoming increasingly homogeneous must be refined to stress the point that only some of the television news programmes will be similar in content and format. That these may be watched by mass audiences is clearly of some concern, especially if information diversity or clarity is reduced for the majority of viewers through over-selection of entertaining content and over-use of entertaining format devices, such as increased pace and concentration on more popular, live and lighter news stories.

Research into the comprehension of news by viewers does not indicate that viewers are particularly engaged or informed by television news (Gunter, 1987). Davis (1990) argues that a news programme must be broadcast at a much slower pace in order to facilitate audience comprehension, and that the most effective way to inform the audience would be for news programme makers to take into account the different educational backgrounds of the viewers, as well as their different interests. Programmes made to accommodate the varying levels of educational achievement would have more chance of engaging the viewer. Dahlgren (1995:57), when considering Davis (1990), concludes that television news producers are not likely to be inspired to slow the pace of news programmes, or attempt to facilitate audience comprehension in direct relation to educational background, simply because this runs 'counter to the logic of television as an industry'.

The main focus of Chapter 2 is on television news in relation to the policy implications of the changing relationship between the public sector and private sector. The chapter closely examines the public interest idea which underpins the regulatory frameworks of both the BBC and the ITV systems, and considers the pressures placed upon their understandings of what served the public interest in the 1990s.

Chapter 3 examines the changing structural and cultural relations of the BBC and ITN during the 1980s and 1990s, placing this analysis of television news within the broad socio-political context of modern society. The key vectors of change affecting the broadcasting environment are identified, namely the politico-economic (and the new commercialisation of television news), technological change and transnational influences.

Chapter 4 briefly sketches out the current television news broadcasting environment and its historical antecedents, values and structures, in order to provide a broad overview of the diversity of terrestrial television news provision in Britain today.

Chapter 5 shows how certain controls, constraints and normative values are the basis of all journalistic practice and are common to all newsrooms. This chapter explores journalistic training; the profession's adherence to acceptance of editorial policy and the assumption of editorial autonomy; the maintenance of a critical distance from a mythical audience; the acceptance and use of wire services and other technological devices; the adoption of a shared set of logistical constraints; and the construction of the newsworthy around a diary and planning, and through the adoption of common television journalistic lores and myths, expressed through formal and informal journalistic language and humour and also through the adherence to objectivity norms in journalistic practice.

Chapter 6 shows in greater detail how a key feature of journalistic practice is formed through compliance with the principle of objective reporting. All television news production is grounded in a shared adherence to and understanding of the need for objectivity as a professional ideology. The chapter explores three key approaches to objectivity: first, the professional adherence to objectivity norms in journalistic practice; second, the legislative requirements of objectivity and impartiality in television journalism; and third, the critiques of objectivity from a variety of academic perspectives. The chapter goes on to show how shared norms of journalistic practice and experiences form a framework within which, through which and by which the journalist can understand and interpret events. These findings support the assertions by many media researchers that a level of consensus exists amongst journalists about what is newsworthy (Gold and Simmons, 1965; Clyde and Buckalew, 1969; Buckalew, 1969; Glasgow University Media Group, 1976; Whittaker, 1981). However, these consensual norms are not always compatible with the communication of complex events and issues to the audience. Norms such as objectivity and fairness superficially appear to be compatible with the journalistic value of accountability to the audience, and the journalist will often rely on the constraint of impartiality to prove his or her fairness and straight-dealing in reporting. Such a defence masks the structured processes which can compromise journalistic scrutiny of events. A case study of the reporting of the ending of the Waco siege in the United States shows how the adoption of objectivity norms reduces information quality.

Chapter 7 analyses the key factor which underpins television news values, namely the construction of newsworthiness. Despite the similarities of practice and common-sense values exhibited in the journalistic process, the notion of newsworthiness itself has a more pragmatic feel. Newsworthiness can be defined as a construct of the journalist's zone and mode of operation, which can be defined in turn as a dynamic relationship between the political, historical, technological and economic macro influences and the organisational, cultural and professional values and practices of the particular television newsroom. The journalist's zone of operation, therefore, is a framework within which, through which and by which the journalist participates in the understanding and interpretation of an event (as a journalist and not just as a neutral individual). This participation occurs by way of the adoption of a particular mode of understanding and via a certain historical consciousness, which in this case is journalistic. This agreement of usage is adapted to the designated style and epistemology of a television news organisation, or television news programme, and is only one way of doing the job (styles or epistemologies are not universal). It follows that this can, and does, result in different television news programmes and therefore a different definition by those journalists of what is newsworthy and what is in the public interest.

Chapter 8 shows how different television news programmes and different television news organisations create their own epistemologies. The concept of newsworthiness is also determined by the particular political considerations of different organisations, different historical considerations such as how and why a similar story might have been reported in the past, and economic considerations. Different organisations' culture and history can result in different considerations and treatment of whatever is deemed to be newsworthy, whilst at the same time identical macro forces (new commercialisation of television news, technological development and globalisation) are now influencing all television newsrooms.

Chapter 9 draws together the analytical themes and the empirical and qualitative evidence from previous chapters and concludes that the ability of citizens to access a diverse range of representative information is vital for a healthy democracy, but the signs are that this is under threat in the current broadcasting environment. The 1998 BBC Programme Strategy Review and the BBC's commitment to twenty-four-hour rolling news (*BBC News-24*, which is shown on a restricted access cable channel or via digital terrestrial and digital satellite television) may be compromising public service broadcasting principles. ITN's uncompromising chasing of ratings and prioritising of service to the contractor, multi-skilling, job compression and desk editing are challenging traditional news production processes. Both the BBC and ITN are operating within a media market which, in general, shows a tendency to move towards global product standardisation, due to increasing pressures from the same forces of economic logic. McQuail (1994:309) refers to this as innovation and 'turnover of product', which is not the same as allowing more room for creativity and editorial independence. The BBC's tendency to differentiate between its own programme types within one channel will not necessarily produce a more diverse range of television news, for instance, if the BBC's *Breakfast News* programme becomes more like an existing programme such as *Sky News*, in terms of its news content. Whilst sophisticated format, marketing, branding and presentational devices may camouflage the lack of informational diversity for a while, the signs are that television news will gradually change through the increased commercialisation of the news product over time, and the standards set over the years by the BBC and ITN may be lost.

The market-oriented drive towards finding niche-markets and product branding, coupled with the different historical antecedents and values of the two main terrestrial news providers, is facilitating the emergence of a variety of television news sub-genres. Whilst the principle of diversity of content as beneficial to the viewer is at the heart of broadcasting policy in Europe, the market-led diversification of products does not lead to the same types of freedom for citizens as that envisaged by public service broadcasting principles.

In British policy the idea of diversity concentrates on the accessibility of pluralistic information for citizens rather than on freedom for communicators to access the media (Hoffmann-Reim, 1987). Access is narrowly defined and promotes one-way communication of television media. Diversity in British television policy is also about presentation of minorities and regions and a variety of cultural tastes in the media. A truly pluralistic television system would apply the principles of diversity in a much broader manner, allowing for access by many voices to the channels of communication. The shift from limited channel capacity to abundance, coupled with the forces of deregulation, has led to refocusing by policy analysts and policy makers on a market-oriented concept of diversity, namely improved choice for consumers based on ability to pay.

McQuail (1992) identifies two useful sub-concepts of media diversity: external and internal diversity. In a situation of maximum external diversity, the full range of relevant differences (social, political, cultural) is mirrored by a range of separate media channels.[9] Each channel represents its own particular interests and topics, leading to a high degree of similarity of content within each channel and a high degree of difference between each channel. As the number of satellite, cable and digital channels increases, there is potential for improved external diversity via narrowcasting. The key issue is that narrowcasting will be commercially motivated and is consequently unlikely to provide 'a more externally diverse television system in political terms' (McQuail, 1992:146). Internal diversity usually arises in conditions of channel scarcity. This means that diversity and balance are needed within the channel. BBC1 and Channel 3 have traditionally worked to a condition of internal diversity. Whilst external diversity improves audience access to niche programmes, internal diversity promotes diversified representation

[9] Ideally each 'voice' in society would have its own channel.

within one channel. Media diversity can be delivered via two basic models, the market model and the public service model. The market model, in theory, should improve access for all voices and produce a supply of content relevant to all consumers. The market processes of innovation and improvement of products should produce a flexible response to audience wants and needs, leading to greater choice for consumers. In practice the flaws in the market model often lead to poor representation of society, via a neglect of poor or marginal groups of media consumers and high access costs, where ability to pay is paramount for access to high-quality information and entertainment.

The public service model generally attempts to redress some of these imbalances by equalising the chance of media access (via policies such as universal service obligation) and by encouraging fairer and broader representation of society via a diverse supply of programming. The main drawback of the public service model (particularly when there are scarce frequencies) is the inevitable limitation of choice for some consumers.

The problems of diversity inherent in both the market model and the public service model of broadcasting have implications for the relationship between the television news media and the public sphere. The media are especially important in large, technologically advanced countries where the citizenry never meet each other. Societies are more fragmented and diversified than in the past, and McQuail (1992) argues that as a consequence greater value than before is attached to diversity and pluralism. The media have a vital role in serving as a type of proxy or co-ordinator for the variety of different debates and public discussions conducted in a complex, liberal democratic society (Herman and McChesney, 1997).

At the political level the media play a part in the well-being of democracies. In the narrowest definition, the role of the media in the public sphere is in providing the space and creating the opportunities whereby issues of importance to the political community can be discussed; in other words, providing information which is vital to a citizen's participation in community life. The public sphere, however, needs to be broader than a political forum, and as such should provide the space and opportunity for issues of cultural and social importance to be discussed and understood. Whilst a democratic society relies on an informed citizenry making good political choices, a complex and technologically advanced democracy also depends upon citizens having a good understanding and tolerance of their own and others' social and cultural duties and needs – citizenship in a broad sense. The duties and rights of citizenship are underwritten within the idea of a common culture and identity. As citizens of nation states we derive our identity from our nationality and our citizenship rights status. Although a common culture is historically grounded it can also be maintained, promoted and developed via the mass media (Harrison and Woods, 1999).

In this regard the media perform many functions in the public sphere and serve many needs at individual, regional, national and supra-national levels.

They can, at the individual level, provide a link to society, thereby helping the individual to develop a sense of connectedness and belonging. This sense of solidarity with the wider society (or in some cases isolation from society) arises in part through an emotional connection provided by the media, through opportunities to express collective sympathy, grief, sadness, pride and other feelings. Televised national and global media events (Dayan and Katz, 1992), such as state funerals, the Olympic Games, the moon landing and the death and funeral of Diana, Princess of Wales (Harrison and Sanders, 1997), can forge a sense of solidarity and connectedness between citizens and can help them to understand other cultures. Production of a diverse range of information and contextual understanding (by both the market and well-funded public service broadcasters) about the past and present, and speculation about the future, enable the media to help to create and nurture a common culture and value system and to contribute to the public sphere or public spheres in a democracy (Harrison and Woods, 1999). It is to the role of television in the public sphere that we now turn.

1

TV news and public spheres, fragmentation and new sub-genres

Television news and public spheres

The role of British television news in the public sphere and its success or fail-ure in serving the public interest can be considered in conjunction with the liberal democratic ideal of cultivating an informed and involved public, to whom established state power is answerable through Parliament and elec-tions, and with whom government is necessarily involved in an on-going dialogue of sorts. Television news is clearly a purveyor of information to the public and therefore has an important part to play in helping people make sense of the world. To do so, television news needs to provide a diverse range of information to foster public interest and participation in political processes in order to perpetuate cultural and ideological plurality and enhance democ-racy (Barnett, 1997). The key concern is to what extent television news can and should be expected to contribute to a citizen's knowledge.

Jurgen Habermas's critique of public communication in modernity is a use-ful starting point. He provides within his analysis of the public sphere a pic-ture of what would constitute an *ideal public sphere* (Habermas, 1989). The bourgeois public sphere which is envisaged by Habermas is ideal not in the sense of its constitution and membership, but in terms of the communicative rationality it represents. Crucially, he believes that human communication is possible without the exercise of coercion or manipulation, and that mutual understanding can thus be reached. This ideal is crucial, as it opens up a space for distinguishing between heavily power-laden communication where democratic communication is blocked, and communication which is com-paratively unrestrained by power-holders.

A key to understanding Habermas's ideas about communication is his use of the concepts of *system* and *lifeworld* (Habermas, 1987). A system is repre-sented by an economy and a bureaucracy, which correspond to money and power. Accordingly these systems are largely beyond most of our everyday understanding and influence. The true lifeworld for Habermas represents the part of our everyday lives which excludes the influences of money and power. It is, however, difficult in the modern world to prevent those influ-

18

ences from infecting the lifeworld. Questions of human value and meaning can be understood via communication, using the medium of language. According to Habermas, in the modern world money and power, imperatives of the so-called system, have infected communication in the lifeworld. McGuigan (1992) points out that for Habermas, the 'new' politics, such as Green politics and popular cultural and social movements that are concerned with the quality of life (and often fight against the influences of money and power), are reinvigorating the lifeworld and contributing to the renewal of the public sphere.

For Habermas (1989) the public sphere is a space which mediates between civil society and the state, and in which individuals and groups discuss and argue about public matters. Within this space, such argument and discussion result in a critical consensus; individuals can change their opinions in the light of reasoned argument and debate. Habermas locates the first signs of the existence of such a sphere in the late eighteenth century and early industrial age. Prior to this, institutions such as the church, the state and feudal landlords had restricted public communication, believing their actions to be for the greater good of social order (McQuail, 1992). The bourgeois public sphere grew from discussion and debate in coffee houses and salons and emerged out of a successful struggle against the oppression of the church, state and feudal landlords. Despite the bourgeois public sphere's limitations as a representative mouthpiece for the whole of society, the coffee-house debates were grounded in the belief of the basic right of freedom of expression. Habermas argues that the bourgeois public sphere created, for the first time, a chance to criticise the authority of the state, which could be called on to justify itself before a potentially informed and rational public (Thompson, 1990).

As the processes of communication developed in the mid and late nineteenth century through the rise of the mass newspaper industry, the bourgeois public sphere declined. During the same period there was a complicated relationship between the growth and development of a mass commercial press and the decline of radical newspapers. This commercialisation of the press resulted in the development of two basic types of newspaper, tabloid and broadsheet.[1] In the tabloid press, which depends less on advertising and more on mass circulation, commercialisation resulted in an orientation to pleasing as many people as possible. The broadsheet press in contrast aimed to attract specific advertisers, by reaching a small target audience which was already wealthy in both information and economic terms. The content of the tabloid press developed to include salacious, melodramatic and entertaining stories. To some extent commercial broadsheet content also developed to include human interest stories and entertaining editorials and articles: the

[1] See Curran and Seaton (1997) for a detailed account of the complexity of the historical development of the press.

Daily Telegraph has long been renowned for its concentration on gruesome crime on page three. Curran and Seaton (1997) argue that the commercialisation of the press has produced consensual journalistic views and a growth of entertainment at the expense of political news, particularly in the tabloid market. The more appealing the nature of the entertainment or the human interest story has become, the more the experience of newspaper readership has changed from one which required effort and political analysis to one which promises private and quite passive enjoyment. For Elliott (1982) this signifies a shift away from people as political citizens to people as consumers in a corporate world. The decline of the bourgeois public sphere identified by Habermas coincided with the development of the commercial press. This press has increasingly been read in private or isolation (silently in a public setting), requiring little conversation or response. This trend is continuing with all manner of media: television, radio, books, magazines and computer games.

The rational–critical public sphere created in the bourgeois salons and coffee houses has been transformed into a mass audience arena, manipulated by commercial production. Thompson criticises Habermas for failing to understand the new type of publicness created by mass communication, which has resulted in a new kind of public sphere. This is despatialised and non-dialogical in the traditional sense; that is, dialogue between members of the public exists not in shared locales, but via electronic means.

For Habermas (1989) commercial media production created a pseudo-public sphere within which a culture-consuming public exists, set in its private consumption pattern. The transformation of the general culture of the public sector in the 1980s and 1990s, which elevated the individual to the status of sovereign consumer, further exacerbated the trend towards the private consumption of cultural goods. As most communication is now forced to channel itself via commercial media, the individual is prioritised as a private consumer, rather than as a public citizen (Garnham, 1990). Thus we need to consider whether it is feasible to talk in terms of the viability of Habermas's ideal of rational–critical public debate (whether the public exists in a common locale or in a despatialised and non-dialogical public sphere) which results in the genuine amendment of opinion. Conversely, we need to consider whether the possibility of such public discourse has been, and will continue to be, irreversibly obstructed by the commercialisation of communication systems.

Instead of the existence of a public sphere, providing for the possibility of genuine consensus formation, it is possible that the contemporary public are offered pre-prepared arguments which do not encourage opinion formation, or public debate and discussion. This daily diet of packaged arguments offered by television news is, it is suggested, aimed at seeking compromise through non-rational persuasion, rather than consensus through rational argument (Livingstone and Lunt, 1994).

The belief in the possible reformation of a British public sphere, in which citizens can actively engage in public debate, is replete with problems, not least the flawed nature of Habermas's bourgeois public sphere. It is important to note that Habermas's critique was a press-oriented analysis of the public sphere in the eighteenth century and that his work has been criticised by a variety of scholars and analysts (Thompson, 1990). Although in principle the public sphere (i.e. the forum for debate in salons and coffee houses) was open to all private individuals (i.e. a truly democratic forum where everybody could have an informed opinion), in fact such fora were open to only a limited section of the population. The informed and reading public in the late seventeenth and early eighteenth centuries was restricted to the male, middle-class and educated, and the bourgeois public sphere was therefore extremely limited as a mouthpiece for the whole of society. The dominant male capitalist class was therefore able to develop its hegemonic position (Stevenson, 1995). This form of bourgeois public sphere is criticised for the exclusion of both the working class and women (Fraser, 1992). Although this exclusion was obviously related to the historical context and the kind of society which existed in the seventeenth and early eighteenth centuries, it is Habermas's failure (when he was writing about and analysing the bourgeois sphere in the late 1950s and early 1960s) to explain the impact of these exclusions upon his *ideal* concept of the public sphere which has been criticised.

Furthermore, Habermas's historical interpretation of the bourgeois public sphere ignores alternative public spheres which may have existed and functioned in parallel with the bourgeois, such as the gathering of radical or alternative groups and associations. Perhaps it is also worth pointing out that any consideration of the bourgeois public sphere must take it into account that Habermas's analysis and his concern for the *ideal public sphere* are part of the Frankfurt School's characteristically pessimistic interpretation of mass society and the mass media's role in the twentieth century. Obviously Habermas's account of the development of the bourgeois public sphere of two hundred years ago could not include an analysis of television – although we can apply it to the role of contemporary media today.

If we accept the tantalising idea that the public sphere is divorced from any type of institutional control and generates the critical consensus which is needed for public participation in democratic political process, then, despite its weaknesses, Habermas provides us with a useful concept which is relevant to today's multicultural and diverse civil society, because it provides an ideal concept against which the democratic process of the contemporary mass media can be judged. The idea of the public sphere has been related to the principles and practices of public service broadcasting (for example, see Curran, 1991a, and Garnham, 1990) and the idea of the unitary public sphere has been defended (Garnham, 1992). But the fragmentary context within which the broadcast media currently work (Stevenson, 1995) in the increasingly pluralistic and multicultural character of British society cannot be ignored

Clearly analysis of the public sphere needs to be made in relation to public service broadcasting and to the fragmentation occurring within Britain as well as in relation to the notion of a European public sphere. Any discussion of the public sphere, the public interest or democracy must take account of and accommodate this idea of plurality at national, sub-national and transnational levels.

It is argued by Mouffe (1992) that both pluralism and the respect of individual freedom are defended by the contributions political liberalism has made to democracy. Modern liberal democracy establishes a particular form of human coexistence where there are distinctions between a public and private sphere as well as a separation between the church and state and between civil and religious law. Whilst Mouffe goes on to argue that it is important to defend pluralism in many areas such as culture, religion and morality, our participation as citizens requires that we also commit ourselves to defending its key institutions. This contention is problematic when it is those key institutions which restrict true diversity and pluralism in the first place. In the mid-1980s, for example, the Thatcher government resisted lobbying for a more pluralist approach to religious education in Bradford schools. The government claimed there was a need for national standards and a national curriculum in education. One of the key problems resulting from the diversification and fragmentation of society is that of how this process can be reconciled with the need for the development of links, understanding and tolerance between individual citizens, to enhance citizenship in a mature democracy.

In the 1990s and the early twenty-first century, minority views are important and to some extent such voices do get heard, although some views are not always represented well by the media. For example, non-radical Muslims have complained that the media coverage of the burning of Salman Rushdie's book *Satanic Verses* reflected a particularly negative version of the Islamic community in Britain (see McGuigan, 1992). A question which arises from the idea of plurality is whether the multiplication of television news programmes and diversification of the television news genre are a symptom or a cause of the fragmentation of the public sphere. More importantly, we need to consider what this means for the current and future value and role of television news. Different levels of 'the public' have developed at the national and regional level and new sub-national political lobby movements have emerged; activities which, according to Dahlgren (1995), have resulted in a plurality of dynamic alternative public spheres. Groups which are forming around particular issues are using the media to protest against the power of the system and to gain publicity and a higher profile. These movements and associations link the family and neighbourhood (the private domain) with political action (the public domain), and often concern issues such as the quality of life and values which belong to Habermas's lifeworld but are challenged and disrupted by imperatives from the system.

Media analysts such as Jameson (1991) and Dahlgren (1995) argue that we are experiencing an increased pluralism and fragmentation of the cultural sphere and the development of a variety of alternative public spheres. A useful reconceptualisation of the public sphere as a multiplicity of forms has been made by Nancy Fraser (1992), who initiates her analysis with a criticism of Habermas's neglect of competing public spheres, which she links to feminist politics in the United States. She shows how the alternative feminist 'subaltern counter public' (Fraser, 1992:123) has confronted and reduced the disadvantage of women in what she calls the official public sphere. The idea of an official public sphere, which includes the mainstream mass media, being in conflict with competing public spheres is important in relation to the role television news plays in a democracy. If it were the case that alternative public spheres were developing and having a significant impact, then we would expect to see alternative political movements mobilising television coverage of their activities in a way which expresses the experiences and interpretations of the group members and which may challenge the status quo. Groups would then have a growing political capacity to transmit their version of events and issues to the existing dominant television outlets by building up power relations beyond the traditional institutions. This activity would legitimate their cause and a wider range of views would be heard in the public domain.

To date we do see a good deal of effort, particularly by the better-resourced pressure groups and lobby organisations such as Greenpeace, to publicise their views and demands via the use of self-produced videos and so on. There is a good deal of optimism about the possibility of counter-cultures and alternative public spheres arising around new media, such as the Internet, and through the growth of new outlets, such as cable, satellite and digital channels. Cheap camcorders should empower previously disempowered people by allowing them to enter the margins of the public sphere (McGuigan, 1992). The rise of ownership of personal video cameras may be a positive development which has the potential to increase citizen activity in the gathering of television news and provide the opportunity for citizens to act in the public sphere. For example, the impact of the Rodney King video in the United States is illustrative of how a citizen can contribute in an important way to the knowledge of his or her fellow citizens, as well as to act in a just and helpful manner (even if money was one of the motivating factors).[2]

At its best, a new multi-channel environment may offer a proliferation of local, amateur-made videos, which contain politically relevant information

---

[2] In 1991, the Los Angeles police were captured on amateur video in a brutal and shocking attack on Rodney King, a black American citizen. Although the video was sold to the media for profit, the video's impact on the public was huge. An enquiry into the racist behaviour of the police was followed in 1992 by riots in Los Angeles.

or provide the opportunity for alternative news programmes such as *Under-currents* (Channel 4, 30 April 1994). However, in the United States there is already a tendency for video vigilantes to favour the recording of the salacious and the dramatic ahead of the investigative and political. Britain is also showing signs that its citizens are prepared to snoop and inform on their neighbours via anonymous hotlines (*Independent on Sunday*, 29 December 1996). Although the Clinton administration in the United States is committed to the construction of an information superhighway, and the European Union, via the Bangemann Report, has shown commitment to an information society, it is doubtful that such policies will greatly improve access to information. In the United States cable technology is restricted to profitable areas, and Europe operates a restricted access policy on non-public service broadcasting material. Nonetheless Rheingold (1994b) theorises about virtual communities being formed in cyberspace, where discussion and communication are comparatively undistorted by power and authority. For Rheingold (1994a) this signals new practices and possibilities of enhanced citizenship.

We may witness an increase in alternative public spheres as some previously marginalised groups gain their own broadcasting or communication opportunities.[3] Whether this will result in the types of programme which empower or even motivate citizens to become more deeply engaged in politics, or to be more fully committed decision-making members of the community, is open to some doubt. As Walzer (1992) pointed out, citizens have too many other things to worry about, not least having to earn a living. Activity in the workplace means that people tend to be more deeply engaged in the economy than in politics or the community. However, this pessimistic view of the motivations of citizens should not discourage any type of broadcaster from his or her social responsibility to offer some opportunity for resistance to certain 'constructions of political identity and subjectivity that take state institutions as the principal sites and state power as the primary object of political struggle' (McClure, 1992:120).

The public sphere (which may be better named the 'meta-public sphere', i.e. the sphere of public spheres) needs to allow access to minority voices and opinions in order to provide a democratic forum from which either compromise or consensus can be elicited. In a truly pluralistic democracy, it is only by giving access to the full diversity of voices that a real, rational debate within the public sphere or spheres can occur. Curran (1996) has argued that creating a democratic public sphere is a more complex issue than simply the dissemination of diverse viewpoints. There also need to be mechanisms in place to facilitate access to, and representation of, minority views

---

[3] Minority languages spoken in Britain such as Welsh, Gaelic and Urdu will be able to find niche outlets via new channels.

in the media. Campaigning organisations such as Undercurrents produce and distribute videos to aid their campaigns, but their material is frequently resisted by mainstream television news. The dominant television broadcasters are usually wary about using such material, and if they do use it they will often edit it heavily.

Whereas some analysts argue that democracy is simply about celebrating differences, others have expressed concern as to whether the public has become so fragmented that collective action is impossible, meaning that consensus and compromise may not be attainable (Livingstone and Lunt, 1994). Gitlin (1998) argues that the unitary public sphere is declining due to the fragmentation of society. At the same time there is an increase in the number of public spheres arising due to pluralism and multiculturalism. Gitlin's concern is that separate public sphericules will emerge at the expense of the so-called unitary public sphere. The problem is that as distinct groups develop and become increasingly organised around different interests, exacerbated by niche channels, this will reduce the existence of *a* public. The decline of *a* public which acts as an active democratic meeting of citizens, who reach across their social, political and cultural divides to agree on an agenda of common concerns and interests, may result in a decline in democratic discussions and debate. Gitlin argues that this could result in a society which is deeply divided.

In contrast, the democratic public service media system envisaged by Keane (1991) aims to allow both argument and disagreement and is founded upon the desirability of a plurality of voices and uncensored media (McLaughlin, 1993). Such a system needs a heterogeneous public to make it work, as well as having structures in place to facilitate public access to public space from which to hold public discourses (Keane, 1991). It has been argued that despite its shortcomings television journalism can, to some extent, do this (Dahlgren, 1995). Since television contributes to people's knowledge, then television journalism can force some minimal accountability from powerful public officials. Indeed, we see revelations and exposures about the wrong-doings of politicians, although these sometimes amount to little more than reporting scandal and gossip. Television news nonetheless has some contribution to make to the public sphere by scrutinising both state-related and private activity on behalf of the public.

Over time, public authority has referred increasingly to state-related activity, and civil society has developed as an area of privatised economic relations established within the realm of public authority. Within, or between, the three realms of public authority, the private realm of civil society (which fights a continual battle to remain free of the system imperatives of instrumental rationality), and the intimate sphere of personal relations, a new sphere emerged. The public sphere is supported by law (the state) and differentiated from the market. Tension lies at all boundaries and we cannot assume that the type of argument and discourse which occurs in the public sphere is both open and unconstrained. In practice the press and the broadcast media, both major institutions of the public sphere, have been subjected to control, regulation and censorship by the state officials, especially during the Thatcher governments (1979–90). Also, the new commercialisation prevalent within the broadcasting media has meant that television has been increasingly exposed to the pressures and rigours of the market place, resulting in more sensationalist reporting, more emphasis on presenter-led reporting and an increase in human interest type stories. For Williams (1962, 1974, 1985) a truly democratic public service could only be achieved through a formal separation of the media from the state and from the market.

Clearly the idea of a democratic public sphere in relation to television news is Utopian (i.e. found nowhere). Despite the philosophy of public service broadcasting which has underpinned the BBC and ITV systems since their birth, both have been consistently criticised for their politics of representation. News cannot be a 'true' representation of reality and has been criticised by a broad swathe of analysts for producing unrepresentative or even biased coverage in a wide range of areas: crime (Chibnall, 1977; Hall *et al.*, 1978), industrial relations (Glasgow University Media Group, 1976, 1980), terrorism (Schlesinger *et al.*, 1983) and race (Hartman and Husband, 1973). Both print and broadcast media have been charged with becoming increasingly powerful since the late 1950s through the concentration of ownership and the reduction of broadcasters' accountability (Curran and Seaton, 1997); with causing information poverty (Golding, 1990); with failing to inform or empower the electorate (Chomsky, 1992); with trivialising news content in favour of entertaining formats (Postman, 1989); and with denying public access to the mass media. These studies have shown how representation of minority interests, political participation, citizenship and active viewer participation have in practice been heavily restricted (Scannell, 1986) and that information for citizens is consequently often constrained.

The fear that the British media are more of a 'fifth column' working against the people than a 'fourth estate' of the constitution can be related to issues such as the ownership of the press and broadcast media (Williams, 1996) or media distortion and intrusion and the systematic use of spin doctors (Jones, 1995). Concern about the media may even be linked to charges of systematic political bias, although the extent and type of political bias in radio and television coverage of the news are strongly debated and contested (Miller, 1991). Increasing commercial pressures on news organisations to provide entertaining stories have resulted in a decline of the examination and scrutiny of politics, which is now seen by journalists to be likely to bore the audience. Instead there is probably greater concentration on the personal, conflictual or human interest elements of politics than on policy issues. The editor of ITN's *5.40 p.m. News*, for example, prefers to broadcast political stories when there has been a 'good punch-up at PMQs [Prime Minister's Questions]' rather than routinely cover political process and debate.[4] Fallows (1996) shows how the growing politicisation and personalisation of policy issues are alienating the American television audience, and Jones (1995) provides an interesting insight into the way that the reporting of events in the House of Commons has increasingly emphasised the entertainment or novel elements of those events. Televised Parliament has become more of a show and a spectacle than an opportunity to enhance the democratic process:

> After an initial burst of enthusiasm, when a wide range of news stories were being illustrated with shots of back bench MPs, speaking or challenging ministers, the editors of peak-time news bulletins also became rather bored with pictures of the chamber. As a result ... unless PMQs produced a spectacular bust-up or ... unexpected outburst, run of the mill Parliamentary coverage rarely made its way into the news. (Jones, 1995:16)

Many communication researchers are concerned that the terrestrial broadcast media do not fulfil a democratic role efficiently in contemporary Britain. Such concern is well founded, since neither commercial nor public service television allows for the emergence or development of a critical public sphere within the television news genre through audience participation and debate. Although BBC1's *Breakfast News* instituted a phone-in opportunity in February 1996 for the public wishing to comment on certain issues, the agenda was still firmly set by the broadcasters themselves, the phone-in was minimally interactive, and it included only a few self-selected audience members. Dahlgren (1995) argues that the increasing commercialisation of the broadcast media, as a result of policies in the 1980s, has resulted in a decrease in diversity, subverting the very principles and goals of public service broadcasting. Dahlgren's analysis, however, ignores the diversification of the terrestrial television news genre and the development of public spheres. It is to these I now turn.

Fragmentation of television news content, production and audiences

The fragmentation and diversification of the television news genre are resulting in the development of a variety of television news programmes. This diversity, which is primarily aimed at gaining and maintaining an audience, also leads to some differences in the conception of newsworthiness and public interest in different television newsrooms and news organisations.

As I have argued, there is already a good deal of change occurring in television news production, selection and output due to a variety of commercial, technological and political pressures exerted on the news providers. These external pressures are also affecting the format and content of television

[4] Conversation with the editor of ITN's *5.40 p.m. News* during a fieldwork visit in June and July 1994.

news output and the process, rationale and mission of newsrooms and news organisations. Different television newsrooms are adopting different newsroom epistemologies or ways of 'knowing' what constitutes television newsworthiness and the public interest, in response to particular contractual arrangements or to audience research.

The increase in satellite and cable, the introduction of digital terrestrial and digital satellite broadcasting, a new terrestrial channel (Channel 5) and twenty-four-hour rolling BBC news are leading to a continuing fragmentation of the television news genre and television news audiences in the late 1990s and early twenty-first century. Tactics are already being adopted by all television news providers to maintain audience share and to make a product which is more popular than that of their competitors. There is an increasing tendency by all television news organisations to adopt a wider range of entertainment values in the production, selection and presentation of news. As Dahlgren (1995) points out, we only need to look back at programmes produced in the mid to late 1980s to see how a variety of entertainment devices has been added to news presentation as a method of keeping audiences interested. Devices such as the increased use of graphics, newsroom redesign, the growth in use of 'star' presenters, warmer and more friendly sets, a greater range of human interest stories, happy endings, dramatic content, personalisation, faster presentation and shorter news stories can be readily identified. Other programmes may follow the precedent set by the British press and differentiate between quality news for an elite audience and tabloid news for the rest. As I have already shown, the BBC's 1998 Programme Strategy Review prescribed differentiated programmes for different audience types. Although this provides internal diversity within BBC1, there is clearly a new priority to provide different levels of information complexity for different audiences. In the press, readership differentiation has similarly led to 'trading down' of some broadsheets such as *The Times* in order to attract tabloid readers. As the price war and readership battle continue to develop, it is probable that the informational quality of newspapers will be compromised. For example, the *Daily Telegraph* appears to be exhibiting a slightly new attitude when it also includes stories about royalty, Liz Hurley and Cheri Blair's new hairstyle.

The future role of the journalist is also changing in parallel with changes taking place in organisations and their news values. Technological developments such as the disk-based video server are creating a new, multi-skilled journalist who is desk-based. MacGregor (1997:211) describes the journalist of the 1990s as rather like a 'battery hen', packaging the news sent into the newsroom from other journalists who are out on location, and who may be working either for their own news organisation or for news agencies. As multi-skilling reduces the numbers of journalists covering news stories, there is a danger that the informational content and quality of news stories will be compromised in favour of perfecting the delivery and repackaging of information. Multi-skilling and desk-editing further separate the distinctions between newsgathering and output and between news content and process. The journalist out on location will gather the information and send it back to the newsroom for processing and packaging. This is different from the practice in the early 1990s when the correspondent was, as he or she still is in some organisations, involved in gathering, producing and editing the news story in conjunction with a producer and a video-tape editor. In the days of tri media, information may be gathered only once, but repackaged in many different ways. Consequently, news content will need to be flexible. The separation of news content and news process may be problematic for the quality of output, because although technological developments may make the mechanics of newsgathering easier, this does not necessarily make journalism or the quality of information better. MacGregor (1997) predicts that technological developments will enable television news to diversify its forms increasingly, offering a wide range of services emanating from a diverse range of repackaging methods.

Given that there is already a limit to the television medium's potential to convey complex and abstract meaning, any move towards dropping informational or pedagogical content is pandering to its natural orientation of being an entertainment medium. The informational and educational content of television news need to be emphasised rather than rejected. Whilst the key to retaining audiences may seem to reside in the newly important news value of relevance, making news programmes relevant to the audiences requires quite a different set of considerations and commitments from the producers of news. To make a story relevant to the audience involves making it possible for the audience to make connections between its own everyday experiences and those which appear on television news. Problematically, television news must be made to matter to a wide variety of subcultures in modern society. There is also a difficulty in over-concentrating on the criterion of relevance as being the key to news values, as it is in danger of pre-defining topics in a way which means that some important developments in society, which are not necessarily relevant to the majority, risk being ignored because they are not perceived by journalists as fitting into people's existing horizons. And yet news journalism needs to be educational, expand citizen's horizons, and not simply resort to reporting what is familiar.

But there is an essential tension in trying to deal with serious issues, given the predominance of the entertainment element of the popular side of today's television journalism. To get a balance between the popular and the socially responsible there must be a wide variety of types of expression; in other words there must be many genres, with each news genre speaking to different socio-cultural groups. The orientation of news provision towards relevance, niche-marketing, multi-skilling, desk-top editing and a faster, racier style of news presentation runs counter to the informational potential of television news.

Clearly, far from slowing down the tempo of television news production and presentation, the development of technology has speeded it up. The use of electronic newsgathering (ENG) has increased the pressure upon news-gatherers to obtain live pictures for immediate broadcast. The increasing stress upon immediacy which ENG and satellite technology can facilitate is reducing the tolerance for 'old' news and thereby promoting the live and dramatic (exciting news) ahead of the important and significant (more complex and boring news). This can lead to a general reduction in complex content and context in favour of the use of simple, visually exciting images, short sound-bites (Gitlin, 1991b) and relatively little information.

Twenty-four-hour rolling news produced by organisations such as Cable News Network (CNN) has already found that ratings go up when a catastrophe occurs, and yet there is a problem in trying to retain viewer loyalty on a quiet newsday. Unlike news programmes which occur at a particular time each day, viewers using twenty-four-hour rolling news programmes do not tend to have particular appointment times when they will sit down and watch the news for half an hour or so. CNN is currently attempting to introduce a more recognisable structure into some of its programming to try to attract audiences at particular times. The loss of appointment viewers also faces the BBC following the launch of its own twenty-four-hour rolling news service.[5]

The advent of digital terrestrial broadcasting may result in a reduction of programme information quality. The debate on the Broadcasting Bill 1996 raised controversial issues in relation to the quality of programming, which were not resolved. The Broadcasting Act 1996 makes no reference to the quality of programming on the new digital channels (this does not include those which will be simulcast by the existing terrestrial television broadcasters). The Independent Television Commission's (ITC) obligations under Section 6(1) of the Broadcasting Act 1990 still remain in relation to good taste and decency of programming. The ITC may choose to apply the broad wording of 'variety of interests' to ensure that some programme diversity is maintained, but this will not necessarily be applicable to news programming. Many of the new digital channels will not contain any news services, offering only an increase in entertainment choice. Such channels would therefore contribute little or nothing to fostering an awareness of the need to be active citizens pursuing the public good. Lack of understanding may, to take a very negative line, be exacerbated if mainstream television news such as the BBC's prime-time news programmes are replaced with rolling news. Viewers may only dip in and out of the news briefly, rather than watch a whole news programme, and may, as a result, have an even more partial and uneven view of the world than before.

The future of the content and format structures of mainstream television news, as well as the importance and significance of broadcast television news

[5] The BBC had to seek permission from the Department of Culture, Media and Sport to distribute the channel via low-access cable.

itself, is being challenged by the kinds of technological development which will allow an individual to choose his or her own news stories. Access may be via the Internet, or through an electronic newspaper, where a menu of news items is constructed personally and contains only news and information relevant to a particular individual. Changes in the press are, however, a little different from those in television (Gilder, 1994). Currently, events are defined as important, significant or interesting by television journalists (to differing degrees) in their role as the custodians of newsworthiness, and, in this sense, they are also interpreters of the public interest. However, if people were left to choose their own television news agenda from a news menu, atrocities such as the mass genocide in Rwanda might go unnoticed by many British citizens. Well-informed citizens may increasingly become atomised individuals cocooned in an individualised media environment, which at worst would be trivial, or at best partial. The danger of these developments is that the reduction or loss of an informative news programme for the masses on prime-time television will result in an information poverty for many (especially those who rely solely on television for their news) and exacerbate the inequality in knowledge and information which already exists (Schiller, 1996).

The BBC and especially ITN are already sensitive to the need for change and diversification of the news product and are creating a range of television news formats. The differentiation of mainstream BBC1 programmes planned in the 1998 Programme Strategy Review meant that audience fragmentation was being exacerbated and a version of information poverty was being constituted by public service broadcasting. Those people who watch only the *Six O'Clock News* would no longer be as well informed about politics and international news as those watching the *Nine O'Clock News*. This was a shift of policy for the BBC, which would show clear differentiation between its breakfast, lunchtime, early evening and late evening news.

In contrast ITN has long defined itself through its ability to provide a diverse range of news formats in response to particular commercial specifications, producing television news for Channels 3, 4 and 5 and Planet-24. Concern has been expressed by media researchers (e.g. Barnett and Gaber, 1993) that the need to boost ratings caused ITN's *News at Ten* to become increasingly 'tabloid' (their word), emphasising crime and human interest stories and carrying fewer political and foreign stories. In 1998 the position of *News at Ten* in the late evening schedules looked very precarious and by 1999 its fate was sealed.[6] The future role and rationale of the BBC as a

---

[6] Shortly before this book went to press, *News at Ten* broadcast its last news programme. ITN also lost its brand name on the news. The reformulated ITV schedule now contains *ITV Nightly News* at 11 p.m., and *ITV News* at 6.30 p.m. It is too early to make any specific comments about the two ITN programmes which have so recently replaced the ITN's long-standing programmes, and this is beyond the scope of this work, but the new ITV schedule will have an important impact on the viewing habits of the audience.

public service broadcaster are being threatened by the current environment of adaptation and change, and the values of public service broadcasting which have traditionally underpinned and defined the commercial broadcasting system are being undermined (Miller and Norris, 1989; McDonnell, 1991). Concerns have also been expressed about the uncertain future of Channel 4. Its privatisation would, according to its ex-chief executive Michael Grade, have a serious effect on its news programme service, leading to more coverage of tabloid stories such as 'Fergie's love tapes' and fewer in-depth analyses of the situation in Bosnia and Afghanistan. Other Channel 4 staff have argued that the analysis, diversity and coverage of foreign news would be compromised if the fifty-minute slot at seven o'clock were reduced (*Press Gazette*, 16 January 1997). Such concerns echo a recurring theme in relation to the commercialisation of television news, namely that, as the American model has exemplified, there is a strong tendency for news programmes to become more populist initially in order to increase audience share quickly (Hume, 1996).

New sub-genres

It is clear that the analysis of television news in Britain in the 1990s is meaningless unless the proliferation of television news programmes is taken into consideration. In 1993 there were fourteen different types of television news programme broadcast by the four British terrestrial weekday television channels, BBC1, BBC2, ITV3 and Channel 4,[7] ranging from *Newsnight* to *Big Breakfast News*.[8] All the programmes analysed have something in common in that they, or their component parts, belong to a specific genre called 'news' and that the core communicative features of the news programmes (or part of the programme) have a distinctive look and sound. Corner (1995) identifies these distinctive features as, first, studio modes relating to the presenter – use of film, stills, graphics, interviews, live two-ways and so on – and, second, location modes relating to the reporter – use of filmed sequences, pieces to camera, actuality, stills, interviews and so on. These basic units, along with familiar logos, introductory sequences, use of music and recognition of presenters, provide a basic communicative repertoire for television journalism. This communicative inventory is immediately recognisable and distinct from other television programme genres and forms.

Producing a precise definition of the term 'genre' is difficult. Its etymological roots in the Latin word *genus* (kind) indicate that genre relates to types, especially literary types; it can be applied to lyric, tragedy, the novel, the sonnet and so on (Dubrow, 1982). Contemporary use of the word 'genre' is

---

[7] This analysis does not include the Welsh national news provider, S4C, on the fourth channel (which has an audience reach of 0.4 per cent), but concentrates only on Channel 4.
[8] When the content analysis was conducted Channel 5 did not exist.

related to popular and formula writing, and it has been used in recent years to categorise film, television and popular fiction.

The use of the concept of genre in relation to popular forms of artistic production is new. In Britain in the late 1960s and early 1970s the concept of genre in the cinema began to be developed (Neale, 1980) and the theory of film was challenged. The assumed excellence of the taste of a few critics and journalism was criticised, as was auterism (viewing the film as the artistic creation of the director), which was the dominant school of serious discussion of cinema (Perkins, 1972). Critical interest was extended to mainstream commercial films, particularly Hollywood cinema. Importantly, the struggle against a specific aesthetics of taste led to a realisation that any form of artistic production was a rule-bound activity which was embedded in social history and which gave an art form a social grounding.

Use of the concept of genre has resulted in a range of problems, notably which characteristics should be considered when deciding which label to give to which literary type (Dubrow, 1982). Defining a genre can be done by subject matter (what is the literary work about?), through a table of opposites, or via analysis of iconography. None of these is enough individually to distinguish one literary form from another. Cawelti (1977) tries to define the characteristics of genres not by the things the literary forms have in common but by attempting to get beneath the surface of the text to see if there is a common, underlying narrative grammar.

Problematically, definitions of genre (such as sci-fi) can be so broad that they can cover almost everything and in the end be too vague to be of use. A more definite way to attempt to consider genre is to make the definition prescriptive, so that certain elements are identified which must be in the film or book in order for it to fit into a particular category. This method seems to be accepted by audiences who find relevance and security in a familiar form. An audience's experience with a particular formula gives it a sense of what to expect in new individual examples.

Analysis of genre definitions tends to imply that a single definition will be sufficient for any one genre because there is a move towards standardisation in modern publishing and film-making (Cawelti, 1977). Yet one often finds that a genre is not one type but a collection of different types, a unity of diversity or a diversity in unity.

Television has now overtaken film as the central mass medium. Television has many different genres: soap opera; drama; quiz shows; chat shows; current affairs and documentary; education programmes; magazine programmes; news programmes and so on. This standardisation of television programmes into different genres has meant that standard conventions have been adopted which enable the audience, the programme makers and the distributors of programmes to identify particular programme characteristics. This enables them to recognise and distinguish particular programme types. One of the most important distinctions between fictional and non-fictional programmes is the way in which information and knowledge are framed. In factual television, programme information is usually framed in direct speech from the presenter to the viewer (Corner, 1995). The presenter-led format of television news is an instantly recognised convention which signals clearly to the viewer what kind of programme he or she is watching. However, boundaries between genres are shifting and becoming increasingly permeable. The distinction between fiction and non-fiction is regularly blurred in the new range of current affairs and fly-on-the-wall programmes and in so-called docu-soaps and docu-dramas (Abercrombie, 1996).

In introducing the concept of the television news genre into my analysis of television news in the 1990s, it is clear that there are problems and difficulties to be faced in trying to define what constitutes a news genre, let alone identify how particular programmes adapt and change within it. Nevertheless an attempt to define the parameters of my analysis of television news is necessary. The categorisation of the structure of television news as a genre shows that such communication forms do not exist by chance, but are controlled and constructed. It follows that different meanings can be derived from an analysis of the different news forms which exist. Identification and analysis of a television news genre allow the pursuit of a central theme, namely that television news is diversifying from a unitary product into different programme types, constituted from a variety of news sub-genres. This suggests that a variety of definitions of newsworthiness and public interest journalism now exists in relation to television news.

The definition of a news genre is further complicated because the concept of news itself is so broad and vague. News is information, the communication of knowledge or the delivery and reporting of a message. The nature, value, importance and structure of each message can vary greatly and have different meanings to different people. It follows that news cannot be classified as a single discrete concept, as it is apparent that the constituent features of the news message are complex and multi-faceted. News programmes can be easily and simply categorised using a variety of devices: the studio and location modes identified by Corner (1995); the time of day the programmes are broadcast; the size or nature of the audience the programmes are transmitted to; or whether the programme is aimed at children or adults, or at a national or regional audience. However useful, this type of classification alone is not adequate for any meaningful analysis of the concept of the news genre.

Broadcasters do try to classify their programmes in terms of a single genre, but again this particular practice is not adequate for any in-depth analysis of television news, since all programmes cannot realistically be described in terms of a single genre (Dubrow, 1982). It was notable when conducting newsroom fieldwork that the broadcasters did not agree amongst themselves about what constitutes the news genre.

As Dayan and Katz (1992) point out, researchers have also shown an uncritical tendency to employ broad categories, such as news, documentary, comedy, soap opera, variety and so on, although little serious research has been done on the constituent features of any of these genres. For example, much attention has been paid to television news, but little effort has been made to map out a working definition of the news genre and its component parts. Even researchers like Williams (1974) and Newcombe (1974), who have attempted to classify television news genres according to a generalisation of what the programmes in each category had in common, fail to analyse patterns of viewing of television in terms of discrete programmes falling into a particular genre.

To try to escape from the strait-jacket of any one particular existing definition of television news, or the prevailing tendency to analyse television news as a single entity, I have formulated an ideal-type model of the news genre (Figure 1). Each circle on the model represents a different genre. The whole field is news-relevant, but only the area in the centre of the circle (the core) is 'pure' news. The core contains the events all news programmes cover, such as election of a new prime minister or the death of a member of

Figure 1 *The television news genre: ideal type generic model*

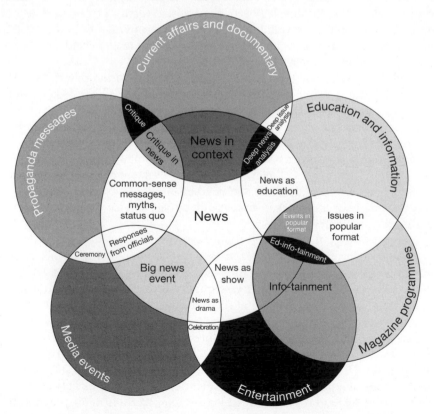

the royal family. Any news programme in the 1990s would also contain one or more of the overlap areas within the news circle, providing a range of possibilities for innovation and variety. The differences between the overlap and the different number of overlaps included provide the basis for the observable differences between news programmes. Each news programme therefore forms its own sub-genres from the television news genre.

When media events such as the death and funeral of Diana, Princess of Wales, VE Day celebrations or John Smith's funeral occur, *all* the news programmes will cover the events. When aspects of these are covered before the media event (such as a state funeral) or when they are repackaged into a news summary, *after* the events have been covered live, the dimensions of the event which are stressed vary from programme to programme. The diverse approach of ITN (providers of news for Channel 3, 4 and 5) was illustrated clearly during the week following the death of the Princess of Wales (September 1997) and during the funeral itself. Instead of filming the funeral service from within Westminster Abbey, Channel 5 filmed the people standing outside. The film was able to capture the crowd's reaction to Earl Spencer's speech (a significant example of the mood of the people and one which may eventually have had constitutional implications). As many people spend time flicking between channels, diversity of coverage of one event is important in providing a variety of perspectives, and in this case in particular ITN was able to show a dimension of the media event which was missed by the other mainstream broadcasters.

Using the above ideal type generic model of the television news genre, the essential features of the television news genre can be illustrated, whereby news may be composed of a variety of constituent parts. It is the presence or absence of aspects of these constituent parts that gives each news programme its own unique characteristics, and it is the endless variety of combinations of the constituent parts which gives each news programme its own peculiarity. The analysis of television news in terms of discrete programmes is vital if we are to understand the degrees of adaptation and change, and the tension between market forces and public service values, that exist within the single news genre.

A way to tackle the problem of what constitutes a television news genre is to define news by what it *is not*, to separate it carefully from other genres and types of programming. It is interesting to discover that any attempt to do so serves to illustrate what news actually *is*. Furthermore, identification of the infiltration of key features of the not-news environment into the news environment actually goes a long way towards explaining the key differences between the different television news programmes. For example, the news genre would, on the face of it, appear to be distinct from the current affairs genre, as current affairs programmes elaborate at great length and in some depth about one particular issue. However, clear distinctions between news and current affairs programming collapse when certain news programmes are considered. *Newsnight* and to a lesser extent *Channel 4 News* deliberately incorporate features of the current affairs or documentary genre. *Newsnight* in particular recruits many of its journalists from current affairs programmes, and the BBC has a policy of providing current affairs-type analysis in its news programmes. Both *Newsnight* and *Channel 4 News* have fashioned their programmes to include the type of analysis of issues that does not appear in the mainstream news programmes. Some aspects of the current affairs or documentary traditions can thus be found in some television news programmes.

News programmes are also different from educational programmes, a distinction which seems obvious if one compares an Open University programme with the *Nine O'Clock News*. Some of the features of educational programming can be detected in many television news programmes, however, which is not surprising when we consider that the BBC's charter outlines its purpose as being to inform, educate and entertain its audience. At their best, current affairs and documentary programmes will intersect or overlap with the education genre, providing a much deeper analysis of issues and events. The best news programmes also contain an element of this type of practice. Journalists at the BBC profess to analyse issues (indeed senior editors in particular discuss this aim at some length in planning meetings), but in reality constraints of time prevent this from taking place in a news programme forum. *Newsnight* has more success as an educational news programme, since it does not have to concentrate on ten or twelve news stories but has the luxury of looking at two or three in some depth, and the programme is the obvious locale for the BBC's analytical approach to news.

The magazine, human interest dimension of television news programmes is increasingly being incorporated into most news programmes. Yorkshire Television's news programme, *Calendar News*, is overtly hybrid in character, combining hard news stories with sofa chats[9] and human interest stories. The BBC's 1998 Programme Strategy Review planned to change the *Six O'Clock News* to a magazine format. Clearly television news is not the same as magazine programmes such as *This Morning* or *Good Morning*, but many news programmes share some of the magazine format and content characteristics. Other national mainstream news programmes are copying the friendly, cosy style of magazine programme presenters, where the X factor has to exist between the presenters, presenters comment on news content, and a light-hearted chat and joke are standard practice at key junctures of

[9] Until 1996 the *Calendar News* set comprised a sofa; later a table was added. In 1996 the set was redesigned and the news from the studio was presented in a more conventional manner, with two presenters sitting behind a desk. From 1996 *Calendar News* was followed by a much lighter entertainment magazine programme, *Tonight*, which took on the sofa and *Calendar*'s original presentational format. However, the content of *Calendar News* was not adjusted and many of the items are still light and human interest-oriented.

the programme. The key to this type of format and content is accessibility, warmth, simplicity and friendliness.

Entertainment programmes such as films or television soaps and dramas manifest obvious differences from the so-called news programmes. However, news programmes are increasingly being forced to compete with entertainment programmes for audiences. As a result some news programmes are consistently incorporating entertainment devices (news as show) into both the format of the programme (e.g. the *News at Ten* spaceship set and other gimmicks) and the content of the news programmes (e.g. 'and finally' stories, or stories of a dramatic nature set to music, dramatic crime reconstructions or live pictures – news as drama). Where entertainment, magazine formats and the education genre overlap, a hybrid concept arises, the so-called info-tainment category. A further grouping occurs, according to Tunstall (1993), where three goals of public service broadcasting merge. He calls this tripartite form ed-info-tainment, which comprises goals from three different genres: education, entertainment and information. This merging of goals is seen in programmes like *That's Life* or the *Antiques Road Show*. Ed-info-tainment originated in a quasi-news programme called *Tonight*, first shown in 1957 by the BBC, which was one of the organisation's first flagship programmes. The *Tonight* programme blurred the traditional distinctions between entertainment, information and even education, and through its informal styles of presentation it broke sharply with old BBC traditions (Briggs, 1995). The producer in charge, Donald Baverstock, 'could see no reason why we couldn't be serious about the state of the British economy ... and in the same programme smile about the hens that were laying bent eggs in Dorset' (Alisdair Milne quoted in Tunstall, 1993:81).

When media events, as defined by Dayan and Katz (1992) occur, they can engulf television news. This was exemplified by the death and funeral of Diana, Princess of Wales. A media event can sometimes start its life as a big news event; for example, in 1994 the death of Labour Party leader John Smith began as a news event, but his funeral was a media event requiring blanket coverage. Television news may incorporate some types of media event as big news events or conversely the whole news programme itself may simply be engulfed by the media event. When media events overlap with the entertainment genre, the celebratory aspects of the event are stressed. A lighter human interest- and entertainment-oriented news programme would concentrate on covering the drama and ceremony of a royal wedding, encompassing details such as the style of the wedding dress, street parties and celebration. A more serious news programme might examine the same media event from a more symbolic or traditional perspective, such as the effect of the marriage on future constitutional arrangements.

Chomsky (1992) identifies propaganda news in American television's reports of US foreign policy. His identification of devices of message control in particular, such as the demonisation of Saddam Hussein and the scant reporting of events in East Timor, have parallels in Britain. A parallel set of concerns is: Margaret Thatcher's criticism and attempts at control over the BBC regarding the reporting of the Falklands War; the scant reporting of events in South America; the consistent representation of Africa as a place of famine and war by the television news media; or the concentration of the television media on the coverage of the activities of the United Nations forces in former Yugoslavia, at the expense of a clearer and more informative picture of the situation there. Such tendencies are a type of propaganda even though they are often unwitting and non-conspiratorial, because they give the audience a particular picture of the outside world. An obvious danger of Chomsky's Propaganda Model is that it can overstate the case, and it is not my intention to imply that propaganda news in a democratic regime is constructed in the same way as the news broadcast in totalitarian states.

Television news contains many implicit assumptions and messages, and particular and problematic representations of race, sex, violence, marginalised religious groups and industrial relations. Murdock and Golding (1973) argue that there is a noticeable tendency in the media to appeal to ideas of patriotism and the national interest, as a way of stressing conformity and isolating outsiders and non-conformists. These researchers also found that British concerns are considered to be more newsworthy and important in Britain than events in other countries. A stress on patriotism, British concerns and the marginalisation of extremism cannot be described as a conspiracy, or even as a conscious intention of the journalist working in mainstream television news. McQuail (1992:193–4) argues that there is a 'typology of news bias' which includes open or hidden bias and intended and unintended bias. McQuail shows us that content can be openly partisan (partisanship), be partisan with bias that is intended to remain hidden (propaganda), have open and unintended bias (unwitting bias), or have unintended but hidden bias that is 'embedded in texts' (ideology). Clearly news cannot be, nor would we expect it to be, value-free. That certain values are of more worth to certain sectors of British society is not generally accepted by journalists, who can illustrate many instances where they have exposed corruption or sleaze in high places and given publicity to the plight of many of those who are powerless to speak for themselves. Propaganda news therefore, in a democratic country such as Britain, is best described in political and ideological terms, as an attempt to form (or to form by assuming the existence of) a consensual public opinion on the topics presented.

Propaganda news can also overlap with media events (see Figure 1). Indeed we often see official spokespersons such as the prime minister or president providing a particular line which is then broadcast by the mainstream news. This official line, which generally reinforces the status quo, is presented as the accepted interpretation of any issue or event. At its best, current affairs or programmes such as BBC1's *On the Record* will analyse and critique such official messages and in the process provide a more balanced and realistic explanation and interpretation of those issues and events. Crucially, these analyses and critiques of official messages and values occur outside the mainstream peak-time television news programmes and have to be sought out by the audience.

The generic model of television news outlined in Figure 1 illustrates core features of the television news genre and shows how influences from the not-news environment can act upon and shape the three dimensions of news: first, the news content; second, the production of news; and third, the possible effects that television news can have on the audience. It also shows how, in an era of globalisation, of converging technology and of commercialisation of television news, the distinction between news and entertainment, news and education, and news and fiction is constantly shifting and adapting (Garber *et al.*, 1993). This ideal type model of the television news genre can be exemplified in its own particularity by each different television news programme, because it has the ability to be flexible and to adapt, modify and mutate. It is the developments resulting from such flexibility and mutation which are of most concern in the current period of change. Different television news programmes and news organisations illustrate marked differences in their formation of sub-genres (see Table 1).

If modification and further diversification of news programmes result in a deterioration of television news quality, this will obviously have serious implications for the public sphere and for democracy. The way the recommendations made in the BBC's 1998 Programme Strategy Review are implemented will indicate the future of public service news. If, by the time this book is published, the BBC has started to produce similar news information to the commercial sector, or reduced the diversity of information provided by further restructuring and rationalisation of its television news provision, then the BBC will be compromising the quality and diversity of its information in order to become more appealing or accessible to audiences. The possibility of a lack of diverse news information should be a chief concern (with that diversity measured not just in terms of consumer choice but in relation to access and representation, and produced via public service broadcasting and not simply through market forces). A reduction in information diversity and a standardisation of content will reduce the variety of representations of politics and the variety of information citizens can expect about their elected officials. This therefore reduces one of the normative rationales of journalism, namely to enhance democratic accountability by informing citizens about political affairs. At its most extreme, citizens could become ill informed and unmotivated, a passive and atomised audience of a medium that mainly provides trivia and sensationalism, allowing prejudice and xenophobia to be nourished.

Current developments in the broadcasting industry must therefore be of concern. Technological advances and government policies to deregulate media control, relax ownership rules and encourage competition obviously

Table 1   *News sub-genres*

Programmes	Primary influences	Sub-genres	Programme type
Channel 4 News at 7 o'clock, BBC2's *Newsnight*	News, current affairs/documentary, education and information, entertainment[a]	News, critique in news, news in context, deep news analysis, news as education, important issues in popular format, ed-info-tain-ment	Results in story plus analysis in one package. News is strongly related to the importance and significance of an event or issue.
BBC news (regional and national): *Breakfast News,*[b] *One O'Clock News, Six O'Clock News,*[b] *Nine O'Clock News, Look North News, Children's Newsround*	News, education and information, entertainment[a]	News, deep news analysis, news as education, important issues in popular format, ed-info-tainment, info-tain-ment, news as show, news as drama	Often results in two packages in a twin-pack format: a story package and a backgrounder. News is strongly related to the importance and significance of an event or issue but with some interest added. The pursuit of audiences has resulted in a move away from the twin-pack, reducing some of the informational background and context provided.
ITN's *News at Ten,* ITN's *12.30 p.m. News*	News, entertain-ment, education and information	News, news as drama, news as show, info-tainment, ed-info-tainment, important events in popular format, news as education	Results in stories and features. News is strongly related to how interesting and important an event is.
ITN's *5.40 p.m. News, GMTV News, Big Breakfast News, Calendar News*	News, magazine programmes, entertainment	News, ed-info-tain-ment, news as show, news as drama	Results in people- and human interest-centred news. Produces hybrid news and entertainment shows. News is strongly related to how interesting and entertaining an event is.

a Some entertainment influences are creeping into the format styles, usually in the form of graphics, live two-ways, new sets, logos, and presenter-led interviews of politicians (rather than more serious interrogation by political correspondents). It is this movement which may result in the increasing homogenisation of the informational characteristics of television news. The BBC has to remain different in order to ensure real informational diversity remains in terrestrial television news pro-gramming.
b May become more oriented to news and entertainment and be situated in the same category as ITN's *News at Ten* and ITN's *12.30 p.m. News.*

have important implications for the future of the quality and diversity of television news information, news content and news format structures. Satellite news formats such as *Sky News* may achieve a competitive edge and seem to be providing a blue-print for successful news production. Copying the *Sky News* formula may instigate a long-term change in the format of television news programmes. The BBC, for example, planned its domestic twenty-four-hour rolling news programme in direct response to the current domination by *Sky News* of this part of the market. Live TV, a cable channel owned by Mirror Group Newspapers, may have set new standards and expectations with regard to television news (such as the introduction of City TV alongside the extreme trivialisation of national news). Until recently Live TV's news programme had a news bunny who gave the thumbs-up or thumbs-down depending on how good or bad it thought the story to be. This kind of trivialisation of television news perhaps marks the first real attempt to bring tabloid news values to the television news format. The format of the show was manic, exciting and gimmicky;[10] the news programmes and headlines had to fit into that format.

These developments are particularly important. As I will show, the content of news programmes (and therefore their informational value) is related to some degree to their format structures (in the extent to which news programmes run at faster and faster tempos, shorten story lengths, increase the use of live two-ways and so on). Developments like these reduce the amount of information transmitted and make it more difficult for the audience to absorb and understand the information they are receiving (Gunter, 1987; Davis, 1990; Dahlgren, 1995). It follows therefore that what appears to be a tinkering with production techniques and format style by news organisations eventually has an effect on news content and the amount of information available, and ultimately on the relationship of terrestrial television news to the public sphere, in serving the public interest and enhancing the democratic process.

---

[10] One newsreader played the cello whilst reading the news. Programme producers are constantly looking for new approaches to news presentation.

2

TV news, the public interest
and democracy

Underpinning this analysis of the news is a recognition of the important role
it can play in a democracy in a direct relation to the information or knowledge content of the public sphere in a modern and complex society
(Dahlgren, 1995). Television, along with a variety of other electronic media,
creates a form of 'mediated publicness' (Thompson, 1990:236) whereby private viewing of public events has replaced the face-to-face interaction of the
nineteenth-century bourgeois public sphere (Habermas, 1984). The scale of
modern society does not allow for a significantly large group of citizens to be
physically present at the same time and in the same place. The mass media
therefore have become important institutions fulfilling the role of the specta-
tor (Dahlgren, 1995). The importance of television in general, and television
news in particular, in relation to democratic processes means that the impact
of the increasing commercialisation of the British television medium, and the
evolution of the public interest idea which underpins both the BBC and ITV
systems, are of significance. Television news in the 1980s and 1990s needs
to be addressed in the context of its changing institutional relationships to
political processes, by having to respond to a variety of pressures to move
from a public service broadcasting model towards a market model (Livingstone and Lunt, 1994).

Television news and the public interest

One of the most important issues in relation to British television news in the
1990s is how the concept of public interest within the context of the public
sphere is served. This idea of serving the public interest is important in both
the theory and practice of modern democratic politics, although it can be
problematic. Public interest can be invoked to support a partisan version of
what is for the general good (McQuail, 1992) and can be used to justify both
public service broadcasting and the freedom of media market forces. As an
ideological device, the concept can be used to obscure unjustified regulation

43

imposed by governments, to restrict freedom of expression, or to justify media intrusion.

The concept of public interest has regularly been used to defend public service broadcasting. A linkage which is understandable as public service broadcasting is often defined in relation to the benefits it is believed to be capable of delivering to society. Until recently broadcasting has been treated rather like the public utilities and deemed to be too important to be left to the whims of the market place. Broadcast media and telecommunications have been dealt with as 'businesses affected with a public interest and subjected to special treatment under law and government policy' (Melody, 1990:18). Values such as equality of access, universal provision, impartiality and objectivity have always been the keystones of the public broadcasting principle in Britain and invoked by the regulators in the name of the public interest. The BBC has traditionally been a public space for people who wish to make high-quality (or even culturally elite) radio and television programmes for their own sake, and not necessarily in order to attract large audiences (Barnett and Curry, 1994). However, in the 1990s public service principles were being challenged at both the BBC and ITN. In the contemporary broadcasting climate the idea of ITN as an organisation with a public interest role is being seriously questioned and some would say compromised. This accusation is further complicated because in practice there is currently little common agreement on what are the essential features of a public service broadcasting system (McQuail, 1992) or what is in the public interest in relation to television news output.

There have been attempts to update the interpretation of public interest in order to try to capture the essence of what is for the public good. The quantity and diversity of information sources, communication opportunities and the growth of media markets have elicited concern, from commentators such as Melody (1990), that developments in the information and communication sector may exacerbate class divisions and inequalities in society. Melody's concern centres on the development of pay-per-view systems, which may be installed in libraries, as well as the increasing significance of the integration of press, print, broadcasting, telecommunications and computers, which may serve to exclude some sectors of the public from accessing valuable and empowering information.

As British society in the 1990s and early 2000s is subjected to a deluge of information from a variety of sources, it is vital that this material is interpreted and presented in a way which is accessible to the whole public (Webster, 1995; Schiller, 1996). But it is unclear whether the most appropriate way for interpreting public information has been defined, or whether the key issue of what the public needs to know in order to function most effectively as a responsible citizenry in a participatory democracy has ever been addressed, either by the interpreters of information, or by the regulators of the broadcast media.

Research has shown that television news is an important source of information for many people. Since the mid-1950s the majority of viewers in Britain have identified television as their main source of world news ahead of the press (Gunter, 1987; Gunter and Svennevig, 1988; Gunter and Winstone, 1993; Gunter *et al.*, 1994). These findings were confirmed by Gunter *et al.* (1994) in a survey of one thousand adults. Ninety-eight per cent of the respondents mentioned television as one of the first three sources of world news. Sixty-nine per cent mentioned television first, above all other media as their main world news source. For local news, newspapers are customarily named as the main source (Gunter *et al.*, 1994; Hetherington, 1989), and even though the circulation of local and weekly papers has decreased over the years, the growth in alternative publications and free newspapers has increased the penetration of local press into homes (Franklin and Murphy, 1991). However, it is only at the most local level that newspapers replace television as the preferred news source. Even at the level of news about the region, television is most often seen as the primary news source (Gunter *et al.*, 1994).

Nevertheless, although television is generally perceived by the public to be its primary news source, this does not mean that the public actually gets the majority of its news information from television. Research has shown that people spend on average less time watching television news than reading a newspaper each day. Furthermore, there is evidence that more information may be consumed from newspapers than from television news (Gunter, 1987).

One of the key features of the audience's perception of television news involves the degree of trust which is placed in it. This trust is not accorded to other media, and is based upon the belief that the broadcast news is not partisan in content. A survey performed by the ITC in 1993 found that, as in other years, only minorities of respondents in the survey perceived any bias towards political parties on the four terrestrial channels (Gunter *et al.*, 1994). The concept of objectivity of television news is an important factor for the millions of people who watch news programmes every day on the assumption that the coverage is fair. There is an important public perception about the significance and reliability of television news as a source of information about the world. Whilst television news does not create a public sphere or public spheres within which rational–critical debate can take place it does, nonetheless, have a significant role to play in providing citizens with political, social and cultural information.

There are clearly questions which arise relating to the public sphere and the sphere in which democratic process occurs. As fragmentation occurs within society at sub-national levels (where a plurality of public spheres may be evolving) and changes occur at the supra-national level (perhaps evolving to a European or global public sphere), the concept of a unitary national public sphere is getting more and more stretched. A unitary public sphere, regulated in the public interest, however, was something that national governments, regulators and broadcasters could contribute to more easily. The significance of television news has always been, and still is, recognised by legislators, who have argued that public control of the media in the public interest is necessary in the form of regulation.

In Britain and other Western European democracies, regulation has been consistently advocated on the grounds of public interest (Mather, 1993) (although equally there are those who advocate deregulation and a further expansion of the free market to be in the public interest; see Horsman, 1997). The particular policy discourse and legislative structure which are developed with regard to broadcast media are illustrative of the evaluative ideas and terms encountered in national culture and politics. Regulatory frameworks articulate what has been deemed to be in the public interest in any particular nation. In Britain, public interest has been delivered both via the public service broadcasting system and via the regulated market. It follows therefore that changes in the politics of regulation of the media and the market affect the public interest.

According to McQuail (1994), the definition or interpretation of public interest by the political system, which is passed to the regulators, is generally arrived at without any recourse to ethical consideration or judgement. Nonetheless, in a liberal democratic state, what generally emerges is a set of principles which are designed to protect particular values assumed by successive governments to be in the public interest.[1]

In Britain, for example, the Broadcasting Act 1990 protects the public from programming which is likely to cause harm, is biased or is acting against the public interest, by ensuring that, 'nothing is included in its programmes which offends against good taste or decency or is likely to encourage or incite to crime or lead to disorder or to be offensive to public feeling' (Broadcasting Act, 1990:6(1)6)[2] and 'that any news given (in whatever form) in its programmes is presented with due accuracy and impartiality' (para. 6(1)6). It is also expected 'that due responsibility is exercised with respect to the content of any of its programmes which are religious programmes' (para. 6(1)6). News output must be 'broadcast ... at intervals throughout the period for which the service is provided, and in particular (except in the case of a national Channel 3 licence) at peak viewing times' (para. 31(1)31). News must also be 'of high quality dealing with national and international matters' (para. 31(1)31).

The Broadcasting Act also charges the ITC with the role of awarding licences subject to a series of guidelines. These are designed to: control the quality and diversity of output; protect children; control advertising; protect minority programming; and more specifically, ensure that television news is

---

[1] See Downs's (1962) description of the pragmatic approach to public interest and Held's (1970) Common Interest Theory.
[2] Exactly the same wording is used in the BBC's Annex to the Licence.

shown live at certain times of the day, is of high quality, contains both national and international news stories, and is impartial and accurate. The Channel 3, 4 and 5 news provider (currently ITN) is bound by guidelines which are clearly designed around the belief that television news has a valuable and important contribution to make to the British public.

The BBC is established by a Royal Charter and Agreement between the BBC and a government. Its charter was renewed for ten years from 1 January 1997, with the licence fee retained as the main source of finance for its public services, originally until the year 2001 (now 2006) when it will be reviewed. The Major government's notion of the nature of public interest and the role of a public service broadcaster was clearly articulated in the White Paper *The Future of the BBC* (Report of the Secretary of State for National Heritage, 1994), and centred upon issues such as diversity and quality of programming. The Major government stated that the BBC should continue to be Britain's main public service broadcaster and that the role of the Board of Governors 'is to look after the public's interest in the BBC' (p. 3). As a public service broadcaster, the BBC must ensure that it reflects the needs and interests of the public, giving priority to the interests of the audiences and providing programmes for minority and specialist as well as majority audiences. The BBC must also seek to 'reflect ... the national identity of the United Kingdom. The BBC should broadcast events of national importance ... enriching the cultural heritage of the United Kingdom throughout support for the arts. The BBC should remain a major cultural patron of music, drama and the visual arts ... nurtur[ing] creative talent' (p. 6).

The high-quality programming which the BBC must provide is linked to a more culturally elite definition of the term 'quality' than is required for Channels 3, 4, and 5 by the Broadcasting Act 1990. Indeed the BBC itself focuses on 'developing services of distinction and quality, rather than on attracting a large audience for its own sake' (BBC, 1993b:84).

A major problem which has emerged for the BBC is how it can reconcile charging a licence fee for services with the probable long-term decline in its audience ratings. It was given a clear directive by the Major government to promote the commercial side of its operation.[3] However, the contradictory and potentially damaging nature of such practice has been criticised in the press. The *Observer* claimed that viewers do not pay a licence fee in order to improve Britain's export performance, but that the fee is there to ensure that the BBC can reach those places commercial broadcasters ignore (14 January 1996).

---

[3] The BBC is not alone in this practice. S4C in Wales has taken advantage of the freedom given to the independent sector in the Broadcasting Act 1996 to enhance its commercial ventures. Like the BBC, it has sought to differentiate between its commercial ventures and its public service remit. It established a self-contained unit as a wholly owned subsidiary company of S4C in order to keep its public service money (annual budget from the Treasury) separate from its commercial ventures. In 1997 S4C was able to transfer almost six million pounds from its general fund to its public service fund.

The interpretation of public interest by successive governments in relation to the BBC and ITV systems illustrates the different type of focus the concept can acquire in a public service context and in a commercial context which also has some public service broadcasting values. The BBC faces great difficulties and challenges in trying to prepare itself for the possibility of an eventual loss of some of its licence fee income, and also has to cope with the commercial legacy encouraged by the Thatcher and Major governments. Nonetheless the Major government perceived and the Blair government still perceives the BBC to have a different role from the ITV companies. It follows that the role of the news output of the BBC and ITN must also be considered in relation to those identified differences in the interpretation of the public interest, formulated by different British governments and put into practice by the regulators.

This interpretation is subjective and flexible and can vary over time. And yet the legislative and regulatory frameworks which embody public interest values do have a positive role to play in establishing a normative framework within which British television news can be examined and analysed (it is less easy to establish public interest criteria in relation to the rest of the EU). This framework, which incorporates the current view of the public interest, serves to highlight how British television news is replete with a complex mixture of values constituted from vague and constantly changing notions of public service broadcasting. These values are being consistently challenged by a new, market-driven philosophy.

The idea of serving the public and the public interest was grounded in the initial BBC charter (and later in the Television Act 1954), and has been consistently evoked as a requirement of broadcasting in a series of government reviews and reports dating from 1926 to the 1990s. In 1926 a public inquiry was conducted. The Crawford Committee examined the status of the BBC as a consortium of wireless manufacturers. It was recommended that the private company be replaced by a public corporation which would act as trustee of the national interest (reported in *Report of the Broadcasting Committee*, 1926). The values embodied in the birth of the BBC stemmed from concern about the American experience, where free enterprise had resulted in unregulated chaos and poor quality programming.

Concerns about the unregulated chaos in America were reported to the Crawford Committee and were probably instrumental in helping to create a climate of opinion which accepted the idea of a public corporate monopoly. The concern with the potential bureaucracy of state ownership was frequently espoused by Reith (McIntyre, 1993) and broadcasting was expected to be conducted in the public interest, an interest not regarded in law or in practice as synonymous with government or state. However, such a clear distinction was blurred during the General Strike of 1926, when Reith and the BBC supported the government (Scannell and Cardiff, 1991). In practice the public duties of the BBC were not really made clear and there was no prescription as to what it was acceptable to broadcast, as the matters of content and social purpose were originally of secondary importance. The requirement for quality and objectivity was prescribed by the Crawford Committee, allowing for a small amount of controversial material to be broadcast as long as it was of high quality and fair (*Report of the Broadcasting Committee*, 1926).

As the BBC developed, the power of the new broadcast media to serve the national interest became inextricably intertwined with the notion of serving the public interest and 'the influence of broadcasting upon the mind and speech of the nation [which made it an] urgent necessity in the national interest that the broadcasting service should at all times be conducted in the best possible manner and to the best possible advantage of the people' (*Report of the Broadcasting Committe*, 1936:7). The 1962 Pilkington Committee, which considered the mixed economy of broadcasting, developed further the view of broadcasting as having a social purpose and suggested that similar principles should govern both public and private broadcasting. It argued that those principles should be ratified in the commercial sector by the Independent Television Authority (*Report of the Broadcasting Committee*, 1962). Broadcasting in Britain, whether a monopoly or duopoly service, depended upon an assumption of broadcasting as a public good. The Independent Broadcasting Authority continued this trend. 'The Authority's first duty is to the public ... we must answer to the public for the programmes of ITV ... [i]f they are unfair, if they are of poor quality, if they are shocking'(IBA, 1974:5).

The Crawford and Pilkington Committees shared a view that public service broadcasting was a way of making society better. The 1977 Annan Report was qualitatively different and was primarily about service delivery. Curran (1998:182) argues that public service broadcasting following the Annan Report was not so much about quality as diversity, 'catering for both cultural mountaineers and couch potatoes'. Paradoxically, the Annan Report did this by being both more culturally elitist and relativistic than its predecessors. As soon as programme quality was relativised, and there ceased to be a universal standard of quality (namely a culturally elite understanding of quality), the way was opened up to allow viewers and listeners to be the best judge of their own and the public's interest. Whilst this was liberating and freed the masses from the imposition of paternalistic and elite versions of quality, it also had the effect of redefining standards of excellence in relation to popularity, with successful programming more often defined in terms of high ratings. I will elaborate on the problems relating to different types of information later in this chapter.

The interventions of the Conservative Thatcher and Major governments into broadcasting in the 1980s and 1990s, the new rhetoric of consumer sovereignty, and the exaltation of the values of individual choice introduced the belief that the public interest and quality in broadcasting were better served by commercial competition than by regulation. The meaning of public interest articulated by the Peacock Committee (*Report of the Committee on the Financing of the BBC*, 1986), the White Paper (Report of the Secretary of State for National Heritage, 1994) and the Broadcasting Act 1990 was more closely linked to concepts such as choice, popularity and diversity than in previous reports. The word 'quality' ceased to have an objective basis in broadcasting and was replaced by planned diversity, elevating service delivery to the consumer in importance.

The BBC was charged by the government in 1994 with the onerous task of exploiting its commercial interests whilst simultaneously protecting its original values, which are enshrined in the principle of serving the public and therefore the public interest. The White Paper stated that the BBC should 'do more to exploit its assets, and to generate income from its programmes ... The Government welcomes the BBC's plans for joint ventures with commercial companies around the world' (Report of the Secretary of State for National Heritage, 1994:2). But the White Paper was at pains to stress that all the BBC's commercial activities should be carried out in ways which were consistent with its public service objectives.

Such an evolution in the ethos and rationale of the broadcasting institutions exacerbates the tensions, uncertainties and confrontations occurring in the broadcasting domain around such issues as what constitutes the public interest in relation to the BBC and in relation to the commercial broadcasting system. However, working definitions of the concept are unlikely to be analysed in any more depth by legislators and regulators in the future, and will continue to be an expedient reflection of the politico-economic realm within which the broadcasting industries are operating. This means that the analysis of the value of television news as a dimension of the public sphere or public spheres will raise concerns which relate to the relationship between television news and democratic processes. The evolution of the changing understanding of public interest over the years is indicative of the changing values relating to broadcasting. It is striking that similar requirements have been a continual feature of both the commercial and the public broadcasting system in Britain and that those requirements have been consistently expressed by the legislators using language relating to serving the public, meeting social purpose, having a public purpose and, in the case of the BBC in particular, serving the nation. We have also witnessed an evolution in some broadcasting values towards the belief that public interest in broadcasting can be better served by commercial competition than by regulation. Thus we saw terms such as choice, popularity and diversity (where diversity is about choice and primarily driven by market forces) introduced into broadcasting legislation and regulatory guidelines in the 1980s and 1990s. These changes have implications for the relationship between the broadcasting organisations' output and their ability to contribute to the public sphere and democratic process.

Television news and democracy

Democracy has been defined as 'a form of public decision-making conducted in public' (Keane, 1991:23). And yet several writers have expressed concern about the tendency towards unaccountable decision-making, and the growing inaccessibility of many areas of public life (Kingdom, 1991; Keane, 1991; Ranson, 1992; Heller and Edwards, 1992; Marsh and Rhodes, 1992; Weir and Hall, 1994; Hogwood, 1995; Marr, 1995). Citizen involvement in single issue politics is increasing (Negrine, 1996), possibly in direct relationship to a feeling of powerlessness in the complex national and supra-national political arena. This activity provides a more immediate and more accessible version of political participation, whilst masking the lack of access to the wider political arena. It has been argued that this inaccessibility of public information is characterised by: the increasing influence of supra-national organisations; the democratic deficit inherent in the European Parliamentary institutions and at the national and sub-national level; the growth in quangos; the privatisation of public companies; and the reform of local government (Marr, 1995). All of these have resulted in 'a new era of political censorship in which key parts of life are structured by unaccountable political institutions' (Keane, 1991:16).

In such an environment, where the tendency is clearly towards increased secrecy and concealment, it is especially important that television news programmes attempt to provide the type of information which enables the public to make critical decisions and assessments of many aspects of public life. This can only be achieved by overcoming the tensions which exist, on the one hand, between the state's persistent tendency to secretiveness and its intermittent interest in direct censorship, and, on the other hand, the simultaneous need to master information overload (Webster, 1995), which is a symptom of late twentieth- and early twenty-first-century society. Only by acting as both rigorous investigator and fastidious interpreter can contemporary journalism hope to overcome the increasing constraints within which it operates. Only thus can the informational content of television news be said to be a truly valuable asset to the public sphere or public spheres. Developments such as multi-skilling, job compression and desk-editing, as well as the impact of competition between news providers, may affect news content and information. The consequences of these developments are as yet unknown. Although the mechanical tasks of journalism will undoubtedly be made easier, such developments may not improve the quality of journalism in terms of information value. As MacGregor (1997) identifies, the enabling presence of technology needs to be supplemented by improved education and training for journalists, a supportive environment which helps journalists to gain a variety of useful experiences beyond those which are simply skills-oriented, and a greater commitment to journalistic content itself and to viewers, rather than an obsession with keeping costs down and ratings up.

However, the main source of revenue for terrestrial independent television is advertising. As advertisers are prepared to pay more money to programmes which are more popular, pressure is placed on commercial television to increase audience ratings. ITN news is not immune from this pressure. Each day, the previous day's ratings for all their news programmes are posted on the newsroom walls, for contemplation. *News at Ten* was specifically designed to retain the audience after the commercial break, and news stories were deliberately advertised before the break as teasers to ensure that audiences returned. Consequently ITN has been accused of over-indulging in gratuitous spectacles, and of relying too much on film and format, such as graphics and presentation tricks, at the expense of informational content (Barnett and Gaber, 1993; *Independent on Sunday*, 22 May 1994; *The Times*, 8 June 1994).

Although there is undoubtedly a wide range of terrestrial television news programming available in the 1990s and early 2000s, the existence of more news programming does not necessarily result in a better-informed citizenry, and may even exacerbate existing social inequality, due to television news's relationship to corporate needs rather than those of the audience. My own examination of British broadcast news shows that there are identifiable differences between the informational value and production of the different news programmes, resulting from the increased diversification of the television news genre (i.e. increased branding of the news product). The flexibility of the television news genre has resulted in differences in *style* and in some cases in *content* of television news across the different news programmes. This also shows how increasing concentration on entertainment techniques and gimmicky format devices to increase audience ratings is jeopardising the breadth of information produced by some television news programmes.

There is still a tendency for some British terrestrial broadcasters to reject some of the more damaging aspects of market-driven journalism. For example, the BBC's corporate ethos is centred on a definition of quality which ensures that a diverse range of issues and countries is still routinely covered. This ethos was maintained throughout the 1990s. The director-general's challenge to this culture in September 1997 by the introduction of five super-editors to oversee clusters of news programmes was resisted. Nonetheless, the planned adjustments to the BBC's mainstream programmes may be a problem (see Chapter 1). ITN news redeems itself with an excellent news programme, *Channel 4 News*, shown on weekdays at 7 o'clock, illustrating clearly that news of a high standard can be produced to a commercial remit, and even though the audience figures are low. Indeed, *Channel 4 News* shows that there are other ways of serving the public interest. Other commercial news providers at ITN's Channel 3 also claim that they are serving the public interest by providing a popular and accessible range of news programmes. The link to mass popularity is achieved via a different interpretation of the public interest idea from either that exercised at *Channel 4 News* or that of the majority of BBC staff. ITN's recent interest in competing in the twenty-four-hour news market, through its bid for EuroNews, may eventually further affect its conception of the public interest. In comparison to the other organisations competing in this market (Cable News Network (CNN), BSkyB, CNBC, Bloomberg and Reuters) ITN is a small player which may run into financial difficulty. This could have serious consequences for its terrestrial television news output.

Criticism of the more negative tendencies of commercialisation is reinforced by the knowledge that it is still possible for a commercial news provider to produce a news programme which is more akin to the traditional BBC public service broadcast news programmes. For example, *Channel 4 News* programmes have played an important role in exposing injustices and inequalities, as when one of their reporters went under cover in China in the mid-1990s to show the British public how deliberate neglect of some female babies led to their death. The domestic revelations are often more circumspect, but nonetheless commercial television news has participated in the exposure of government sleaze and scandal, corruption in government, unacceptably high salaries paid to the chairs of the privatised utilities, the growing power and unaccountability of the quangos and so on. Nevertheless, academics, sectional interests and minority groups have cause to criticise the selective content and informational weakness of all television news and the obvious problems inherent in the concept of objectivity, since both commercial and BBC television news journalists do not always provide useful information to the public (see Chapter 6).

Whether the more human interest-type stories, such as long-running royal family sagas, are serving the public interest is more debatable, even amongst journalists themselves. Journalists working at ITN's Channel 3 would view many of the general everyday activities of Fergie or the late Princess Diana as newsworthy, whereas those working for *Channel 4 News* and on some programmes at the BBC would be much less likely to broadcast general royalty stories, unless they had constitutional implications. Despite the increasing tendency towards sensationalist and human interest reporting, television news journalists have not yet resorted to making up stories, an activity which seems to be seen as an acceptable practice in some sections of the British tabloid press (Chippendale and Horrie, 1990), or to introducing 'meaningless trivial "Hey Dorris!" factoids as a way of disguising lack of indepth coverage' (p. 150).

On a more positive note, popularisation of information programmes generally can be credited with some success in the increasing democratisation of the public sphere. For example, political debates conducted in a television studio do make political activity more open; hitherto it would have been hidden from view. Similarly, broadcasting has cultivated a type of style of discussing politics which makes it more accessible to the public than the debates conducted at Westminster (Sparks, 1991). Sparks also argues that a more aggressive style of interviewing politicians is more conducive to the democratisation of the public sphere. The director-general of the BBC, John Birt, however, criticised BBC presenters like Jeremy Paxman and John Humphreys for this activity, as unnecessary and not conducive to good political journalism (*The Times*, 4 February 1995; *Media Guardian*, 17 July 1995).

The basic human and democratic rights of freedom of expression and freedom of opinion are curtailed by the current (one-way broadcast) structure of the television medium itself. Because the notion of public interest is largely determined by the government and the regulators, it is questionable whether television news produced in the public interest can really provide the type of information which empowers the citizen, enhancing his or her civil, political and social rights. The inevitable acknowledgement by the Annan Report that a consensus no longer existed about what constituted programme quality initiated a different system of valuation of broadcasting products, based on consumer choice. In practice this has led to increased popularisation of news programmes and a weakening of consensus on public service broadcasting values. Given these constraints, the value of television news, as one dimension of the public sphere, obviously remains limited. In principle the concept of democracy carries with it a basic right of freedom of information, and this can provide a moral and legal basis for journalism and therefore for television news (Dahlgren, 1995). In practice this needs to be institutionalised through a Bill of Rights and a Freedom of Information Act, and is institutionalised in this way in most Western societies. Unfortunately at the moment in Britain we do not have either, although the current Blair government says it is committed to addressing these issues.

Clearly there are some problems inherent in the role of the television news medium in serving the public interest in a democracy. The limitations of the public interest as developed through the regulatory system, which underpins journalistic values of objectivity and newsworthiness, has been contrasted with a normative assessment of what role the television news media should play in enlightening and empowering a citizen to act morally and knowingly for the public good. Such limitations should not be understood to be occurring in a temporal vacuum but must be considered in the context of recent social change.

The 1980s and 1990s were characterised by a new relationship between government and the state. The nature and role of the state, a wide collection of institutions over which government has control (Kingdom, 1991), was radically changed by the Thatcher and Major Conservative governments. These changes were made intellectually coherent by New Right theorists. Political credibility for these changes was gained from the alleged failure of the interventionist policies of the governments of the 1960s and 1970s (Farnham and Horton, 1993). Thatcher used radical measures on most policy fronts to attack post-war social democracy, corporatism and consensus politics. The aim was to reduce the public sector by spending less on the welfare state, abandoning Keynesianism and releasing market forces. A new politico-economic philosophy dominated the public sector, centred upon the belief that consumer demand would drive competitive market forces and ensure that consumers would get what they wanted (Gunter, 1993). Undoubtedly free-market philosophy has been a theme of British television broadcasting since the creation of the ITV system in the 1950s. In the past the balance of state policy was weighted against it through regulation of the ITV system and support for the BBC. In the 1980s and 1990s this balance was changed and is now weighted in favour of the application of a free-market philosophy to the whole broadcasting industry. Such a change has initiated broad debate about the role of public service broadcasting in Britain and has threatened its future security (Barnett and Curry, 1994). Public service broadcasting was seen by the Right as a producer-dominated institution that presented vested interests as the public interest. Concentration on the individual and on individual consumer choice and sovereignty as the priorities of public life has infiltrated, and until recently influenced, governmental and popular conceptions of citizenship and the public interest. In practice commodification can result in the individual believing he or she is the sovereign consumer, masking the effect of a commercial and economic hegemony (Stevenson, 1995).

It is commonly argued that Thatcherism as a political ideology for governing a nation state was flawed and contradictory (Held, 1989). It professed to be reducing the size of the state and the role of the government whilst simultaneously becoming increasingly interventionist and centralist in a wide variety of state activities. In the 1980s, the broadcasting industry felt the effects of the government's contradictory ideology. In the new era of the free market, the BBC was threatened both by a hostile interventionist government and by new commercial competitors. It was forced to respond to such pressures, and to change its ethos and culture by introducing an uneasy mix of Birtian reforms, which included what MacGregor (1997:214) has referred to as the 'shotgun wedding' of current affairs and news (both requiring different skills) and the introduction of the internal market and new managerial practices in order to guarantee the renewal of its charter and licence fee (Barnett and Curry, 1994; Horrie and Clarke, 1994). The replacement of BBC chairman, Marmaduke Hussey with Sir Christopher Bland from London Weekend Television (LWT) ensured continuity of the practices introduced by Director-General John Birt. Birt and Bland were old friends, which was predicted to be damaging to the BBC and likely to perpetuate the Birtist regime (Brookes, 1996).

Political changes to broadcasting were formalised by the establishment of new legislative frameworks. The government White Paper of 1988 was recognised as instituting an enormous shake-up in television which would have important repercussions (*Observer*, 13 November 1988). The Broadcasting Act 1990 which followed created an auction for ITV licences, which were only protected from the rigours of pure market forces by the last-minute addition of a quality threshold. Although the ITV system was, and is, a commercial system, it was required from its birth to operate within some public service rules. The principles of geographic universality, catering for all tastes and interests and producing high-quality programmes, in theory, are still key ITC requirements of the ITV licensees. The ITC must ensure that licensees provide a wide range of services throughout the UK and that the services are of high quality, are not offensive to public feeling, and appeal to a variety of tastes and interests (ITC, 1994). These principles are being compromised by the mergers and take-overs of ITV companies, the acquiescence to the pressure to move *News at Ten* to provide more time to show films, and the chase for ratings, which is marginalising minority interest programming and is influencing television news programme content, quality of news information and news format structures. The ITC, as regulator, will have an increasingly difficult task in defining programme quality and standards within the strong commercial environment which now exists in the ITV system.

Intervention by the Conservative governments 1979–97 was aimed at increasing competition, encouraging the development of new technologies and new services, and providing the consumers with more choice and diversity. In practice it has served to challenge the future role of the BBC as a public service broadcaster, as well as to elicit a growth in concern about the implications for the standards and quality of the services provided by both the BBC and its commercial competitors. With or without Conservative government policy, the BBC would have been challenged by new technological developments and economic pressures. Even with a strong political commitment to public service broadcasting, it is likely that public broadcasters were bound to face major funding constraints as a result of competition (Foster, 1992). The lack of support for public service broadcasting by the recent Conservative governments has simply served to exacerbate this crisis.

This market-driven broadcasting philosophy has resulted in a diversification of the British television news product. The television news genre has become increasingly flexible and dynamic in response to the need to produce a wider market choice and range of programmes, in the context of a more competitive broadcasting environment. The idea of increased choice and diversity of service has been one of the most beguiling, as it presents free-market commercial broadcasting as able to respond directly to the wants of the public. A major concern is that increased competition from new, non-terrestrial services and from digital broadcasting multiplexes will reduce audiences and advertising revenue for the terrestrial commercial broadcasters, and also reduce audiences for BBC television. While increasing quantity of programming, this may lead to a lowering of its informational quality.

To date there is no operational framework which a broadcast regulator can use to monitor programme or information quality effectively (McQuail, 1992; Gunter, 1993), despite several attempts to provide a consensus view which would clearly define quality television (Brunsdon, 1990; Broadcasting

Research Unit, 1989). In practice, broadcasting quality has been linked to a culturally elitist view of programme quality. Some commentators (e.g. Mulgan, 1990) have recognised that such a definition may not be applicable in the 1990s and early 2000s, as quality is not the exclusive property of highbrow programming, but can be found in other genres such as soap operas (Gunter, 1993).

This evolution of the concept of quality in television programming is important. These developments lead us to ask what constitutes information quality and whether we measure the quality of informational programming via audience appreciation, or via some more objective and scientific standard. If we wish to apply the latter, we invite the question of what measures can be used and whether they are sufficient to determine whether one news programme is providing good-quality information whilst another is not. Informational quality is related to some extent to the format structures of programmes and the features which reduce the utility of the information provided. Of relevance are the increasing proliferation of magazine-type news programmes; the use of format devices to increase entertainment value, such as the over-use of graphics and other gimmicks and the increase in the use of live two-ways (Channel 4, 1994); the shortening of television news stories and sound-bites (Barnett and Gaber, 1993); and the extent to which news programmes run at faster and faster tempos. These are just a few developments which have been heavily criticised in recent times for reducing programme quality. Developments like these reduce the amount of information transmitted and make it more difficult for the audience to absorb and understand the information they are receiving (Gunter, 1987; Davis, 1990; Dahlgren, 1995). Also related to information quality is the degree to which a diverse range of issues and voices is represented and has access to television news programmes. The shortfalls in the information value of television news may simulate democratic debate while actually disempowering and disenfranchising the viewer.

Whilst the 1980s and 1990s saw an unprecedented growth in the power and diversity of media technology, in practice greater access to information does not necessarily correlate with a more knowledgeable and informed public, and may even have the negative effect of obscuring information by exceeding the interpretative ability of the viewer. As Baudrillard (1983) argues, although there is more information, there is less and less meaning. McLuhan (1964) began the concern for the cultural consequences of new communication technologies with his pioneering analysis of the role of television as a medium. The negative impact of the modern media in terms of the information overload they can produce was first noted in studies which Daniel Bell published throughout the 1960s, culminating in *The Coming of Post-Industrial Society* in 1973. These developments were further analysed by popular authors such as Alvin Toffler in *Future Shock* in 1970 and *The Third Wave* in 1980, and in arguments about the social effects of the new media, which have developed alongside technological innovations (Neuman, 1991; Ferguson, 1990).

A clear concern for the relationship of television news to democratic process is that, as the producers of raw material for international news and the owners of regional and global television are becoming increasingly concentrated, the content of international television news in particular is becoming ever-more similar. Indeed television news organisations compete with each other but are all dependent on the same news agencies. Reuters Television World News Service (WNS) and Press Association TV (PATV) dominate the television news agency market and are in heavy competition with each other. Increasingly television companies are refusing to take feeds from both agencies, so the market is being divided in two. Also, television companies are demanding more and more that they should be allowed to purchase the stories they want to run instead of the full package of ten or so stories sent in a routine feed. This may encourage differentiation of international news between different television companies. Contrary to popular myth these agencies do cover and offer political, economic and human interest news about third world countries, but claim there is no market for them in the Western world, and generally sell them back only to the third world countries. Consequently, Western viewers still tend to see the third world news solely in relation to famine, war and disasters.

As Western democracies which have long existed in an international political and cultural order become increasingly interdependent, television services have begun to play a role in international politics. Gurevitch (1991:187) uses the *Washington Post*'s term 'telediplomacy' to refer to this. Although the power of news agencies can be overstated, global information flows have played a major role in events such as the 1989 revolutions in Eastern and Central Europe (see Kent, 1996; MacGregor, 1997), as citizens watching events on television in other countries, such as Romania, reacted by taking to the streets. Given the increasingly important role television news is playing in our awareness of global events, it is of concern that financial commitment to overseas news stories is having to be reduced in most news organisations.

At ITN some international bureaux have had to be closed, and resources have been rationalised due to financial difficulties in the early 1990s. Its move to a purpose-built headquarters at Grays Inn Road proved problematic when ITN found it could not immediately find tenants to help to pay the high costs of the building. ITN also allied itself with the unsuccessful bidders for the new Teletext and breakfast TV licences in 1991. Coverage of major world events such as the Gulf War and the capsizing of the car ferry at Zeebrugge cost it a great deal of money; the banks refused to lend the company money before the ITC had selected ITN as the sole news provider in 1993; and the ITV companies were reluctant to pour more money into a company which they would no longer be allowed to own fully. ITN finally had to make four hundred staff redundant in 1991–2, in an effort to claw back a deficit of ten million pounds. The company also had to renegotiate another five-year contract with the ITV companies to supply news at a cheaper rate, make cuts to its number of international bureaux and aim to become profit-making by 1993 (ITC Press Releases, 1993).

On 31 December 1992, ITN was taken over by a consortium comprising Carlton Communications, LWT Holdings, Reuters and Central Independent Television, later joined by Granada Group, Anglia Television and Scottish Television, and a new contract with the ITV companies was agreed. Each company owned 18 per cent of the shares, except for Anglia and Scottish Television, which owned 5 per cent each. In 1995, ITN made a profit of fifteen million pounds for its shareholders. Mergers and take-overs between Carlton and Central Television and between Granada and LWT resulted in shareholders Carlton and Granada owning 36 per cent of ITN each, meaning that they profited substantially from ITN. Under the terms of the Broadcasting Act 1990, no single shareholder was allowed to have more than a 20 per cent share in ITN beyond the end of 1994. ITN has continued to come under pressure from those ITV companies which are no longer shareholders but which have to pay a high price for the ITN product. Although the ITC favourably reviewed ITN in December 1995, the company was forced by the ITV companies to reduce its charges to them for its news product. The new contract between the ITV companies and ITN ensured that ITV would pay five million pounds less for news in 1998 and up to seventeen million pounds less each year 1999–2000 inclusive, under a five-year contract from 1 January 1998 (Deans and Armstrong, 1996). Further reductions in ITN income are likely to affect its news production quality, as quite serious job cuts and restructuring are likely. ITN has pledged to reduce profits first and foremost rather than investment in the news, but it is unlikely that the news process will remain unscathed, particularly as it had already been thoroughly streamlined and rationalised in the early 1990s. The BBC has made similar adjustments by redesigning and rationalising the BBC World Service. This activity is contradictory when we consider the increasingly important role international news has as a result of transnational shifts, with international affairs becoming more important to the nation.

At the same time the sense of nation has become less intelligible. Due to the process of globalisation the nation appears to be less self-sufficient and therefore is more dependent in international terms (Leca, 1992). It therefore becomes more difficult for the state to explain its political, economic and social position convincingly unless it can use the international context as its referent. Rationalisation and reduced commitment to international news, as in the proposals for BBC's *Six O'Clock News*, represent a blinkered and unreflective approach to television news selection and newsworthiness, in the context of news production in the 1990s and early 2000s.

The pressures which have been inflicted upon broadcasting institutions have had profound implications for the concepts of public interest in relation to television news, and of the relationship of television news to democratic processes. This is exacerbated as the rationale and ethos of public service broadcasting in Britain are increasingly weakened, as both the BBC and ITV systems drift away from their original and founding remit. The market-driven philosophy of the recent Conservative governments encouraged a diversification of broadcast products, in the name of consumer choice. This development coincides with, and complements, the emergence of demassified, consumerist and post-Fordist society in the late 1980s and 1990s (Hall and Jacques, 1990; Harvey, 1990). The decline of mass society and the emergence of consumerist and post-Fordist society are associated with changes in work practices, the decline of traditional political parties, the waning of national traditions, the changing structure of the family, and changes in the technology of the media (Stevenson, 1995). Only major news stories or media events tend to bring the nation back together again as a unitary public with a common public interest (Dayan and Katz, 1992). These developments raise questions about the value of terrestrial television news in a democracy. Katz (1996) argues that the decline of mass television viewing is actually weakening the foundations of liberal democracy in Israel. People are no longer connected to each other through the mass media, which have, until recently, acted as a kind of central meeting ground and shared public sphere. Instead the public is being dispersed by the growth of a multitude of channels. Katz argues that public service broadcasting is being damaged through a reduction in civic programming in favour of programmes aimed at increasing ratings, and that the separation between television systems and nation states is weakening national identity. Although Curran (1998) argues that Katz's assumptions are not borne out by the experience in Britain, he agrees that Katz's reading could be true in the future if public service broadcasting continues to be placed under combined commercial, political and ideological assault.

And yet, given that the majority of the public perceive television news as their primary source of information about the world (Gunter and Winstone, 1993), there is actually little motivation for either the public themselves, the journalists, the regulators or the government to lobby for a truly democratic forum for public debate and contribution, within the context of British broadcast news programming. This lack of motivation leads us to consider more carefully what the role of terrestrial television news should be in a democracy and what the future forms of audiovisual information should be.

Television news and audiovisual information should play an important part in enabling the public to participate and judge. Curran (1998) suggests that public service broadcasting needs to be protected via increasing distance between the BBC and ministers; that the licence fee should rise, to ensure financial independence; and that the charter should not need renewing, as the lead-up to the renewal makes the BBC more vulnerable. Curran goes on to argue that the advent of digitalisation needs to be explored to extend the repertoire of public service broadcasting in the future. Access and representation to and by the broadcast media need to be improved. Social access to the television media needs to be upgraded via serious, as opposed to trivial, chat-show-type, audience participation. Representational diversity needs to be widened and protected via a pluralism requirement.

Television journalistic practice charges journalists with the role of working with public concern, by analysing and interpreting the data which exists 'out there' on behalf of the public. Institutions such as academia in general and journalism are an important part of the public sphere and have a role to play in interpreting and presenting information to the public. A critical difference is the time-scale to which such agencies work. Journalism has to work to a short time-scale and is therefore restricted in the depth of analysis, in the rigour of research methodology, and by the format constraints of the programme structure. The very nature of television journalism is thus multiply constrained and should be perceived as only a restricted source of selective information. Whilst it has a useful role to play in society as an important and valuable provider of some types of information about the world, it must be recognised for what it is. What is disturbing for the relationship between the terrestrial television news medium and democratic processes is the trend towards further restriction of the informational potential, and the increasing relativisation of the concept of quality of television news through the growth in the number of news programmes and the increased commercialisation of broadcasting institutions. Despite the potential of digitalisation, the development of new forms of audiovisual information appears to be set to continue the worst practices of existing popular forms of television news and information, thus further damaging its already flawed relationship to the public sphere and its ability to serve the public interest.

3

BBC and ITN: a changing world

Much of what occurs today in television newsrooms is grounded in their history, their public service broadcasting values and the complex, multi-causal origins of the television news organisations. A good deal has been written about the origins and structures of both the BBC and the ITV systems and on public service broadcasting. It is not necessary simply to reiterate historical analyses here (though see, for example, Briggs, 1961, Burns, 1969, 1972, 1977; Schlesinger, 1987; Seymour-Ure, 1991; Cox, 1995; McNair, 1994).

One of the first challenges to the public service broadcasting duopoly occurred when Rupert Murdoch's Sky Channel, the first satellite television programme channel in Britain, began transmission in 1984. It became clear that regulation of a huge number of news television channels, which were transmitted from Luxembourg, would not be easy. Furthermore, the increasing proliferation of cable and satellite channels has resulted in their being exempt from some of the regulatory programme requirements which the terrestrial companies have to meet. Cable and satellite only have to adhere to consumer protection requirements such as taste and decency and rules on due impartiality. This inaugurated the debate about the future of quality[1] television in Britain.

Of key significance in the 1990s are the tensions which exist between commercial pressures, the values located in the ideal of public service broadcasting, and the structural pressures inherent in the BBC and ITN. Clearly, news by its nature is a constantly changing form and is shaped and defined by the issues and events it represents. It is the changes in the broadcasting environment and the effects that these have on the production context

---

[1] The notion of quality is absent from cable licence requirements, and notably the Broadcasting Act 1996 contains no quality requirement in respect of the new terrestrial multiplex agreements (except for the existing terrestrial channels, which must be simulcast by the BBC and ITV companies).

within which journalists work with which this chapter is concerned. This is not to imply that news itself is a fixed, constant form while the political, economic, organisational and technological factors affecting it can change. The intention of this chapter, however, is to consider some of the external forces which have affected the newsroom cultures at the BBC and ITN.

The BBC

Many of the BBC's current troubles began in 1984 with its announcement that it wished to see an increase in the television licence fee. This poorly timed announcement resulted in the BBC being granted a compromise figure but also drew attention to the issue of its funding. A Committee of Inquiry into BBC finances, led by Professor Alan Peacock, was set up. The intention of Margaret Thatcher, prime minister at the time, was to introduce advertising to the BBC. But the 1986 Peacock Report rejected the replacement of the licence fee with advertising. In 1988, however, the licence fee was linked directly to the retail price index (RPI), which had the effect of reducing the BBC's real income. Since then, the future viability of the licence fee has been a consistent source of debate in the multi-channel age. There has been an eight-fold increase in the supply of news available to consumers with over two hundred and forty hours a week now available to some.[2]

In January 1987, Thatcher's appointee Marmaduke Hussey (chairman of the BBC) dismissed Alisdair Milne from his post as director-general after a series of well-publicised clashes between the Thatcher government and the BBC. Milne was subsequently replaced by Michael Checkland. The early replacement of Checkland with John Birt (causing a furore in the BBC, especially as public service broadcasting gurus such as John Tusa were not even approached by Hussey) in 1992 heralded a new era at the BBC. Birt and Hussey brought in a management team from the private sector and began to reduce staff numbers and to import private sector values into the system (O'Malley, 1994).

In 1992 the Major government published a consultation document in response to the conflicting attitudes and political debate which had emerged on the future of the BBC. The debate centred on the issue of whether the BBC should continue to be funded from the licence fee or should become a commercial body with a reduced public role. In response to the Major government's scrutiny, John Birt set about reforming the BBC's culture and aimed to persuade the government that the BBC's charter should be renewed in 1996, and that the licence fee should remain the main form of funding. Birt and Hussey's remodelling of the BBC was centred upon ensuring that the Conservative government would recognise that the BBC was becoming an institution which it could support. What this meant in practice, of course,

[2] URL <*http://www.bbc.co.uk/info/news/newsfuture/res_page4.shtml*> accessed 10 October 1998.

was that Birt would push the BBC as far into commercialism as it could go as a public service broadcaster, in order to reconcile its past inflexibility and inefficiency (real or otherwise) with the commercial vision of some of the members of the Conservative government. 'The BBC began a review of the entire range of BBC activities, "thinking the unthinkable", so that the Corporation would be ready for any questions the Government might throw at it' (Horrie and Clarke, 1994:203).

The transformation of the BBC was particularly symbolised by John Birt's introduction of Americanised management-speak, the internal market rationale of producer choice, and major internal reorganisation. In the period 1991–4, well documented by the press and by The BBC Charter Review Series (Barnett, 1993; Harvey and Robins, 1993; Mulgan and Paterson, 1993; Shaw, 1993; Stevenson, 1993, 1994), Birt tried to reconcile the need for diversity and quality of programming with efficiency and effectiveness. This was followed by restructuring and a commitment to digitalisation and competition in the new media market place. Both strategies of digitalisation and competition caused problems. BBC television news producers were due to move into a purpose-built digital newsroom in November 1998, although the BBC would not be operating a fully digital newsroom until 1999. The attempt to reconcile a number of contradictory forces and to make a lot of changes very quickly created difficulties for the BBC, culminating in a spate of technological problems in 1998 caused by a new newsroom computer system, which caused programmes to be interrupted. The BBC's commercialisation plans were opposed by disillusioned staff who threatened to go on strike. They wanted the BBC to abandon plans to make production crews compete in the private sector. The ITV Network Centre also reacted angrily to reports that the BBC planned to spend one billion pounds on digital television and radio from 1998 for five years. The key problem for competitors was that the BBC was straying too far into the space occupied by commercial sectors, whilst being protected from market forces by a licence fee subsidy. In 1998, BSkyB instigated a European Commission investigation into the BBC's *News-24* programme, arguing that it presented unfair competition to *Sky News*.

Clearly there have been several phases of changes at the BBC. In relation to the news, the first change was to reclaim the 'high ground' in news and current affairs in order to ensure that BBC News was far superior to any of its competitors. This vision had begun in the mid-1970s when Birt and Peter Jay wrote a series of articles bemoaning the state of news reporting on British television. Their important contribution to the news values of the BBC revolved around what became known as the Birt–Jay thesis, which subsequently became the blue-print for wholesale changes in BBC journalism (Birt and Jay, 1975a, 1975b; Barnett and Curry, 1994). These changes centred on two main priorities: first, to provide the kind of intelligent news analysis identified by Birt and Jay; and secondly, to break with the two main antecedents of television journalism, which Birt and Jay identified as traditional newspaper operations (the newsroom model) and documentary film-making (the movie model). In a newsroom model, the dramatic or unusual (and personalities) are given prominence over other values in the news. Birt and Jay argued that these values are not problematic when they are applied to simple stories of human interest, but are inadequate or even dangerous when they are applied to social, political, economic and international forces. Birt and Jay identified a tendency for journalists to report complex issues as separate stories or discrete facts, so that budget stories led on the price of beer rather than a commitment to full employment. This, they argued, was due to the uninformed journalist being unable to explain issues because journalists are trained simply to report straight every crime story they come across. The second model, the movie model, also draws attention and effort away from analysis of issues. The tendency is for such programmes to work to film requirements and to see a story as an excuse to make a film rather than film as an aid to explanation.

Birt and Jay's prescription for the malaise in British television journalism was to unify the News and Current Affairs Departments in order to emphasise the issue rather than the event (1975b). This would result in a daily flagship programme, broadcast from 10 o'clock to 11 o'clock, with only five or six stories placed in the fullest context possible. It was envisaged that this would be the most important programme and would have priority over the department's pooled journalistic resources. The staff would be organised into two parallel echelons under a head of department. The first group would consist of programme editors and producers exercising the editor's delegated responsibility, and the second would consist of journalists organised into subject teams (specialist units), each headed by a different editor, such as a foreign affairs editor, industrial editor and so on. This, Birt and Jay argued correctly, would be much easier at the BBC than at ITV, as the BBC's News and Current Affairs Departments were both already under the same management, whereas the ITV federal system enables individual companies to pursue their own programme philosophies.

The application of the Birt–Jay thesis from the late 1980s onwards, along with the introduction of other new management techniques, did not result in an immediate response from the Conservative government. In the end Birt and the BBC had to wait until the government issued the 1994 White Paper on the future of the BBC, which was granted both a continuation of the licence fee and a charter renewal. The national press considered that the BBC had had to pay a price for such a victory (Harrison, 2000).

Since 1994, as Birt has pushed the BBC even further towards a commercial, quasi-privatised model of broadcasting, questions have been raised about the future of the BBC as a public service broadcaster and the future of its news product.

The BBC and public service broadcasting

Consistently, legislators have lacked clarity on what constitutes public service broadcasting or what its purpose actually is. Most research and legislation is guilty of taking the concept of public service broadcasting as somehow given without actually trying to define it. At the BBC, the concept of public service broadcasting has been codified in the *Producers' Guidelines* (BBC, 1993c), which guide programme makers and journalists to work to a formula imbued with certain values and ethical constraints.

The Broadcasting Research Unit (BRU), 1985–6, provided evidence for the Peacock Committee on the financing of the BBC, and identified eight basic principles of public service broadcasting: geographic universality; catering for all tastes and interests; catering for minorities; concern for national identity and community; detachment from vested interests and government; direct funding of one broadcasting system by the body of users (that is, via a licence fee system); competition in relationship to good programming rather than in increasing audience numbers; and guidelines which liberate programme makers rather than restrict them.

In contrast, John Reith had conceived of public service broadcasting as having four facets: it should be protected from purely commercial pressures; the whole nation should be served; there should be unified control (public service broadcasting should be organised as a monopoly); and there should be high programme standards (McDonnell, 1991). Obviously, one of the major problems in trying to use such a complicated concept is that it can be redefined at almost any juncture to suit almost any purpose or belief. The Independent Television system dented the Reithian vision of public service broadcasting by breaking the monopoly held by the BBC of British broadcasting; nevertheless, the ITV system was set up along most of the public service principles outlined above.

If public service broadcasting is a term which can be affected and changed by vested interests, then clearly there are problems in defining it in the context of a comparison between the BBC and the ITV system in the 1990s. What follows is an attempt to provide an analysis of the ways in which commercial pressures have influenced television news values and agendas in the 1990s, and the way in which these have in turn corrupted some of the founding principles of public service broadcasting.

The principles of geographic universality and of catering for all tastes, interests and minorities should still apply to the existing system of British broadcasting, as the requirement is written into an annexe attached to the BBC licence in 1964 and underpins the Television Act 1954. The BBC itself believes it should inform the nation by expressing British culture (BBC, 1993b) and that 'there should be broader coverage of the cultural life of the nations and the regions of England' (BBC, 1994a:14). The last Conservative government before 1997 endorsed this view, stating that the BBC should be 'providing diversity and choice in its programmes' (Report of the Secretary of State for National Heritage, 1994:6) and 'ensuring that the rich cultural heritage of all parts of the UK is represented in its programmes' (p. 6).

Even though public service broadcasting has been weakened in Britain (Curran, 1998), it is vital not to lose sight of the important role the BBC has to play in relation to British national democracy. Notwithstanding the difficulties involved in defining public service broadcasting, the British government has ruled that the BBC will 'continue as the public service broadcaster in the UK' (Report of the Secretary of State for National Heritage, 1994:6), and from 1926 to the present day public service broadcasting values and the notion of serving the nation have evolved to accommodate competition and change (McDonnell, 1991). The structures of public service broadcasting are still standing and are a dominant but weakened feature of British terrestrial television provision: in 1998 public service channels still commanded the largest audiences, and the Internet service BBC On-Line, a public service website, claimed eighteen million hits in March. As a public service broadcaster the BBC has a remit to provide useful information to citizens in a participatory democracy. This commitment to provide information which will enhance the constitution of the public sphere and encourage communicative competence of the citizen is a key factor in defining the relationship the BBC has to serving the public interest and national democracy. The role of the BBC is grounded in a rationale of defining national identity and being a public service broadcaster. The former has historically been undertaken by serving the public sphere of a nation state and providing a focus for national cultural identification (Morley and Robins, 1995); the latter is often understood in terms of serving the public interest (McQuail, 1992).

The BBC and national identity

Throughout its history the BBC has clung to a particular sense of national identity. This has been achieved via an adherence to public interest values that were the embodiment of a set of a particular type of political and cultural value. These originated in the authoritarian and paternalistic distrust that John Reith, the first director-general (1924–38), had of the public's ability to determine the public interest responsibly (McIntyre, 1993). For Reith, news and other programmes should be what those in control of the BBC thought listeners should hear (Garnham, 1973). The BBC was perceived as a way of educating and improving the masses.

The BBC traditionally maintained national identity via radio in the 1930s and through the coverage of the Second World War, and via television from the 1950s onwards. The organisation has also occupied an important cultural location in the world and has therefore played a role in defining and promoting British national identity in the former British Empire and colonies. In the 1990s and early 2000s, the BBC *World Service News*[3] still has a brand

---

[3] Although its audience is diminishing in India and the former colonies.

name which is instantly recognisable throughout the world and stands for impartiality, authority and veracity.

The BBC occupies an important cultural location in defining a particular type of national identity in Britain, although the notion of a British nation state is problematic.[4] The idea of a 'British' national identity has evolved, and is one which is usually evoked in relation to constitutional arrangements, 'the British Parliament' or 'the British Empire' (Kearney, 1991). The qualities which the British share bring the British together at times of war (Hoggart, 1995), as in 'the Battle of Britain', or in representation of the British nation by 'the Brits abroad'. Even this idea of Britain, generally ignores the multinational nature of the British Isles, as common qualities are not necessarily the same as a common culture. Kearney (1991) argues that perhaps the British do not have a single national history or a single national past and therefore perhaps do not have a single national image. In reality there has been dominance of Britain by England, which has been exacerbated by urbanisation, increase in population, the electoral system and parliamentary representation. Further, British history has tended to produce a partial, self-regarding and divisive account (Hoggart, 1995) which has concentrated on English history. The BBC has long subscribed to this parochial view of Britain and Northern Ireland from London and the Home Counties, and the notion of national identity to which it contributes and promotes is replete with English values and expectations and does not reflect the whole of Britain and Northern Ireland. And yet, the BBC in terms of its structure represents England, Scotland, Wales and Northern Ireland, through its Board of Governors. The Board is responsible for maintaining standards in England, a responsibility which is shared in Wales, Scotland and Northern Ireland with National Broadcasting Councils. The BBC divides Britain and Northern Ireland into six regions, three in England (North, South and Midlands) plus Scotland,[5] Wales[6] and Northern Ireland.[7] But the BBC's headquarters is in London.

In principle, the structure of the BBC appears to reflect the BBC's public service broadcasting, which was founded upon the premise that it should contribute to the public and political life of the nation (defined as England, Scotland, Wales and Northern Ireland) and should help to construct a sense of national unity (Morley and Robins, 1995). In 1927 the BBC emerged as a corporation with a mandate to promise a national service. From then on it expanded and consolidated its institutional position within the established

[4] It has proven difficult to determine what actually characterises a nation, nation state, national identity or nationalism, and numerous definitions have been produced. Discussion and analysis of these studies are beyond the scope of this book (see Oakeshott, 1975; Anderson, 1983; Alter, 1985; Crick, 1991; Schlesinger, 1991; Calhoun, 1994; Diamond and Plattner, 1994; Gellner, 1994).
[5] BBC Scotland is based in Glasgow; the daily news programme is *Reporting Scotland*.
[6] BBC Wales is based in Cardiff; the daily news programme is *Wales Today*.
[7] BBC Northern Ireland is based in Belfast; the daily news programme is *Newsline 6.30*.

political and social order. The BBC was established as patron of the whole nation's cultural resources (Scannell and Cardiff, 1991). The construction of national identity via symbolism, ritual, ceremony and pageantry was a priority of early BBC radio, followed by BBC television. Both have traditionally broadcast royal events such as anniversaries, visits, births, deaths, marriages and the Christmas message from the monarch. The BBC has also traditionally transmitted a variety of ceremonies and historical occasions such as VE Day, VJ Day, Remembrance Day, the eightieth anniversary of the Battle of the Somme and so on. These ceremonies and others like them invoke memories of a golden age in which the nation can locate itself (Smith, 1986). The cultivation of this particular type of national identity was enhanced by the BBC's ability to formulate and design a set of precedents for reporting events it deemed to be in the national interest. The BBC had a special function in the Second World War, helping to develop a national self-image of cheerful patriotism (Harrison and Woods, 1999).

However, the BBC's role as a public service broadcaster will be increasingly less representative of the multicultural and varied audience of Britain and Northern Ireland if it continues to protect the public interest, and what it deems to be the national interest, by patronising children and adults with a 'no blood policy' (BBC, 1993c, 1996b); if it continues to have a London and south-east domination of news agendas; and if it promotes a particular type of cultural nostalgia and retains its image as the nation's 'Auntie'. The growth of multiculturalism and pluralism challenges the BBC's version of national identity, rendering it outdated and parochial. It is questionable whether the British viewer can continue to be addressed in such terms. Exporting national identity abroad is similarly constrained because the BBC is not European or pluralistic in terms of either its ethos or its values, and especially as the values and identities which are exported tend to be predominantly English, rather than British. The process of Europeanisation and the possible cultivation of a European public sphere (Schlesinger, 1995) centred on the European Union may offer a strong cultural challenge and even threat to the role of the BBC as a national public service broadcaster.

Similarly, as regions and provinces strengthen and develop, the people living within them are likely to form stronger regional identifications and more cross-national alliances on issues of common concern. This process is likely to be aided by the development of stronger, regionally based, non-BBC media. Prior to 1982 only a small number of the Welsh programmes which were produced were shown on BBC1 and ITV. The advent of a fourth channel in Wales, which had a distinct broadcasting role, means that S4C plays an important part in reflecting and reinforcing Welsh cultural identity and language. The advent of digitalisation will greatly improve this trend, and S4C's new digital channel, S4C Digital Networks Limited (SDN), will facilitate greater production and broadcasting of Welsh programmes in Wales and across the rest of Britain and Northern Ireland. Importantly, S4C has exported over ninety programmes to almost one hundred countries world-wide and is proving to be adept at exporting its own culture.[8] If links are forged between regions and the European Union's supra-national institutions, national governments and administrations will be by-passed (Marquand, 1991). Given the BBC's (and other national news organisations') predilection for closely following and reporting the activities of national governments and agencies through a strong tendency to cultivate sources at a national level, journalists are finding it increasingly difficult to access information which transcends state boundaries (Marr, 1995).

The BBC in particular will need to adapt and change far more than it is doing if it is to survive as *the* viable British public service broadcaster in the twenty-first century. It must be committed to serving and empowering the citizens of Britain with sub-national and improved national coverage and representation, with international information relevant to the 2000s, and possibly with contributions to the sense of regional and European identity. The signs are that it will not do so, due to several related factors.

The main problem the BBC has in its adherence to a nostalgic, historical, sentimental, English, white, male, middle-class sense of national identity is that it is simply irrelevant in an era of multiculturalism and pluralism. This is nowhere more apparent than in the newsroom, where these values are at variance with the political correctness which has recently permeated the culture. Journalists at the BBC may drop a news story because they know it has a south-east bias in favour of a story which originates outside London and the south-east. This is ironic, since the BBC's stated mission, 'to report impartially in all circumstances', is compromised by a political correctness which seeks to compensate for the sentimental values the BBC traditionally feels at home with. Of course political correctness has only a limited success rate. In either case news values are distorted.

The definition of public interest and national interest is often seen in news values; for example, *BBC News* broadcast the state opening of Parliament as a lead story on the same day as ITN led with a coach crash which killed several children. Many would question whether this adherence to a ceremonial event occurring in London is relevant to the whole of Britain and Northern Ireland, or as important as the deaths of children. The different news values exhibited by a public service and a commercial broadcaster show how the maintenance of public service broadcasting and national identity is problematic. The former is constantly squeezed by the new commercialisation of the broadcasting industry; the latter is equally squeezed by the fragmentation of society and the development of globalism and localism as a means of communication and dissemination of media images and messages. The

[8] URL <*http://www.s4c.co.uk/corfforaethol/e-cyflwyno.html*> accessed 17 March 1999.

national message can appear inappropriate and not particularly relevant at certain times.[9]

Public service values relate to serving the whole nation in the national interest and to regulation in the public interest. Such control of public service broadcasters in Britain and in other countries traditionally has been about diversity and choice. Current trends towards globalism and localism are about pluralism and fragmentation. A citizen in the early 2000s needs better and greater knowledge of international affairs, and better knowledge of local affairs (and still requires useful information about a broad range of national affairs). At the BBC, the continued development of the internal market and the quest for efficiency have resulted in the splitting of the broadcasting and production functions, output and newsgathering. It has also resulted in the merging of radio and television news services (bimedia) and controversially the incorporation of *World Service News*[10] under one management structure. The changes to the World Service in particular have been criticised as counter-productive, reducing the creativity and diversity of *World Service News*, which has traditionally exhibited very different news values from BBC national news. It is unclear whether it will continue to remain as distinctive.

In an era of plurality, developing a structure which encourages homogenisation of news content appears to be short-sighted and ignores the possibility of a development of different and important spheres of communication, such as the supra-national and sub-national. It may also reduce the possibility of the development of a critical regionalism (Frampton, 1985), in which a local regional culture sees itself (and is perceived by the media) not as self-communing, but as an expression of global culture.

These challenges which are being faced by the BBC are also being faced in different ways by many state-financed national broadcasting organisations in different European countries. Although the BBC is unique in the power of its global reach, its case illustrates some of the same sorts of issues facing other national broadcasters. For example, the state broadcasting company RTVE in Spain is facing serious problems in relation to loss of advertising revenue since the privately owned television stations (Antena 3 De Television, Tele 5 and Canal Plus Espagne) began broadcasting in 1990.

Although supporting and maintaining a national identity via a national television company is at variance with trends towards regional cultural diversity and transnational corporate integration (Waters, 1995), it reflects

[9] Following the death and funeral of Diana, Princess of Wales, in September 1997, the BBC began to reconceptualise and reorganise its planning for television coverage following the death of the Queen Mother, in the recognition that its planned obituaries are not relevant to a large percentage of the population.

[10] Although the BBC does not publicly admit to any diminishment of the status or position of *World Service News*, it is significant that the director of *World Service News* no longer holds a position on the management board and is represented by the director of news and current affairs.

the early nineteenth-century elevation of the nation as a central value, providing meaning and justification for the political, social and cultural activity of its citizens and rulers. In a nation state national interests provide the yardsticks of political thought and action (Alter, 1985). Such a strong sense of nationalism and national identity, which exists throughout the world, is not likely to, and is not expected to, disappear suddenly (Anderson, 1983; Gellner, 1994). Although television news agendas in the 1990s appeared to be under pressure from a need to be both regionally sensitive and internationally relevant, there is a future for the BBC as a national public service broadcaster, whilst information via the mass media is still controlled at the national level. This point was noted by the European Commission (Commission of the European Communities, 1984).

Fortunately for the quality of BBC programming, the Peacock Committee argued that one main broadcasting organisation should continue to be funded by the licence fee so that broadcasting could continue to be structured around the principle of good-quality programming, rather than around the principle of seeking audience numbers (Broadcasting Research Unit, 1985). However, the publication of a broadcasting White Paper in 1988 challenged the idea of good-quality programming through the proposed replacement of the Independent Broadcasting Authority (IBA), with a lighter-touch Independent Television Commission,[11] and through the award of Independent Television franchises by competitive tender.

ITN

When Independent Television (ITV) was compelled in 1954 to inform, educate and entertain, it was accompanied by the formation of a separate news provider, Independent Television News. ITN was jointly owned by all the new television news channels. The Beveridge Committee, which reported in 1951, made no direct recommendation for commercial television (Davidson, 1992), but saw no contradiction in advertising within a public service system. Furthermore, the Independent Television Authority (ITA) was established to supervise and regulate the new television companies by ensuring that the priorities of revenue from advertising did not override the need for quality content of programming. The model for the ITA was based upon the structure of the BBC's Board of Governors and was a public corporation. Unlike the BBC board, the ITA selected applicants from different would-be television companies and awarded them seven-year franchises, subject to their compliance with ITA regulations.

Although ITV was set up as a direct competitor to the BBC, and was able to sell advertising in order to acquire revenue, it was nevertheless set up

---

[11] Professor Barrie Gunter, formerly head of ITC research, says 'it is not true to say that the ITC has a lighter touch than the IBA. The touch can still be heavy, it's just that it is implemented differently' (personal communication, 25 March 1995).

upon some of the same public service broadcasting principles as the BBC, to be a provider of quality, high-standard programmes, which served to inform, entertain and educate the audience. The excesses of market forces were further tempered by a strong and powerful regulatory body to regulate in the public interest, which, unlike the current regulatory body (the ITC), could view and condemn programming in advance.

Importantly, ITV offered regional programming, a distinctive feature of the new system. In principle this was deemed to enhance the public service values of the ITV system. In practice, however, this principle was diluted by the forces of the market place as ITV came to be dominated by four and later five large regional companies (Seymour-Ure, 1991). Although ITV was initially set up as a commercial competitor to the BBC, it came to be recognised as enhancing and complementing the programme output and quality of British television, and the two channels slowly were perceived 'as part of a *single* public service system' (p. 69), an acceptable duopoly.

For ITN and the ITV companies, the Broadcasting Act 1990 was a watershed in their history. The Act introduced competitive tendering as a principle of licence application. A quality threshold was belatedly added which included an obligation for prospective broadcasters to provide certain types of programming. This addition followed successful lobbying by broadcasters to ensure quality safeguards were introduced into the proposed legislation, so that franchises were not simply sold to the highest bidder. The selection process of applications and the subsequent award of licences is well covered by Davidson (1992), but the losers in the new process were either those licensees who were refused a renewal of their licences, such as Thames Television, TVS, TSW and TV-am (which were replaced by Carlton, Meridian, Westcountry and Sunrise), or those existing licensees who overbid, such as Yorkshire Television (YTV). The former stopped broadcasting and YTV became debt-burdened and ripe for take-over. First YTV merged with Tyne-Tees Television and then the merged company was taken over by Granada.

The post-Broadcasting Act 1990 era has been one in which the original public service-oriented ethos of an Independent Television has been consistently diluted in the face of increasing competition and deregulation. Indeed, one of the main principles of regionalism has been compromised by the introduction of a central network which controls and allocates network programmes to the regional companies (*Guardian*, 3 August 1992, 5 October 1992). The ITV Network Centre, which was established to meet the requirements of the Broadcasting Act 1990, is owned by the ITV companies. Its role is to commission, purchase and schedule the programmes which are shown across the whole ITV network, taking the power of scheduling away from the regions. Also, the subsequent take-overs of smaller television companies by larger companies from 1994 have compounded concerns for the future of regional television with the concentration of power in the hands of fewer and fewer large television companies.

When ITV was first formed in 1954, ITN was nominated the sole news provider and was owned by all the regional television companies. After the Broadcasting Act 1990, the role and security of ITN were placed in jeopardy, especially during a period when the ITC considered whether it would nominate ITN again as the sole news provider to the television companies. During 1990, the ITV companies also began to consider the implications of a radical restructuring of ITN, to protect their own interests from new government policy. In future, ITV companies would be able to own only 49 per cent of ITN; the rest was to be owned by private shareholders. In the end, due to a consortium take-over by a variety of ITV companies and Reuters, the ITC nominated ITN the sole news provider for the ITV companies for ten years from 1993, but also built in the proviso that the television companies could reconsider ITN as their news provider after five years in 1998.

Financial difficulties in the early 1990s, coupled with the new relationship with the companies ITN serves, have changed its ethos and rationale. ITN's aim of providing excellent news coverage has now to be reconciled with making profits for shareholders and with increasing ratings.

The weakening of public service broadcasting

The ability of Britain's public service broadcasters to adhere to their remit to deliver a diverse range of information to the public in the 1990s can now be seen to be compromised as follows:

The BBC has begun to make decisive moves towards increasing its commercial income from its 1997–8 base of 5 per cent of total revenue, and towards reducing production costs. It has restructured World Service Television, and made global satellite deals in 1994 with Pearson[12] and Foxtel,[13] in 1997 with Flextech[14] and in 1998 with the Discovery Channel.[15] The BBC has also strengthened its own internal market by introducing producer choice and splitting the production and broadcast functions. It is now required to ensure that 25 per cent of output is by independent producers (Broadcasting Act 1990) and through co-productions, reducing the presence of the BBC ethos and tradition in all its output. The BBC has reduced its production staff and the scale of its production facilities since the early 1990s

---

[12] Pearson is thinking of selling out of the BBC's two loss-making European channels (news channel, BBC World and entertainment service, BBC Prime).

[13] The BBC has a 20 per cent shareholding in UKTV, an Australian entertainment subscription channel with Pearson and Foxtel.

[14] The BBC's Worldwide Division and Flextech have a pay-TV joint venture, UKTV. This is the first BBC-backed network to carry advertising. Its four channels are UK Arena, UK Gold, UK Horizons and UK Style. Due to the dependence on advertising revenue, the BBC does not attach its name directly to UKTV material which promotes the venture.

[15] The £500-million deal with Discovery Communications Incorporated is the biggest step that the BBC has taken so far towards commercialisation. The deal involved the launch of an American cable channel, BBC America, and global channels Animal Planet and People and Arts.

(Report of the Secretary of State for National Heritage, 1994). And it is still uncertain how such changes will ultimately affect the culture and values inherent in a national public service broadcaster.

The BBC is aiming to be completely digital by the year 2001. Despite ITC and Labour Party pressure to include an improved diversity and quality clause to govern the new multiplex operators for digital television, the Broadcasting Act 1996 reflects the Conservative Party's free-market stance. According to the BBC's director-general, it is a case of whether the BBC adapts or dies (Hargreaves, 1996). It is the manner of adaptation and its consequences which are at issue. Multiplex channels offered by the BBC in the future may not be of public service broadcasting standard or contribute in any way towards defining sub-national, British or international identity, especially given the BBC's tendency to define national and cultural identity as English.

The BBC's current practices belie any real commitment to fostering regional and international identity. Although the BBC's new *Six O'Clock News* programme will contain more regional stories, it remains to be seen whether the news programme will provide balanced geographic representation and access. Analysis of television news in the 1990s needs to consider how well terrestrial television news serves both sub-national and transnational frameworks of democracy. In relation to the coverage of international or transnational affairs, there is a noticeable tendency for *all* news organisations to ignore certain sectors of the world (Wallis and Baran, 1990). For example, British journalists covering the EU do not scrutinise or examine the role of the European Parliament. We have seen little sign of any British television news coverage which highlights the undemocratic nature of the institutions of the EU, and we are not witnessing coverage of world regions in any consistent manner. Similarly, a unified global capital market has evolved, which can, due to technological developments, work in real time (Castells, 1996), and yet it is unclear how terrestrial television news organisations can keep up to date with the flows of information circulating the globe. It is also uncertain how the complex legal rights of television viewers can be dealt with in a trans-border broadcasting environment (Porter, 1993). It is questionable whether the BBC could ever contribute usefully to defining a European public sphere and the 'European interest', as a European public service broadcaster (given the problems inherent in the BBC) and notwithstanding the difficulty of trying to identify what constitutes European and, indeed, national identity. It would appear that the BBC's immediate future is that of a national broadcaster (despite some of the problems with this idea noted earlier). But if the BBC remains a committed *national* public service broadcaster it will mark the end of its chance to be pluralistic, to compete abroad or to contribute to European or global public service broadcasting.

The principle of sub-regional diversity is also being challenged by structural developments occurring within the ITV system itself. In 1991 the ITV network consisted of fifteen ITV regions in addition to Channel 4, GMTV and Teletext. Relaxation of ownership rules in the Broadcasting Acts 1990 and 1996 (in particular from 1 November 1996) have led to companies merging or being taken over. This has resulted in the development of 'the big three' ITV companies, United News and Media, Granada and Central. Although all the ITV companies still retain individual licences, the concept of regional coverage is being challenged by mergers, take-overs and the reduction of the ITV system's federal structure. Since 1990, Carlton has taken over Central Television and Westcountry Television; Granada has taken over LWT; YTV and Tyne-Tees merged to avoid collapsing under the weight of their enormous franchise bids; Granada Media Group has taken over Yorkshire Tyne-Tees Television; and Meridian has merged with Anglia Television.[16] It is of concern that such changes will bring about a reduction in the commitment to regional identity and distinctive programming.

The restructuring of the managerial system at the BBC appeared to be leading to a homogenisation of the BBC's culture, although recent resistance to change there indicates that there are limits to which the values of a public service broadcaster can be subverted to market forces. The attempt by Director-General John Birt in September 1997 to introduce five new executive editors to oversee clusters of individual (currently distinctive) news programmes was seen by the majority of BBC staff and media analysts as an attempt to save money and to centralise production. The key criticism levelled at the policy was that such a move could lead to homogenisation of the BBC's news values, resulting in a reduction of the BBC's creativity, diversity, pragmatism and commitment to serving the nation. Such homogenisation appeared contradictory in the face of the fragmentation of the cultural sphere, which is resulting in the emergence of different levels of 'the public' at the national and regional level. The 1998 Programme Strategy Review has reversed this trend towards much clearer distinction and differentiation between programmes but has done little to reduce the centralist structure of the BBC.

The introduction of the BBC's twenty-four-hour rolling news[17] has affected its existing mass audience news programmes, the *One*, *Six* and *Nine O'Clock News*, which have lost funding and staff to support the BBC's *News-24*. Furthermore, concern was expressed by viewers in a BBC survey of public opinion that its twenty-four-hour rolling news programme should not simply be repetitive bulletins broadcast at twenty-minute intervals, but should provide in-depth analysis in the style of current affairs-type programmes (BBC,

---

[16] This was more or less a take-over, and the company that owns Anglia and Meridian is itself a composite of Lord Hollick's MAI and United Press, United News and Media. The company has now bought almost 30 per cent of HTV to try to stop Carlton–Central from acquiring HTV following its purchase of Westcountry Television.
[17] The BBC's *News-24* programme began broadcasting in November 1997 at a cost of £30 million per year (according to the *Media Guide*, 1999).

1997b). As the BBC's News and Current Affairs Directorate is a mix of the two genres it is, in theory, singularly well placed to provide news plus analysis in a twenty-four-hour format. So far the BBC's *News-24* has not been perceived as being particularly in-depth. If investment in a twenty-four-hour rolling news format were to compromise the funding, resources or status of the *One, Six* and *Nine O'Clock News* it would obviously be an issue which would need to be addressed seriously. The solution which is implicit in the 1998 Programme Strategy Review is to be all things to all people by having a range of programmes which appeal to a variety of audiences. Such differentiation is an odd step for a national public service broadcaster that has traditionally provided a consistent style of news to the audience on a mass audience channel.

Under its powers derived from the Broadcasting Act 1990, the ITC issues guidelines for licensees which charge ITV to cater for all tastes and interests. Both the BBC and ITV systems still have regional outlets or companies situated around Britain and Northern Ireland, which should in principle be catering for a variety of tastes and geographical distinctions. But the ideal, upon which basis the ITV system was constructed, of one regional television company per region has been challenged through the relaxation of rules on cross-media ownership. These developments are diluting the public service broadcasting principle of catering to a variety of tastes and interests. Both the BBC and ITV already have a questionable commitment to this principle.

The chase after ratings, particularly by ITV, is further diluting the principle of catering for all tastes by marginalising minority interest programmes to parts of the schedules which will not affect advertising revenues. Before the Broadcasting Act 1990, for example, ITN's *News at Ten* was basically an immovable object, even though the only requirement of the franchise holders was to broadcast a news programme some time between 6.30 p.m. and 10.30 p.m. However, in the increasingly competitive climate of commercial broadcasting, pressure to move *News at Ten*[18] to an earlier or later time in the evening was a regular ingredient of a heated debate (Harrison, 1997). The proponents have been the ITV companies, whose position in an increasingly competitive commercial environment centred their interests on the issues of scheduling, ratings and commercial expediency. The defendants have generally been politicians and public opinion leaders, who make claims relating to the damage to democracy and public service broadcasting.

One key public service principle, of retaining one broadcasting system which is directly funded by the licence fee system, has been protected until 2006. However, it is still the case that the BBC will increasingly have to justify charging a licence fee as its audience share drops. The BBC's *Report and Accounts 1993-94* admits that the BBC's share of viewers and listeners fell in 1993–94 by 2 per cent to 48 per cent of the audience share (BBC, 1994a).

---

[18] *News at Ten* broadcast its last programme on Friday 5 March 1999.

The former chief executive of ITN, David Gordon, argued on *Newsnight* that the BBC 'has its cake and eats it with a licence fee and commercialism' (BBC2's *Newsnight*, 6 July 1994).

This contrasts very heavily with the kind of adaptation to commercial pressures that ITN had to undergo in the 1990s. Indeed, BBC news and current affairs were initially spared the worst internal market pressures, as resources had been invested into them in the early 1990s in order to meet John Birt's initial demand for news programming which 'reports, analyses and debates the main *issues* of the day' (BBC, 1993b:83). However, in 1995 a rein was put on news and current affairs expenditure, and plans to launch a twenty-four-hour television news channel raised questions about whether the BBC's other news services might be weakened by the new drain on resources (*Media Guardian*, 17 February 1997). Nevertheless the BBC's News and Current Affairs Directorate still has staff budgets unmatched elsewhere in the media industry. Whilst it is feared that the BBC may have to abandon some of its higher aims and principles in the new financial climate, ITN has no pretence to such grandiose ambitions. In contrast, ITN acknowledges that it is commercially oriented in its remit to be a news provider. Interviews[19] with the then editor-in-chief of ITN and the managing director of news at the BBC illustrate fundamental differences in their contemporary mission statements. ITN's remit is geared to an improvement of audience ratings and a good relationship with ITN's customers (the contractors), and the BBC's is committed to the principles of building a consensus around a mission to broaden the news agenda and to analyse issues. 'It is necessary to continue to change the news at the BBC, to broaden the agenda, to cover parts of the world which are not currently being covered' (managing director, BBC News and Current Affairs). In contrast ITN's 'priority is to our audience and our audience is the ITV company or the contractor of the programme, not the viewer out there' (editor-in-chief, ITN).

Different principles of public service broadcasting and commercialism, or the compromise between some of the competing aspects of both of these, result in some differences in television news philosophies, news values, news agendas and what is deemed to be newsworthy in different television newsrooms. Different conceptions of what serves the public interest arise in different news organisations, and affect and differentiate the relationship of the BBC and ITN to the public sphere and democracy in the early 2000s.

[19] I interviewed Tony Hall at the BBC and Stuart Purvis at ITN on the same day. They were asked the same questions, namely their view of the mission, rationale and culture of their organisation and the remit of their news departments. The contrast in their replies was striking.

4

TV news diversity:
structures, practices and forms

News production at the BBC has developed as a result of several historical phases and sequences, and has retained some elements from each transitory period. The Reithian mission to give the public what they needed, and not necessarily what they wanted, was echoed to some extent by the Birt–Jay thesis and has clearly underpinned the BBC's policy towards news and current affairs in the early 1990s. The uneasy marriage between current affairs and news now has to exist within an unprecedented commercial BBC environment. The 1998 Programme Strategy Review has refocused and reinforced the audience's relationship to BBC news in an attempt to give the audiences more of what they want, namely greater choice in the digital age. The neo-Reithian ethic of recognising that audiences have diverse views and needs is adhered to at least in the BBC's current philosophy of diversity and choice, although the motivation for such rhetoric is entirely different from that of the 1940s and early 1950s. ITN has had to rationalise its news production process in response to financial stringency imposed upon it throughout the 1990s. ITN's philosophy of diversity and choice is related directly to its contractual obligations, although it is still regulated in the public interest by the ITC. News and current affairs at the BBC, at ITN and in the regions have, as I shall show, complex origins and values which are reflected in the structures, practices and forms of their news production processes and news content.

The structure and process of the BBC's news and current affairs

Complexity is inherent in the BBC's structure, which traditionally has been large and bureaucratic (see Figures 2 and 3). Currently there are two terrestrial network television channels, BBC1 and BBC2, five network radio services and eighteen regional television services. Overseas radio broadcasts, for many years, were made by the World Service, and its radio audience was the biggest for any international station in the world. World Service Television

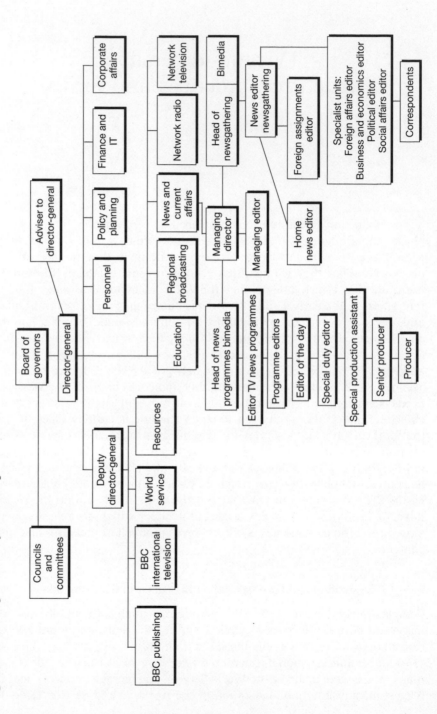

Figure 2   *The organisation of the BBC pre-1997*

Figure 3 *The organisation of the BBC post-1997*

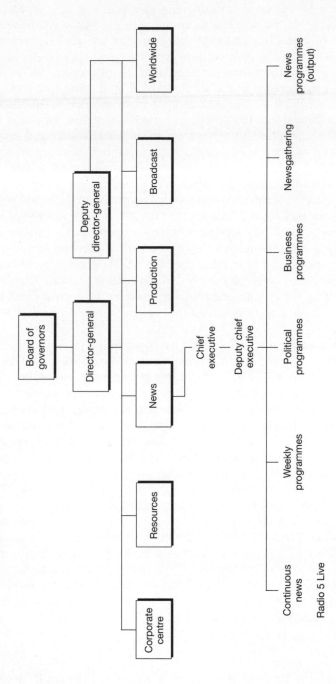

Note: All Directorates have sub-divisions. Only news is listed.

began broadcasting in 1991 and was incorporated in 1994 into the new directorate responsible for generating income at home and for the World Service, BBC Worldwide. Its remit is to co-ordinate the BBC's commercial activities in both broadcasting and publishing[1] and its international broadcasts. It is responsible for the joint venture with Flextech (UKTV); the joint venture with Communications Incorporated Discovery, BBC Prime; an entertainment channel for Europe; and a 20 per cent shareholding in UKTV, a subscription channel in Australia, alongside Pearson and Foxtel. Six directorates have been formed and the production and broadcasting functions at the BBC have been separated. BBC Broadcast schedules channels and commissions services for audiences; BBC Production runs the in-house radio and television production; BBC News is responsible for a combined television and radio news operation across the range of BBC news and current affairs services; BBC Resources provides the facilities and expertise to serve and support BBC programme makers and broadcasters; BBC Worldwide is responsible for generating income and the Corporate Centre is responsible for personnel, finance, IT, policy and planning, and corporate affairs. These new structures replace three original directorates: the output directorate made programmes (news and current affairs were part of this); the second directorate supplied services to the output directorate and was controlled by the deputy director-general; and the third directorate consisted of the corporate and policy directorates.

The BBC is still controlled by a Board of Governors whose twelve members are officially appointed by the queen, which in reality means the prime minister. Any prime minister who abuses the power of patronage can ensure the board is composed of government sympathisers and is unrepresentative of British society. In 1992 eight out of twelve BBC governors had been to Oxford, Cambridge or London universities (Curran, 1998). The governors' responsibility for the BBC is shared in Wales, Scotland and Northern Ireland with National Broadcasting Councils, whose members are appointed by the governors. The governors also appoint the General Advisory Council, regional advisory councils in England and local radio advisory councils. The Board of Management in practice makes many of the important decisions at the BBC. It consists of the director-general, deputy director-general, adviser to the director-general and the heads of the BBC's directorates.

The new BBC News Directorate is controlled by its directorate head, the chief executive, who is also a member of the Board of Management and therefore actively involved in BBC policy decisions. Below him is a variety of middle managers who control the administrative affairs of the department, and the senior editorial staff who head up various parts of the television news process. There is a deputy chief executive, a head of News Programmes, a

---

[1] BBC Worldwide has twenty-three titles including the *Radio Times*. In 1997, the BBC earned £118 million from its magazines (*Media Guide*, 1999).

head of Newsgathering; a head of Business Programmes; a head of Political Programmes; a head of Weekly Programmes and a head of Continuous News (which includes Radio 5 Live, twenty-four-hour UK news, BBC World, Ceefax and other multimedia services). Below each section head are individual programme editors and heads of Special Units, and beneath these people is a stream of more junior editors, senior producers, producers, correspondents and technical staff. The programme editors of the *One O'Clock News, Six O'Clock News* and *Nine O'Clock News* at the BBC rank immediately above the editor of the day, who is classed as a senior producer. The programme editors have long-term goals with regard to their programme's objectives and play a more managerial role, with an overview of the programme identity, a long-term view in planning, and aims for distinctiveness of coverage[2] and organisation. In contrast, the editor of the day is mainly concerned with the programme output for that lunchtime or evening.

One of John Birt's main policies was to convert the already huge news operation into an even bigger one by, first, merging the News Department with the Current Affairs Department and, secondly, merging radio and television news. Morale was deemed to be at an all-time low at the BBC in the mid-1990s when radio personnel based in central London were told that they would have to move out to west London to work with their television colleagues (*Media Guardian*, 19 June 1995). Members of staff had to try to reconcile the problems of having two parallel command structures resulting from the introduction of bimedia news and current affairs. One journalist working in Newsgathering described how he had eight immediate bosses in the middle management (not counting the managing director and above).[3]

Observation of the BBC showed how recent change in the newsroom, namely the greater separation of the department's newsgathering operation from the output processes, reflects a move to separate newsroom process from content. This change initially increased the power, resources and importance of the Newsgathering section over and above the Output section. Consequently there is a tendency for Newsgathering staff to present stories to the programme editors or editors for the day as a *fait accompli* which the latter have to accept. This has the effect of taking away a good deal of editorial choice. Director-General John Birt, in an effort to create clearer lines of organisation and accountability, appointed an overall head of each news programme, the programme editor. The programme editors were allocated their own programme budget, which meant they could commission stories from Newsgathering and did not simply have to take what it offered, shifting the power back into the Output department and to the individual programme editors. As the *Nine O'Clock News* programme had the biggest budget, the programme editor was in the best position to distinguish his programme

[2] It is this position which was challenged in 1997 by the director-general. John Birt proposed to introduce five executive editors to oversee several news programmes at once.
[3] Conversation held during my observation fieldwork at the BBC.

slightly from the *One O'Clock News* and the *Six O'Clock News*. Programme editors could therefore hold several stories in reserve and drop them at will if something more newsworthy happened. The forward planning meeting held by Newsgathering therefore became increasingly important as a forum in which the programme editors could tell Newsgathering what they deemed to be newsworthy. The development of subtle programme differentiation at the BBC occurred primarily as a reaction by programme editors to the new power of the Newsgathering department to determine the newsworthy stories of the day.

However, the budget for news and current affairs, which was protected in the early 1990s from the BBC's internal market, is now coming under more pressure. For a while it appeared that editorial freedom to commission stories would be affected, reducing the prospect of differentiation between the *One, Six* and *Nine O'Clock News* programmes and therefore changing the content of BBC news. The attempt to introduce five executive editors would have further reduced the power of individual programme editors to carve out a distinctive look for their own programme. Following pressure from BBC staff in September 1997, Chairman Christopher Bland indicated that the programme editors would not lose their ability to shape their own distinctive programmes and would work alongside executive editors.[4] The future of the individual programme editor for the moment looks safer, especially following the 1998 Programme Strategy Review, which will celebrate programme differentiation.

It remains to be seen whether the financial pressure facing the BBC in its determination to compete with cable, digital and satellite services will prove to be irreversibly damaging to its public service remit. According to the media analyst Rob Brown, BBC staff believe that senior management are obsessed with the growing commercial competition both at home and abroad, which means that they are steadily transforming the corporate ethos of the BBC itself into that of a commercial business. Journalists do not share the same view and tensions are therefore mounting (*Independent*, 22 September 1997).

Senior members of Newsgathering also hold weekly look-ahead meetings to go through the prospects and decide which forthcoming events will be covered. This has tended to result in a uniformity of coverage, as the *One O'Clock News, Six O'Clock News* and *Nine O'Clock News* will generally cover most of these stories (although some small differentiation in coverage was always retained via programme editor budgets, as the *Six O'Clock News* takes fewer international stories than the *One O'Clock News* and the *Nine O'Clock News* etc.). Of course this will be greatly exacerbated by the forthcoming news programme changes.

[4] *Daily Telegraph*, 19 September 1997:1, 4, 28; *Guardian* 19 September 1997:1, 10; *Media Guardian*, 22 September 1997:6–7.

Figure 4   *The BBC newsroom,* One O'Clock, Six O'Clock *and* Nine O'Clock News

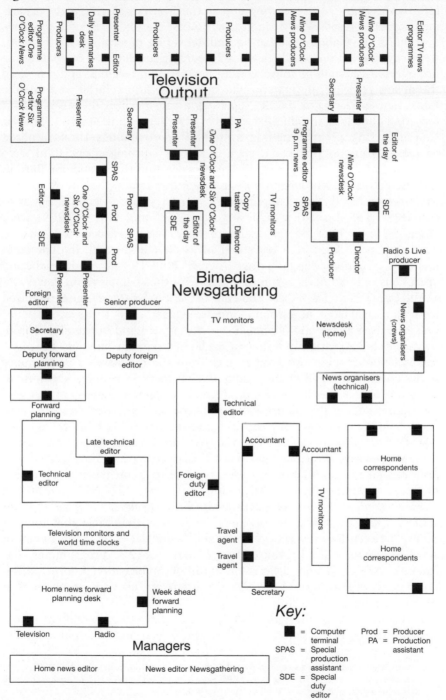

The BBC newsroom at Television Centre in London (see Figure 4) is divided into two sections, Newsgathering and Output. Newsgathering is the department which is responsible for industrial process (i.e. the logistics of the news operation): the planning, gathering and delivering of all the BBC's network news coverage on radio and television; providing the diary; co-ordinating the use of resources such as crews, editing and location facilities; and providing the means of delivering material via radio cars, link vehicles and satellite feeds. Newsgathering at the BBC operates as an independent business unit reporting directly to the chief executive of BBC News. In the early 1990s the Newsgathering department had a staff of approximately three hundred people, two hundred of whom were broadcast journalists; one third were based at Television Centre, one third at Broadcasting House and one third in the regional centres or foreign bureaux (one hundred of these were specialist correspondents). Newsgathering cost over forty million pounds a year to run (BBC, 1994b). When Schlesinger (1987)[5] and Burns (1969) were observing at the BBC, the newsgathering operation was called Intake, which defined its role. Since John Birt's arrival as director-general, the operation has been renamed Newsgathering. In April–May 1994 the newsgathering operations of radio news began to merge with those of television news.

The *One O'Clock*, *Six O'Clock* and *Nine O'Clock News* programmes produced from one television newsroom, and broadcast from the same studio.[6] *Children's Newsround* and *Newsnight* on the other hand are produced from two separate newsrooms and share a studio in a separate building. The physical isolation of these two programmes from the mainstream programmes may account for some of the traditional diversity of content and format. *Breakfast News* at the BBC is also produced in a different newsroom, but uses the same studio as the mainstream news programmes. There has been constant dialogue between *Breakfast News* and the *One O'Clock*, *Six O'Clock* and *Nine O'Clock News* journalists. Often journalists working on pieces for these programmes say '*Breakfast News* want this piece too', or the daytime programmes take pieces from the *Breakfast News* programme which are included in the prospects list from the beginning of the day. Neither *Newsnight* nor *Newsround* has this type of relationship with *Breakfast News* or the *One O'Clock*, *Six O'Clock* and *Nine O'Clock News*. It is noticeable that there is rivalry between the *Nine O'Clock News* and *Newsnight* with regard to film or stories commissioned by the editors of either of the programmes. For example, *Newsnight* may deliberately withhold information from the computer network system until the *Nine O'Clock News* has gone on air, so that the latter cannot spoil a story.

It is important to understand the physical geography of the newsroom structure as an organisation as well as the formal and informal dynamics

---

[5] Schlesinger conducted his observation period in the BBC newsrooms in the mid-1970s.
[6] This was set to change in 1998–9 as the BBC relocated both its radio and television journalists to a new digital newsroom at White City in west London.

created by this environment. Often these are good indicators of the perceptions held by journalists working on those programmes, regarding their role, function and objectives. Once the structure and hierarchy of newsdesks and newsrooms are clarified, it is easier to understand the rationale behind much of the activity in the newsroom. Sitting with the editor and observing all the activity from that perspective is one of the most useful ways of understanding the complexities of newsroom activity, as the editor is the only one with an image of the overall programme. Seemingly arbitrary decisions regarding a news story are often based on a set of logistical or political considerations which are not apparent to other journalists working on the same programme. For example, the relationship of the television newsroom to the rest of the organisation and senior management must be understood, along with the historical origins and development of the informal relationships and processes operating between senior management, middle management and the journalists. Meetings between editorial staff and middle management staff are particularly informative, as many of the organisational tensions and differences are evident in such a forum.

A television newsroom appears to be undisciplined and chaotic, and the newsroom staff structure at the BBC is no exception. The newsroom there is complex. Some journalists are correspondents and some are specialist correspondents. Some of the former work on a variety of general stories, but the specialists work within one of the four specialist units (Politics, Economics, Foreign News and Social Affairs), which were set up by Director-General John Birt in an effort to improve the quality of journalism at the BBC, and to perform an investigative role. The aim of the specialist units is to broaden and deepen the stories which are covered and to ensure that priority is given to the consideration of issues, rather than just straightforward reporting of an event. BBC's Newsgathering operation's investment in specialisms has been designed to provide context and analysis which enable viewers and listeners to make well-informed judgements (*BBC 1996d*). This has traditionally been a keystone of the BBC's philosophy on news and current affairs. The 1998 Programme Strategy Review indicated that the BBC will use specialist correspondents in a different way in the future, namely associating them with one programme only and, by allowing regular appearances, ensuring that they become familiar to the audience. This is a deviation from former plans and will result in a reduction of the bimedia commitment of some correspondents, possibly reducing the efficiency of use of material in some cases.

A producer is allocated two or three correspondents each day, and is the main link between the correspondent in the field and the programme editor or editor for the day. This important role is centred on reconciliation and compromise between the programme editor's requirements, logistical possibilities, time and cost constraints and the artistic temperament of the correspondent. The special duty editor sits next to the programme editor and is his or her eyes and ears for the day, following up loose ends the editor may have missed, and sub-editing a lot of the reports coming in from the correspondents via the producers. The special production assistant (SPAS) helps the special duty editor (SDE) in his or her role. At the BBC, each news programme, such as the *One O'Clock News*, *Six O'Clock News* and *Nine O'Clock News*, has a programme editor who also has an office away from the newsdesk. Sometimes the programme editor edits his or her (the majority are men) programme, but usually this is done by more junior staff who are senior producers, and are acting as editor for the day. These senior producers operate to a rota which involves them in editing or being the special duty editor or the special production assistant.

The presenters sit opposite the editor and the special duty editor. Each presenter has a different style and mode of working: some like to be very involved with the activity of selecting and producing the news, and write their own introductions to stories and so on, whereas some assume a more passive role and simply spend the day reading through the stories as they come in and talking to the editor about them. The director of the programme ensures that the programme is broadcast without a hitch and occupies a key and important role in the gallery during transmission, in liaison with the technical production staff and the journalists. The director is aided by the production assistant in the gallery, who ensures that the programme does not overrun. The role of the presenter at the BBC is about to change as it adopts the USA model of the anchor system. Following the United States' tradition the BBC will use a much smaller pool of presenters, building up viewer recognition and familiarity, a policy which is ultimately aimed at ensuring greater programme loyalty from the audience.

The copy taster works a full newsday from nine o'clock in the morning until nine o'clock at night, watching the wires, watching television news, listening to the radio and reading the papers in order to alert the editor to any changes or developments on stories, or to give him or her new ones. Often the same information comes in from the Newsgathering part of the newsroom. This is because the role of the copy taster has changed since newsrooms became electronic. All journalists have a computer terminal and access to the wires and are all in a sense acting as gatekeepers.[7] The copy taster's most important time is from about one hour before transmission, when the editor is busy. When it is a long time until transmission, copy tasters will pass on even marginally interesting stories to the programme editor or chief sub. However, as it gets nearer to transmission time the copy tasters have to exercise more judgement and pass on only things which are directly relevant to the programme, avoiding bothering the editor with trivialities.

[7] White (1950) used the gatekeeper concept pioneered by Lewin (1943) and applied it to the study of news selection by wire editors. See also the challenges to White's research by Bass (1969), Snider (1967), Donahew (1967), Robinson (1970), and Bailey and Lichty (1972) and the recent reconceptualisation of gatekeeper theory by Shoemaker (1991).

Changes in the content of the BBC's news in the recent past is of interest. From 1987 until 1990, the BBC had a distinctive programme structure, generally covering only about four or five news stories in depth, and usually in the form of the so-called twin pack. This invention resulted from the Birtian philosophy of ensuring that stories were first told straight in one package and then analysed in a backgrounder or second package. In the second package an issue was extracted from the event for further consideration and was often followed by an appropriate interview with an expert. In response to falling ratings, however, programme editors began to commission a more diverse range of coverage (via their new editorial budgets), doubling the news stories in each bulletin and reducing the opportunity to include the more esoteric but boring twin packs.

One of the main problems which was identified by numerous BBC staff was the slow and ponderous way decisions are made by their senior managers. One producer drew the analogy of the BBC being like a huge oil tanker that would take ten miles just to stop. The view that the size of an organisation affects its internal structure is confirmed by business writers such as Handy (1993). When an organisation is as large as the BBC, it must have a clearly defined hierarchical structure to provide careful controls for consistency, news accuracy and decision-making. One of the main ways control is maintained at the BBC is through the translation of abstract public service ideals into written guidelines (BBC, 1996b), to construct a consensus of aims and goals in the absence of the profit motive. The *Producers' Guidelines* have recently been updated to include new problems which are being faced by BBC journalists relating to payment of witnesses. No other broadcasting organisation codifies its practice to such an extent.

One apocryphal tale illustrating the BBC's difficulty in making fast decisions concerns the death of Stephen Milligan MP.[8] Stephen Milligan was found dead at his home on 7 February 1994. Reporting the circumstances of his death proved to be more problematical for the BBC than for ITN. ITN led with the story that evening and all the next day, whereas the BBC placed the story fourth in its running order on 7 February, but led with it the next day. The problem which the BBC journalists faced related to the circumstances of the death. At the BBC a policy ruling by senior News and Current Affairs staff was issued in relation to the story content and 'the wording of the story' (BBC editor, News and Current Affairs). The reporting was therefore delayed whilst senior staff considered how the circumstances of his death should be reported. In contrast ITN broadcast the story, agreeing quite easily to a corporate line on taste and decency, but 'the BBC management couldn't make up their minds' (BBC senior producer, News and Current Affairs). The major problem related to taste and decency, and there was

---

[8] Stephen Milligan, Conservative MP, was found dead in his home by police. He had been practising auto-erotic sex by using a drug-soaked orange and self-asphyxiating (by placing a bag over his head and tying a flex around his neck), and was wearing stockings and suspenders.

debate as to whether there should be any mention of the orange in Stephen Milligan's mouth and whether there could be any mention of the way in which he was found. In the end the BBC allowed its journalists to mention 'women's underwear, the flex and the bag' once. The word 'orange' was not mentioned, and only the *Nine O'Clock News* was allowed to mention 'stockings'. At ITN, reference was made to the circumstances of his death, but at the prospects meeting the editor of ITV programmes said that there should be a restraint on the reporting of all the details, and requested that the orange was not to be mentioned.

ITN had no problems at all in choosing the Milligan story as the lead, because, as a BBC producer pointed out, 'they tend to go for the more scandalous and sensational stories and we don't' (BBC producer, *Nine O'Clock News*). ITN justified leading with the story because 'it was a puzzle and a mystery and potentially damaging to the government' (ITN producer, *News at Ten*). The main difference between the two organisations was that there was a good deal of doubt at the BBC about whether the story was important enough to justify it becoming a lead on the day it broke, or whether a story about Bosnia was more important (BBC producer, *Six O'Clock News*). At ITN there was agreement on the Milligan story being the lead story (ITN correspondent, *12.30 p.m. News*).

The differences in the news priorities of the two institutions is instructive. At the BBC, Stephen Milligan's death led to a disagreement in relation to news values, which delayed the reporting of the story. Some journalists argued that his death was not as important as the atrocities occurring in Bosnia. They believed that whilst the death was quite important, the only reason it had become so newsworthy in other newsrooms was because of the salacious details. In contrast, some other BBC journalists argued, in the same vein as ITN's journalists, that Stephen Milligan's death was of public interest and should be reported. That this divide exists between the two news organisations and within the BBC itself reflects some of the differences in television news philosophies.

Problems in reporting some news stories also occur in the regional newsrooms. The relationship of the regional news centres to the BBC in London is based on control and some tension. There is a great deal of referral upwards from the regions. For example, a correspondent who was unsure whether it was appropriate to interview a 14-year-old boy following a stabbing in a school first referred to the programme editor, who then referred to the editor of News and Current Affairs, who at this stage could have referred either to the head of Broadcasting for the North, or to the head of Editorial Policy in London. When asked about the regularity of the referral-up process, a senior News and Current Affairs journalist and manager at the BBC's *Look North News* replied, 'Frequency of referral, it depends if you're talking about formal referral processes or the informal process, which happens all the time.'

A further control placed upon the regions is via the scrutiny and review of mistakes by the BBC centre in London. The editorial policy controllers visit the regions and hold seminars where the reporting of crime and other issues is discussed and the BBC's central view on this is communicated to the regions. Finally, all journalists working in the regions have a copy of the *Producers' Guidelines*, which is referred to on a regular basis. As Schlesinger (1987) noted, referral up, which is supposed to be an indicator of editorial autonomy, is actually fictitious. Indeed the frequency of referral up from the editorial staff at the BBC's *Look North News*, on an 'informal' basis, serves to compound the view of voluntary compliance. In fact an obvious power relationship emerges whereby the regions seek constant confirmation that they are not breaking the BBC's rules and guidelines.

The structure and process of ITN's Channel 3 news

The structure of ITN is much more streamlined than the BBC's. The need to reduce staff numbers by almost half, and to become profit-making and efficient with fewer resources in the 1990s, has produced a company which is run along the same lines as a commercial enterprise. However, ITN does become more complicated than the BBC when one addresses issues such as its relationship to advertisers and to the other television companies. At ITN staff are reminded of such obligations by senior editorial staff in daily posters containing ratings and viewing figures. These are compared with those of the BBC and with those of the day before. At ITN ratings and audience viewing figures have been taken more seriously than at the BBC. ITN has been shaped to work more efficiently and effectively than the BBC, which has far more personnel and resources. The relationship between Intake and Output at ITN's Channel 3 and Channel 4 is very close and is much more integrated than the one between Newsgathering and Output at the BBC (the separation between news process and news content is not yet so distinct at ITN). This close relationship is in large part due to the financial constraints. The Home and Foreign Intake desks are situated next to the two main Output newsdesks. Therefore, the editors of Intake and Output are able to shout across to each other constantly, as well as to laugh and joke with each other.

The whole process of newsgathering and selection at ITN is more flexible and pragmatic than at the BBC. At ITN, the programme editors have more influence over the stories and types of story they would like to cover. ITN Intake journalists have to be completely sure a story is required by the programme editors before a correspondent and camera crew are committed to it. 'There is more consensus at ITN early in the day than at the BBC, and more integration between Intake and Output' (ITN senior editor). Journalists working for Channel 3 in particular at ITN do not spend a great deal of time considering whether a story is serving the public interest or not, but rather rely on their experience and expertise as journalists to tell them what is newsworthy and what is interesting enough to prevent the audience from switching off their television sets.

The newsroom at ITN is much smaller than the one at the BBC (see Figure 5). Even the architecture of the buildings which house ITN and the BBC is markedly different. The open and airy, glass and steel, Norman Foster building within which ITN is housed contrasts markedly with the warren of corridors, lift shafts and closed doors at the BBC. ITN was so pleased with its own building that it even featured it in the opening sequence of ITN's *12.30 p.m. News* and *5.40 p.m. News* in the early 1990s. At ITN the studio was placed on the edge of the newsroom. In this way the journalists can be made to feel far more part of a whole news process than at the BBC.

ITN's Channel 3 has both general reporters and correspondents. The general reporters, as their title implies, are sent out on a variety of stories and gain no particular expertise in any one area. The correspondents, on the other hand, are often more senior, have their own specialist areas and belong to bureaux. The bureaux at ITN are similar to the specialist units at the BBC, but cover some different specialities such as health and sickness, diplomatic news, business news and home affairs news, indicating differing areas of newsworthy priorities.

ITN, in common with the BBC, has producers, who work with and 'look after' the correspondents and reporters and who liaise with the programme editor. At ITN the individual who helps the editor is the chief sub-editor. His or her role is the same as that of the special duty editor at the BBC. One difference is noticeable: at ITN the chief sub also spends the morning editing the summaries, whereas there are other staff dedicated to this task at the BBC. ITN has fewer resources than the BBC and ITN producers often look after more correspondents and reporters. They also have to fight for more limited editing suites and graphics facilities. Furthermore, there is no special production assistant at ITN; the producers and senior producers have to help the editor as requested. Unlike at the BBC, there is no rota whereby three or four different people take it in turns to edit the programme; at ITN the programme editor usually edits for four days a week and spends one day planning and attending meetings, whilst the chief sub edits the programme. News programmes at ITN have acquired certain editorial quirks which are related solely to the personality of the programme editor, who interacts with the staff every day of the week in a journalistic role. For example, the *5.40 p.m. News* may often feature animal stories because 'Paul likes dogs'. No such identification seems to be apparent at the BBC, where some of the programme editors are away from the Output desk at meetings for hours or days at a time.

As at the BBC, ITN presenters sit opposite the programme editor, and some are more involved in the process of news selection and production than others. For example, Trevor McDonald as presenter of *News at Ten* attended all the editorial meetings and conferences and consistently tried to exert some influence over the handling of certain stories. Several times during my obser-

Figure 5   *The ITN Channel 3 newsroom*

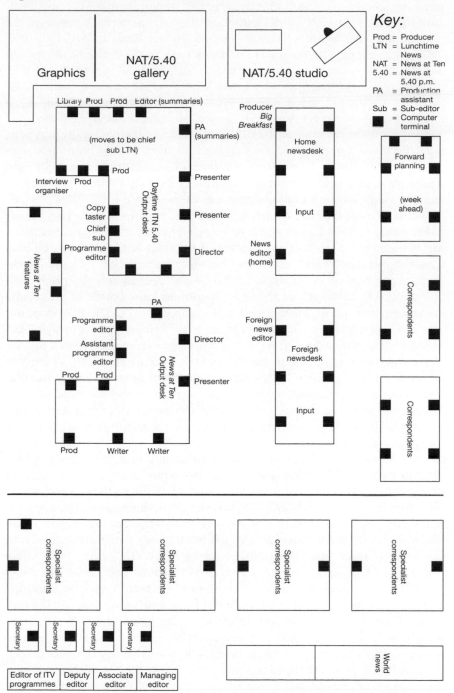

vation period he made comments that a sports story should be broadened to consider racism in sport. This was never undertaken during my visit, although in February 1995, following the televised clash between the English and Irish fans at a football match in Ireland, *News at Ten* did an 'analytic' piece asking why there were no black faces in the crowd at the match. Several black citizens were interviewed in the street, all of whom said they would not go and watch a football match because of racism on the terraces. Enthusiasm for such subjects only seems to be aroused in the senior editorial staff when there is a so-called 'fat peg' to hang it on. At ITN there are far fewer presenters than at the BBC and a form of viewer loyalty has been built up towards presenters. *News at Ten* has affectionately been known as the *Trevor McDonald Show*. It is this type of familiarity, accessibility and friendliness, common to ITN and American news programmes, that the BBC aims to adopt for some of its programmes in the future.

The director of the programme, as at the BBC, ensures that the programme is broadcast without a hitch and is aided by a production assistant. The director is under more pressure at ITN than at the BBC, because a news bulletin has to finish exactly on time due to the advertisements immediately following the programme, or during it, in the case of *News at Ten*. The production assistant (PA) has to ensure that the programme runs exactly to the second to prevent the advertisements suddenly cutting into it. The BBC does not have this same problem; a news programme is often allowed a leeway of several seconds either way, and when it is running over by more than a minute the editor can negotiate with the Presentation department for a little more time. It is not uncommon for the editor for the day to ring 'Pres' at the BBC and negotiate a returned favour (e.g. perhaps he or she has filled time for them by running an extra story earlier in the week). Of course these different relationships to programme length have some bearing on the flexibility of programme content.

At ITN there are a large number of regular and routine meetings which help to structure the newsday and allow the senior editorial staff, including the programme editor, to instruct the journalists about their requirements and their vision. Like the BBC, ITN encourages both senior and junior journalists to contribute ideas at meetings. At both organisations, senior editorial staff quickly dismiss any ideas which waste time or are too radical. Thus, each of the three news programmes produced by ITN's Channel 3 has a slightly different structure, but a predictable format. The *12.30 p.m. News* usually comprises eight or nine news stories of approximately one minute and forty-five seconds each, and contains one or two live interviews. The programme usually ends with sport, followed by city news. The *5.40 p.m. News* in contrast starts with the most newsworthy story, which is made more dramatic by using several devices: the lead-in words are spoken in a dramatic tone by the presenter; the first story is run before the rest of the headlines; the amount of time devoted to the first story is usually longer than the time granted to the rest of the stories in the bulletin; and the story is often accompanied by a live two-way or other interviews. The *5.40 p.m. News* is notorious at ITN for its dramatic lead-in, and the journalists sometimes occupy their spare time writing spoofs. The rest of the *5.40 p.m. News* programme comprises five or six stories, each lasting approximately one minute and ten seconds only. *News at Ten* is the most structured programme of the three. The structure varies from other mainstream television news programmes shown on ITV's Channel 3 and on the BBC, and changes little from day to day, keeping the same or a very similar format (Table 2). This is because the journalists have all day to consider which stories to include, and do not generally have to rush to get the story ready in time, thus paying more attention to the structure, flow and running order of the programme.

Table 2   *The structure of ITN's News at Ten*

Bongs
Item 1
Item 2
Item 3
Item 4
Item 5
Pre-commercial break teaser ('Precoms')
Commercial break
Item 6
Item 7
Newswrap
Special report
Sport
Headlines
And finally

News at Ten always leads with what is considered to be the most newsworthy story, but other newsworthy stories are highlighted by the headlines, read to the dramatic chimes of Big Ben. These headlines are known in the newsroom as 'the bongs'. The editor and the senior editors spend all day considering which stories will become the bongs, and a short film is prepared to accompany the presenter's words. The bongs are usually recorded in advance of the programme as it is difficult to get the timing precisely correct. The headlines have to be decided an hour or so before the news programme. The bongs usually contain a 'teaser' for a story which occurs in the second half of the programme, after the commercial break, to try to keep the audience interested for the whole programme. As research has shown that viewers often only stay with the programme for Part One, *News at Ten* has been redesigned so that important and interesting stories are included in Part Two. This structure differs from that of other news programmes, which endeavour to run the stories in order of their criteria of newsworthiness. It is the practice at *News at Ten* to place a very interesting and important story second in the running order. Sometimes this may not be the most newsworthy story, but is likely to contain a live two-way or an interview and is often a subject which affects many people, such as pensions or a rail strike.

Advertisements of stories to come after the commercial break are called the 'precoms'. These are, according to the *News at Ten* editor, vitally important as they advertise stories which are interesting enough to keep the audience loyal throughout the commercial break. The precoms therefore have a rather dramatic tone, such as 'and coming up after the break, the Hollywood star suspected of murder. A dramatic development tonight' (*News at Ten*, 23 June 1994). After the commercial break the editor aims to have two or three hard news stories saved for Part Two; these are presented individually and as a 'newswrap'. This is primarily to avoid the criticism that the second half of the programme is simply devoted to human interest and feature stories. Often a *News at Ten* special report is included about eighth or ninth in the running order. This will have been commissioned in advance by the programme editor and could take several days to film and edit. In a traditional sense this story will not be particularly newsworthy, but it will deal with interesting issues or events in some detail (often four minutes are dedicated to this slot). Storylines are often about unusual events or happenings, such as the mystery of corn circles, animal cruelty, or rhino hunting in Africa, or pseudo-issues such as whether tennis was more boring to the public in June 1994 than it was ten years earlier. None of these specials is particularly investigative and they are not particularly newsworthy or important, but deal with issues which might be found in a magazine or Sunday newspaper supplement.

The specials are usually followed by sport and a reminder of the day's headlines. The 'and finally' piece ends the news programme and is designed to cheer the audience up. ITN research has shown that the audience prefer the programme to end on a high note, and some time and effort are devoted to fulfilling their wishes. These stories are generally of a very light human interest nature or are about famous people.

The different structures and format requirements of the news programme go some way towards determining the content priorities and criteria of newsworthiness which are accorded the plethora of events and issues available during a television newsday. In contrast, the BBC's prime-time news programmes, the *One O'Clock News*, the *Six O'Clock News* and the *Nine O'Clock News*, transmit stories in order of their newsworthiness (using an inverted pyramid format).

The structure and process of ITN's *Channel 4 News*

In 1982 a new fourth channel was introduced to the British airwaves and S4C became the national broadcaster in Wales, reaching 0.4 per cent of the British audience. Following content analysis and newsroom observation, this account concentrates on *Channel 4 News* in London only.

The Channel 4 newsroom in London is smaller than that for Channel 3 at ITN (see Figure 6) but is still divided into similar work desks, such as the home newsdesk and foreign newsdesk (Input), summaries desk, Output desk, correspondents, producers and specialist units. The correspondents at *Channel 4 News* are usually involved in working on a story which has been well planned in advance, and do not really approve of being assigned stories by the programme editor. These correspondents are similar to the specialist correspondents at the BBC, as they prefer to offer stories rather than be allocated them. *Channel 4 News* correspondents produce stories of four or five minutes in length, and unlike the BBC they routinely attempt both to tell and to analyse the story in the same package. Therefore the producers at *Channel 4 News* have a different role from those working on Channel 3 news programmes. The latter are more like administrators, sorting out and organising correspondents, ensuring that all the Astons (words on the screen which denote name and title) occur at the right time, finding pictures to drop into pieces the correspondents have already partially prepared in the field, updating scripts and ensuring that the programme editor's wishes are complied with. At *Channel 4 News* the producers are much more involved in the story content and have more of an editorial role in producing the packages. Also, general producers move around quite a lot, perhaps acting as assistant editor on the newsdesk on one day and editor of the summaries the next. Thus, producers at *Channel 4 News* are much more in tune with the editorial role as well as its constraints and problems than those working on Channel 3 news programmes.

Channel 4 News has overseas bureaux in Washington, South Africa and Moscow, but is poorly resourced in comparison to the BBC, which has over fifty overseas bureaux. However, *Channel 4 News* has an Independents Fund, with which it can commission freelance journalists to help cover international stories. At *Channel 4 News* any coverage of foreign affairs usually has to be planned well in advance, therefore editors tend to consider very carefully the types of foreign story they will cover. For example, on 28 June 1994 the editor of Channel 4 programmes suddenly decided that it was imperative that *Channel 4 News* should cover the vote of the Legislative Council in Hong Kong on Chris Patten's democratic reforms the following day. He felt that the implications were enormous if Patten's plan was rejected, as it would undermine his role in Hong Kong, and if it was accepted it would still be an interesting story. The foreign correspondent was despatched immediately so he could arrive in time for the vote. What was particularly interesting about

Figure 6   *The ITN Channel 4 newsroom*

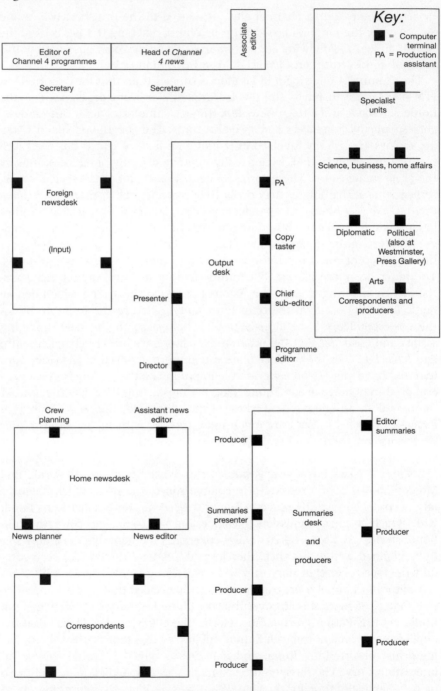

this story was that no other news programme bothered to cover it in any depth at all.

On 4 July 1994, *Channel 4 News* sent Jon Snow, the programme's presenter, to Jerusalem to cover Yasser Arafat's inauguration, and twenty-three minutes of the programme were presented from Israel. A senior figure at the time pointed out that 'Had that been the BBC's *Nine O'Clock News* there would only have been room for two or three quick stories and then they would be off the air, as it's a half-hour programme, whereas we have still got twenty minutes and we can do lots of other things as well. That is a great benefit, a great advantage.'

Channel 4 News can deliberately aim to cover different types of international news story and issue, on the basis that it has a longer time in which to do so. Mainstream overseas news stories which go into the newsbelt (the section of the programme in which the main news events of the day are quickly read by a second presenter) are often based on Channel 3 film, which itself may have been obtained via Eurovision, with a *Channel 4 News* voice-over done in London. *Channel 4 News* has also developed a Part Three to the programme which is designed to take a longer, more unusual feature piece. This was a positive decision by an editor of Channel 4 programmes, who described *Channel 4 News*'s remit as being 'a programme of news and analysis. It's meant to be a programme which has space for specialist reporting, which has a wider range of foreign coverage than is available elsewhere and which treats news in a serious and analytical way.'

Channel 4 News is the most rigorously planned of all the terrestrial television news programmes. This, in part, is due to the length of the programme, but also relates very strongly to its relatively small financial resources and its remit to be different. As the longer and more unusual pieces do not follow the mainstream news agendas, the programme has to commit its resources to initiating a piece from the beginning and cannot share the costs with Channel 3. Also, because its pieces are longer and more complex it often takes two or three weeks to produce some of the packages (the notion of the immediate does not apply to all stories as a criterion of newsworthiness at *Channel 4 News*). Planning can be divided, broadly speaking, into short-term and long-term. Short-term planning concerns the day-to-day decisions, such as which news event has to be covered and how, and what resources and facilities will be needed to do this. Obviously, every potential story cannot be covered to the same extent, so some events are deemed to be more newsworthy than others. One of the major conditioning factors on this process is the effect of decisions made regarding long-term news planning. This is necessary due to the structure of the programme, but once long-term planning has tried to pin-point likely areas of newsworthiness, the journalists have in effect created their own momentum. In other words, if resources have already been allocated, there is pressure to use them and to some extent this is regardless of what else is happening.

The *Channel 4 News* programme has a very distinctive structure. It is divided into three parts and contains two commercial breaks. Similarly to *News at Ten*, programme planners try to retain audience loyalty throughout the programme. Unlike *News at Ten*, *Channel 4 News* has only a very small audience (about seven hundred thousand viewers, down to half a million in the summer), most of whom are dedicated *Channel 4 News* watchers. The programme makers do not have to seek to be quite so single-minded in their quest to retain high viewing figures (at least it is not spoken about so often).

Part One of the programme always contains two packages and a live interview. If stories one and two are similar in terms of newsworthiness, then the editor tends to lead with the story which contains the interview. Part Two contains one package, which is usually something quirky or interesting enough to keep the viewers after the break, followed by the newsbelt, followed by another package. Part Three contains one package. This is known in the newsroom as 'a Part Three piece', which marks it out from the rest of the packages and the newsbelt. Part Three will not necessarily be based upon a topic which is currently in the news, but may be devoted to something which interests one of the specialist correspondents or the senior editors. For example, such pieces might be a story about a mutant virus affecting plants (4 July 1994); a profile of Margaret Beckett, when everyone else was looking at Tony Blair as a possible leader of the Labour Party (5 July 1994); or a profile on open-cast mining (7 July 1994). The Part Three pieces give *Channel 4 News* a distinctive style which has differentiated it from the other mainstream news programmes on ITV's Channel 3 and BBC1.

The *Channel 4 News* newsroom is thus very different from that for Channel 3 at ITN. In some respects the relatively low audience rating of the *Channel 4 News* programme has given it poor standing in the eyes of the Channel 3 journalists producing the mainstream programmes. Indeed, unusual overseas news items which appear on the wires are often referred to by Channel 3 journalists in a derisory fashion as a '*Channel 4 News* story'. It seems appropriate therefore that Channel 4's *Big Breakfast News* programme is produced not by the *Channel 4 News* team, but by journalists working for Channel 4 and housed in the Channel 3 newsroom.

The structure and process of regional television news

Regional television news broadcast from Leeds exhibits some interesting and distinctive features when compared with national news, although the similarities between the BBC in London and in Leeds is marked.

In his study of the seventeenth and eighteenth centuries, the thinker on the Scottish Enlightenment George Davie (1961) identifies one of that Enlightenment's central themes as a recognition of the fundamental role of the principle of common sense, that is, that other people's opinions should not be so uncritically accepted that they become the basis of those people's control over or use of force on us. In the seventeenth and eighteenth centuries this was a radical view; today it is one that Chomsky (1989) believes should be at the heart of an individual's relationship to the news. To some extent there has always been a diversity of opinions found in a variety of avenues of expression, from the parish pump, the pamphlet, books, local newspapers, magazines and so on, even though some groups were exclusive, such as those occupying the bourgeois public sphere in the late eighteenth and early nineteenth centuries. Those reading the radical press were often excluded from voicing their opinions, as they challenged the status quo. Nonetheless these were the traditional avenues that led to the forum of the challenge and counter-challenge of opinion. Davie (1961) argues with David Hume (the eighteenth-century Scottish philosopher) that the diversity of the free and unregulated exchange of opinion was the antidote to despotic and military governments and tyranny.

Today many new, electronic avenues of expression have arisen, and much of the forum for debate and formation of public opinion is wired. Newspapers survive, local television and the Internet have emerged. In the early 1990s, however, local or regional television was still in its ideal form, the most likely guarantor of the diversity of opinions, simply because it still had a position in the peak-time schedules and continued to attract audiences which matched or exceeded those watching early evening national news programmes (Cottle, 1993).

The fundamental *raison d'être* of local or regional television in a democracy is to ensure the expression of the diversity of opinions within a given area of cultural, economic and political identity. Local services such as the weather report or economic factual information must and do assume a sense of the regional. This important role is not to be underestimated, as citizens gain their citizenship first as members of their local community (city or region), and secondly as members of the nation, or rarely as members of a transnational state. Citizenship is primarily grounded in the local and regional. Regional television is about this first-order sense of our citizenship. Local or regional television is thus the natural forum (wired or not) for the free exchange of opinions, opinions closely based upon our citizenship. But, as I go on to show, the format, content and production regimes of local or regional television news reflect the same constraints and shortcomings as the national news. This means that the possibility of local television news occupying a space for the free exchange of views is as problematic.

Simon Cottle's (1993) analysis of Central Television's regional television news coverage of local and regional problems of urban distress clearly indicates how the professional pursuit by regional journalists of popular programming affects the representation of serious issues. Cottle analysed regional coverage of the Handsworth riots which occurred in Birmingham in 1981. His hypothesis was that national television news cameras provide only a fleeting and fragmentary response to regional concerns, because the national television medium was usually attracted to the latest outbreak of violent disorder, before moving on to the next national and international story. In contrast, regional television news should enable more in-depth and extensive coverage of issues, and encourage a diversity of opinions and views about inner-city conditions and causes of the riots. Crucially, regional television should provide the forum for these issues to be addressed and sustained over a longer period of time. Cottle found that the regional television news coverage of the riots by Central Television privileged a conservative understanding of the events, not through explicit explanation by the journalists but through their use of narrative structures, keywords, the agenda of issues and the types of image used to tell the riot stories over time. The regional news values therefore portrayed the riots as a criminal outbreak of lawlessness, requiring law and order to control it. For Cottle regional television news values mirrored those of the national news.

Regional television news should not simply be a replication of national news provided by BBC1, BBC2 or ITN. Indeed, the idea of regionalism at the BBC is embodied in the charter, in the licence and agreement and in the ideal of public service broadcasting. The BBC has a duty to cater for all tastes and interests and those include the regional audience. Similarly, the federal ITV system was set up on public service broadcasting principles and a belief in the importance of regional broadcasting. One of the key principles of public service broadcasting which underpins both the BBC and ITV systems is the principle of geographic universality and of catering for all tastes, interests and minorities.

Both the BBC and ITV systems have regional outlets or companies situated around Britain which should in principle be catering for a variety of tastes and geographical distinctions. Although television news should act as a guarantor of diversity of opinions, closer scrutiny of its content by Cottle (1993) has shown that such a belief is optimistic. There are serious challenges to the principles upon which regional news was originally built.

In Chapter 3 I showed that it is unlikely that the BBC will be able to adapt and accommodate to the truly diverse range of national and regional identities which exist in Britain, let alone in Europe. Programmes relating to the rich cultural heritages of Scotland, Wales and Northern Ireland are rarely broadcast by the BBC to those countries, except for speciality programming which is scheduled well out of prime time. Crucially such programmes are not simultaneously broadcast in England.

Although the BBC pledges that a third of its programme output will be produced in the regions (BBC, 1994a), this does not necessarily mean a change in the content or values of regional programme production. The Royal Charter does not have requirements on production quotas outside London, and this pledge can be met simply by London producers making some programmes in other parts of the country. Furthermore, programmes made outside London by people living locally do not need to be confined to reflecting local material. In spite of the licence agreement requirement that the BBC's regions contribute to the network output broadcast throughout Britain, it is the regions which are often neglected in terms of both programme content and speciality programming. Scotland, Wales and many of the regions in England outside London and the Home Counties are underrepresented in news broadcasts (Harrison, 1991a, 1991b), and Northern Ireland has generally been covered in relation to violent activity. 'Today regionalism, in BBC parlance, refers to a substratum of national programme services. It no longer has, as it once enjoyed for a few years before the Second World War, an independent existence as a real alternative to national broadcasting' (Scannell, 1993:37). It will be of interest to examine the contribution the new *Six O'Clock News* will be able to make to regional coverage. It is the BBC's latest pledge to 'mobilise the BBC's unrivalled regional and network resources together to reflect the increasing diversity of the UK in a way that no other single broadcaster can reach'.[9] It remains to be seen if the planned 'regular live report from a UK town or city focusing on the issue of the week'[10] will constitute adequate regional representation.

Indeed it has been the BBC's own policies which have increased coverage of London in relation to political reporting. Huge expenditure by the BBC on resourcing 4 Millbank (the studio and newsroom opposite the Houses of Parliament) has resulted in the situation where political correspondents are expected to produce something every day to justify such investment (Jones, 1995). As Roger Bolton (1995) argues, this might account for the overkill on British political stories and their endless recycling.

Such concentration of resources in the capital's political headquarters often produces news which is artificial and concerned with minutiae. This is similar to the news in the United States, where there is a strong tendency to politicise news stories in terms of their potential for reflecting political conflict (Fallows, 1996). If high investment in political journalism results in inconsequential political reporting, it would be better, and more clearly reflect the values of public service broadcasting, if resources were redeployed to the neglected regions, with coverage of a wider variety of European, international or neglected areas of the news agenda, such as the plight of the homeless or disenfranchised. Cottle (1993) found that although *Central News* did seek to inform, it also aimed to address the ordinary viewers and affirm their preoccupation and concerns with the privatised world of their family, leisure and consumption and not with the social issues underpinning urban distress. By following such a strategy ITV regional news cannot contribute effectively to public debate and engaged criticism.

Yorkshire Television was one of the highest bidders for a regional licence and pays £37.7 million per annum to the Treasury for its licence awarded

---

[9] URL<*http://www.bbc.co.uk/info/news/newsfuture/prog_page4.shtml*> accessed 9 October 1998.
[10] *Ibid.*

for the period 1993–2002.[11] The large licence bid resulted in financial stringency at YTV, which merged with Tyne-Tees Television; Yorkshire Tyne-Tees Television is now owned by Granada. YTV covers Yorkshire, Humberside, Derbyshire, part of Nottinghamshire and Lincolnshire. *Calendar News*, Yorkshire Television's daily news magazine, is a hybrid programme of hard regional news in the opt-outs (see below) read straight, and softer magazine items presented from the studio. Tyne-Tees Television covers north-east England and North Yorkshire. Granada covers north-west England.

Although YTV is based in Leeds, it obviously covers a wide geographical area and has the problem of making regional news applicable to the diverse audience it reaches. Lincolnshire news is not particularly interesting to people living in West Yorkshire, for example. *Calendar News* attempts to solve this problem by having 'opt-outs' whereby part of the programme goes sub-regional, aided by access to two different transmitters from Belmont and Emley Moor. The sub-regional opt-outs occurred twice in each programme in 1993, but the format and presentational style of the programme were altered several times between 1993 and 1999. In 1997 *Calendar News* operated with two separate opt-outs from the programme, during which three different variations of local news were broadcast from three separate locations, Sheffield, Leeds and Humberside. The rest of the news programme, approximately twenty minutes in length, is common to the whole region. *Calendar News* has been praised by the ITC for attempting to serve the region via sub-regional news opt-outs which cover news which is more applicable and relevant to people living in different areas of the so-called Yorkshire region.

The newsroom layouts in regional television news organisations are more compact than their London counterparts and less well resourced. BBC's *Look North News* is also bimedia and houses Radio Leeds. Obviously there is no foreign desk and the Intake or Newsgathering process is much more integrated into the whole process of news selection than in the system at the BBC in London. At both *Look North* and *Calendar News* the Newsgathering editor or Intake editor sits opposite the Output programme editor at the same desk. Also, staff often move around between the different roles. For example, the editor for the day at *Look North News* variously acts as the Newsgathering editor and performs a forward planning role, and other journalists take it in turn to plan ahead or to produce the short bulletins which occur throughout the day. This rationalisation of human resources at a regional level means there are no great divides between the different sections of the newsroom (or between content and process), although personality differences and differences of opinion between editors and producers obviously exist. *Look North News* is particularly interesting to study because the national influences from the BBC newsroom are apparent, such as the adherence to the policy of having specialist correspondents. Also, the system of referral

---

[11] The licence-holders were able to renegotiate with the ITC in 1998.

upwards is more apparent in the region than in London. It appears that the regional editors are more cautious about offending BBC managerial sensitivities than are the editorial staff in London.

The specialist correspondents at *Look North News* in Leeds reflect the different type of news covered by a regional organisation, specialising in education, transport, community affairs (mainly ethnic), health, business and industry, and environment. The role of these correspondents, as in London, is to seek out and generate stories and to provide in-depth analysis of the issues surrounding events. In practice, the correspondents generate few such stories and are often allocated stories to cover via the Forward Planning Desk or the Newsgathering editor. The rest of the journalists in the *Look North News* newsroom are called either regional journalists (generalists), who fill in, act as fixers, report a variety of news stories and forward plan, or reporters, who have their own geographic patch to cover. There are three main presenters at *Look North News*, and a main summaries presenter. In common with *Calendar News*, other regional journalists occasionally present bulletins.

At *Calendar News* the programme producer looks for two good stories to lead the programme, a chatty feature-type story which will lead into the break, and lighter pieces breaking up the local and generally more serious news opt-outs. The criterion required for the lead at *Calendar News* is different from that of *Look North News* in that the story does not necessarily have to be serious, and can be developed into a three-minute piece. News values at *Calendar News* depend upon which part of the programme the story is aimed at. Illustrative of the difference in news values and priorities at the two organisations is the fact that journalists at *Calendar News* watch *GMTV News* in the morning and *Look North News* journalists watch BBC1's *Breakfast News*.

The programme structure at *Look North News* still reflects the Birtian philosophy of the twin pack, in which the top story is always told straight in one package and then analysed in a backgrounder or second package. In the latter an issue is extracted from the event for further consideration and is usually followed by an appropriate interview with an expert. Often journalists struggle to fill a regional news programme with something interesting, and to try to extract the important issues behind such events can be difficult. However, *Look North News* has been rather less flexible in approach to its own particular interpretation of Birtian philosophy than have the London newsrooms, where there has been a pragmatic easing of the heavy approach to news in response to both journalistic and perceived audience wishes.

The programme editor at *Calendar News* is called the programme producer, and he or she is flanked by two news editors. Because the programme operates an opt-out system, both news editors are needed, one to cover the stories in the Emley transmitter area and one those in the Belmont area. The programme is much more complicated to produce than *Look North News* due to the opt-out facility, and therefore several technical staff sit at the main newsdesk. The studio, as in ITN in London, used to be in the newsroom, and because of the style of the programme, which has a magazine format, the presenter was at times even more integrated into the newsroom area; he or she wandered around and often sat on the edge of a newsdesk to present part of the programme. The rest of the newsroom is devoted to regional programming, so the area given to news alone is relatively small and compact and has a different layout from other newsrooms.

The differences between the layout and rationale of *Look North News* and *Calendar News* manifest themselves in both the content and the format of the programmes. *Calendar News* sometimes seems to struggle to reconcile hard regional news with the softer magazine items, and the programme set in 1994 was a curious hybrid of potted plants and computer terminals. The studio set was redesigned in 1996 and the programme currently has a slightly more conventional style. Nonetheless the presenters sit closely together behind a desk and the programme uses a format similar to that used by *Sky News*, in which the two presenters laugh, joke and interact with each other during the programme. In contrast, *Look North News* takes its remit directly from its London headquarters, aiming to impart information and explore issues, and so far its styles of presentation have been rather traditional. Although *Look North News* updated its studio and introductory sequence in 1995, it still follows a traditional format and has not deviated markedly from its original style of presentation.

There is undoubtedly a diverse range of terrestrial television news formats, news philosophies and news values in Britain in the early twenty-first century. This can be clearly related to the different television news programmes and organisations. These differences also apply to television channels, where, for example, BBC2 and Channel 4 both have a higher commitment to international news output than BBC1 or ITN on Channel 3 (see Chapter 7). Sometimes different news programmes can have different interpretations of the news value potential of the same event and can extract different stories or storylines from that event. While there are some substantial similarities between all television news programmes, it is clear that different news programmes do have different levels of commitment to explanation of complex issues, with programmes such as the *Big Breakfast News, GMTV News,* and ITN's *12.30 p.m. News* and *5.40 p.m. News* telling the story straight, without elaboration or diversification. This causes some concern for the informational quality of these television news programmes and for their lack of contribution to empowering their viewers to participate competently in the public sphere.

In contrast, *Newsnight, Channel 4 News* and BBC1's *Nine O'Clock News* in particular are less inclined to offer such simplistic explanations for an event, preferring to explore other relevant issues. However, *Newsnight* was reinvented during the late 1990s. In late 1998 it was relaunched following further changes (which include an update of the day's news at eleven o'clock) recommended in the 1998 Programme Strategy Review. The traditionally aggressive style of the programme has been softened since 1997. The BBC's rationale for this is that such change is necessary given that the current Labour Party is adept at manipulating and using the media, and that the Opposition is currently weak. Traditional modes of confrontation are, according to the programme editor, outdated and ineffective. Critics of the BBC argue that it should not suspend its critical faculties and give the current Blair government too easy a time. Many will see this as a sign of the BBC's reduction of its 'mission to explain' philosophy in favour of different priorities such as commercial enterprise, digitalisation and so on.

Both *Newsnight* and *Children's Newsround* tend to follow a different news agenda from the other news programmes, and *Channel 4 News* tends to report international news in fewer but longer sequences than domestic news. Chapter 3 and this chapter have also indicated how the different organisational values and structures can be used as indicators of their particular criterion of newsworthiness, and can show how different notions of what is public service broadcasting and what serves the public interest are at work in different television newsrooms. It is the maintenance of diversity of choice, representation and access which is at risk in the current broadcasting environment, due to the compromise being forced between public service broadcasting diversity and market-oriented choice, a compromise that the BBC in particular is finding challenging.

5

A shared culture

In spite of the differences that exist between numerous television newsrooms, I propose to analyse the similarities in news production and content exhibited by the different television news programmes and organisations. These similarities are grounded in the sharing by journalists of a set of extant formulas, practices, normative values and journalistic mythology passed down to successive generations (of journalists) – in short, a journalistic culture. This culture results in the perpetuation of common-sense values, lores and journalistic myths in all newsrooms. A shared belonging to a journalistic culture obviously provides journalist professionals with a clear and identifiable set of skills, practices and expectations within which they work.

Practices and routines

Such homogeneity within the practice of journalism is acceptable in the same way as homogeneity of medical or engineering skills is used to ensure a professional standard and quality. Thereafter, however, the similarities between the professions stop. Journalism, unlike medicine or other skills-based professions, contributes directly to the knowledge-base of society (rather like educational institutions but to a much shorter time-scale). The information which is produced by journalists generally, and television journalists in particular, is therefore automatically imbued with the potential to educate and inform or, problematically, to mislead and confuse. Given the constraints of the practices of the profession itself, it is only through offering a diverse range of news items at different times of the day that television news can attempt, in some small measure, to contribute to the pluralistic nature of Britain in the 1990s and early 2000s.

Any journalist, regardless of where he or she works, will already have, or have to acquire, a notion of what is newsworthy. This understanding of newsworthiness is intrinsic to being a journalist. Although all journalists, and indeed the general public, would recognise that the death of Labour leader John Smith was newsworthy, it is claimed that in general only a seasoned journalist has 'a nose for sniffing out the news' from the plethora of events and issues crowding into every working day. This acquisition of the knowledge of what constitutes newsworthiness, the ability to identify the newsworthy story and the skill to cover it are the factors which allow trainee or would-be journalists to 'join the club', and which keep the observer or the critic of journalism out. This mystique of the journalistic role is something which permeates aspects of its practice and teaching.

Journalistic practices require great expertise and precision and the acquisition of skills which allow journalists to master a brief quickly, not only to understand the complex array of facts and issues they may be facing, but to convert them quickly, succinctly and correctly into a package which will be meaningful to the audience and acceptable to their peers. Such skill is sometimes underestimated by some academic analyses, which dismiss it as being simply a formulaic response to a set of demands. In fact all the journalists working in national and regional television newsrooms have to reconcile contradictory pressures of good intention and creativity (particularly at the BBC) with the more prosaic time and cost constraints, contractual obligations and commercial imperatives. Many journalists are fairly good at analysing some of the shortfalls of their own profession, but of course some are not.

Newsroom study and observation of journalists at work, especially in particular national newsrooms, highlight the complexities involved in describing journalistic culture. Furthermore, newsroom observation highlights that in order to study the production of television news from within a newsroom, one must immediately dispel any notion that it is possible to explain the production or selection processes simply in terms of monolithic issues such as the influence of government or owners, or in terms of the routine nature of journalism or news factors, or simply via the measurement of television news output. Newsrooms are dynamic and sometimes frenzied; they are replete with tensions, pressures and constraints (see Breed, 1955; Bantz, 1985; Soloski 1989); and, in common with all organisations and institutions, they have their own codes and conventions.

Other comparative studies have pointed to similarities in news processes and output. However, most of these studies have either concentrated on news output only, using content analysis, or have simply analysed one or two newsrooms. The following claims to similarity in news production are based on the study of a broader range of newsrooms than hitherto analysed.

Bell (1991) identifies homogeneity in the format of all news stories, and writes generally about the similarity of the use of the lead or the lead paragraph and its structure, the use of headlines, the use of news sources, and journalistic devices such as the who, what, when, where, why and how, which ensure that all news stories basically contain a certain type of information. Also, the reliance on facts and figures, which all journalists use to illustrate and supplement the story, goes some way towards creating some uniformity of structure and content of broadcast journalism (Tuchman, 1978).

Chibnall (1980:86) points out that 'you can put six reporters in court and they can sit through six hours of court verbiage and they'll come out with the same story'. Journalists would prefer to see this as evidence of objective, skilful reporting rather than the 'triumph of formulaic narrative construction' (p. 86). Therefore rhetorical, structural and format devices which pepper the practice of journalism are often denied as such by journalists, who prefer to see them as methods to ensure that accurate, fair, impartial (and 'objective') information is conveyed as efficiently as possible.

Different studies of individual television newsrooms have highlighted similar types of procedure, structure, routine, pressure and constraint (see Burns, 1969; Epstein, 1973; Tuchman, 1978; Schlesinger, 1987). Empirical studies of television news output have pointed to similarities in news content. Research in the United States showed news editors' judging patterns to be nearly unanimous (Buckalew, 1969; Clyde and Buckalew, 1969). News selection patterns among daily newspapers in Iowa were interpreted by researchers as either representing similarity of news judgements or showing the pattern of emphasis of the wire service (Gold and Simmons, 1965). Whittaker (1981) argues that news in Britain is disturbingly similar in content and structure, leading towards a common set of assumptions which are taken for granted by the media. Such assumptions create a uniformity of discourse in the media.

It is possible to observe the similarity of format and structural devices at work in all newsrooms. For example, if a big story occurs, such as a major air crash or five policemen being shot dead in the Orkney Islands, the Input or Newsgathering news editors (the newsdesk) would know straight away that this was a good story and that the programme editors would want it for their particular programmes (i.e. they would 'know' their market, just as the programme editors 'know' their audience). Camera crews would be despatched to location X or location Y; programme editors might intervene at this point and ask if a crew could be despatched to location Z. Subject to logistics and resources this would be done. It is implicitly understood in all newsrooms that Input and Newsgathering editors have to be able to judge a newsworthy event and to react with speed in order to allocate crews, and as such cannot afford to waste too much time negotiating with Output. Both Newsgathering and Output programme editors are able to discount the potential news story which is hard to cover due to logistical difficulties and which is not worth specifically sending a crew out to. For example, twenty journalists all agreed that the three policemen who were accidentally injured on the Isle of Man whilst watching the TT races were not worth allocating a crew for, but if a crew had already been there then the accident would have been covered (ITN programme editor, *12.30 p.m. News*).

When this process becomes less clear cut in all newsrooms is if the story is not so obviously newsworthy (i.e. it is a mid-ranking story) and is of interest to some programme editors and not others. For example, ITN's *5.40 p.m. News* wanted to cover a story about some children being attacked and burnt by a man with a flame-thrower whilst in school, but *News at Ten* did not want to cover that story (ITN, 17 June 1994; see Chapter 7). Such differentiation in newsroom conceptions of newsworthiness contradicts the view that all news output and process are very similar. Even within the same organisation the fragmentation of the news genre has resulted in a plethora of possible combinations of different news sub-genres, which in turn allow a variety of news programmes to emerge, all of which do show diversity in their assessment of newsworthiness.

Philip Gaunt (1990) argues that journalistic images and practices are in large part the result of journalistic traditions which are shaped by history. In his comparative analysis of journalism in France, Britain and the United States, he argues that traditions are created and developed in accordance with the laws, economic constraints, political pressures and social dynamics of the culture in which they exist, as well as technological developments. He believes that the stereotypical image of the journalist in each country is different. In France, for example, the journalist is often seen as a tough intellectual who is politically motivated. In contrast, Gaunt's version of the American journalist is the stereotype produced by 'Humphrey Bogart's newspaper reporter in *Deadline USA*, a shirt-sleeved hero with typing fingers like meathooks, eager to fight corruption in high places and defend the cause of TRUTH' (Gaunt, 1990:20). In Britain, Gaunt argues that it is Evelyn Waugh's novel *Scoop*, which portrays 'the London reporter as an unscrupulous news hound in pursuit of a good story, or as a nail-bitten, nicotine-stained fingered hack bashing out his story on a battered old typewriter' (p. 20), which is most accurate. Whatever the true image is of the British journalist, it is interesting to note, in fiction at least, that it is very different in tradition and style from his or her French and American counterparts.

Sparks (1991) laments the loss of the hard news reporter symbolised by Hildy Johnson in the 1930s play *The Front Page*. Hildy Johnson's great triumph was to expose a corrupt city administration and to save the life of a murderer, whilst almost losing the chance to marry his fiancée. He is an attractive image of the investigative and tenacious journalist, whose role is often referred to in debates about citizenship. Such concerns with journalism and citizenship highlight the impossibility of there being an enlightened citizenry if the press and the broadcast media simply report what they are spoon-fed by the government and other authorities. Hildy, therefore, has become a metaphor for press and broadcasting freedom. As Sparks remarks, rather sadly, the modern Hildy Johnson 'no longer dreams of bringing down the mayor or the government in the wake of a great scandal. That only happens in the movies' (Sparks, 1991:72).

Journalistic training and socialisation

In Britain, the image of journalism variously as a trade or as a profession has been related in part to its education and training, and to the different routes into journalism, via university, via college, or up through the ranks starting in the regional press. The method of entry into journalism often, but not always, reflects the type of work the journalist will undertake. Most journalism training is industry-driven, in the sense that journalists are expected to acquire certain skills which will enable them to identify newsworthy facts so they are able to produce a newsworthy story and to work within the constraints of the law and professional codes of practice.

The National Council for the Training of Journalists (NCTJ), for example, usually produces reporters who will work on regional or weekly papers, who often move on to the national newspapers later in their career. The NCTJ course is formulaic; journalists must complete a set of examinations, a shorthand test, and a final proficiency test in order to pass, studying subjects such as law and public administration as well as learning how to write a news story. The acquisition of National Vocational Qualifications (NVQs) and on-the-job training stresses the practice of journalism, and its status as a trade.

Other courses which attempt to reconcile such skills with an academic grounding in the issues and dilemmas facing journalists have emerged once again in universities (some provide NCTJ accreditation). In the same way as the BBC encourages its home-grown graduate trainees to become thinking journalists, higher education is encouraging would-be journalists to evaluate critically both the profession and the role of journalism. In a recent survey of print, agency and television journalists, researchers found that the proportion of journalists that go to university or college has increased enormously since around 1980 to 69 per cent.

Once the trainee journalist has entered the newsroom, then a further learning process begins. Assuming that at this point all journalists have acquired the rudimentary skills of their trade, through whatever means, they will now be faced with the daunting task of putting them into practice. New recruits have also got to learn about the organisation and newsroom for which they are working. Often this occurs through assimilation of newsroom mythology and socialisation (Shoemaker and Reese, 1996), which is communicated down by experienced journalists. These veterans of journalism often make assertive statements about their profession which no one can prove to be correct or incorrect, but which can be incredibly confusing to a novice or an observer. One such example occurred in the *Look North News* newsroom. A female correspondent complained that a rape which occurred in broad daylight had not been covered because it happened in Cleethorpes and not in Leeds. Whilst this claim may have had some basis in truth, it is clear that story coverage also depends on many other variables. This seemingly cathartic admission of the shortcomings of BBC journalism is a reflection of BBC journalists' sensitivity to criticisms levelled at them by academic research and journalists in other organisations, as well as a result of the politically correct values of the corporation. The problem is that the internalisation of such criticism can then become a catch-all explanation for non-coverage of stories. All senior or experienced journalists issue a wide variety of such polemics from time to time about the inadequacy of the organisation, apocryphal tales of stories which were missed or handled badly, examples of really great moments, criticism of bad journalists and so on; the junior recruits watch, listen and absorb, and mythologies are continued.

In every newsroom there are generally several new journalists. The novices tend to be young and ambitious and have faced a good deal of competition to get to their position. In most cases there is also an inherent desire to please the senior journalists – not to rebel and shock, but to conform and contribute. All the new journalists are quickly schooled into understanding that investigative journalism is basically a myth and that their success is strongly related to their accuracy and skill in applying journalistic techniques and formulas. At the BBC inexperienced journalists are treated quite harshly, given the least exciting stories and left to muddle through. The routine of any newsroom is one of spasmodic hyperactivity, and when an exciting news story breaks or transmission time gets close, the young journalist often finds that he or she is ignored. Senior staff appear impatient and tense, making it difficult for the trainee to ask questions or to get guidance at particular times of the day. If he or she has been pushed into the situation of having to meet a deadline when everyone is far too busy to help, then the trainee must very quickly learn how to cope. All newsrooms are full of these tense, stressed and inexperienced journalists. Those who survive the pressure are, by the nature of their work environment, socialised into a (best) way of doing things which is in total accord with the rest of the news programme or news organisation. In effect this results in a conformity of production and selection.

Uppermost in the new journalist's mind is survival (similar to Peter Woods' (1986) survival strategy of teachers), whereas the other, more experienced journalists appear to have other concerns, such as beating the opposition and making sure that their own news report and coverage is better than the rival company's, as well as showing a broad grasp of the subject. In all newsrooms, but especially in a forum such as *Channel 4 News*, *Newsnight* or BBC1's *Nine O'Clock News*, a journalist who has not thought a subject out thoroughly or is not able to express a degree of cynicism or lateral thought about an event or issue is often humiliated by the other journalists who know better. Some journalists cope with this by becoming news junkies totally immersed in news and current affairs, whilst others who take it less seriously never move on. A journalist would probably defend such immersion as a professional tactic to ensure that the public gets the best possible news coverage, but it is also an expedient way of avoiding embarrassment or humiliation by his or her peers. In other words, the demands of the news-room and other journalists require that a journalist is able to discuss exist-ing or potential news stories intelligently, or to critique them, with fellow journalists. On listening in to such a conversation one will often hear jour-nalists expressing doubt or looking for an angle, or saying things like 'there's something odd about this killing' (ITN correspondent, *News at Ten*).

Once a journalist gains experience of the demands and pressures of jour-nalistic culture, he or she can move beyond simply surviving the newsday and be more able to contribute to the ebb and flow of newsroom discourse, humour and journalistic analysis of the stories and events covered. By that time the journalist will have learnt the nuances and techniques of news selection and production according to the particular journalistic culture and values in operation in the particular television newsroom.

Some values permeate all newsrooms and are the same wherever a jour-nalist works. For example, all journalists are inherently driven by the quest for the good story, the telling of which will impart some information to the audience. (Although the definition of a good story may differ from newsroom to newsroom, it is nonetheless a guiding principle of every newsday.) A jour-nalist who cannot identify what is newsworthy, whether it is the identifica-tion of certain newsworthy facts to complete or update an existing story or the recognition of a new newsworthy issue or event (according to the crite-ria the programme uses), will strive to learn. One who repeatedly suggests stories which are not newsworthy will not be humoured for long. A jour-nalist must learn how to work to deadlines and other format and legal con-straints, which he or she must respect and obey. (Again, this requirement is the same in all newsrooms even though the specification may be different.) So much depends on clear and precise communication, often in journalistic jargon or other codes, that a journalist must learn the value of trust in fel-low team members and learn to be an efficient and reliable member of that team. In all newsrooms journalists talked in terms of having to trust their fellow news personnel, and it is one of their key values.

Therefore, the values one would find in any television newsroom can be summarised as awareness, acceptance and trust; that is, awareness of what constitutes newsworthiness, even if a journalist cannot articulate it in any other way than 'a gut feeling', or as 'having a nose for a good story'; accep-tance of the logistical, legal, organisational, economic and political con-straints of news selection and production; and being able to be trusted oneself and to trust one's colleagues. Any journalist who fails to acquire these val-ues will have a difficult time surviving in any broadcast newsroom.

What does this tell us about conceptions of newsworthiness in different television newsrooms? Undoubtedly, journalists are all schooled to develop a good news sense. Furthermore, television news does concentrate to some extent on the same news stories, illustrating the 'me too' aspect of journal-istic practice, where journalists follow stories because their competitors are also following them. However, the market-driven diversification of news programmes is, to some extent, allowing television news journalists to escape the strait-jacket of copying the opposition (although this commitment to diversity really only applies to a percentage of the news stories broadcast). As always in any form of journalism, big news stories, such as the Lockerbie plane crash, the death of Diana, Princess of Wales, election results, general elections and major government reshuffles, or dramatic events such as the ending of the Waco siege in Texas result in a 'feeding frenzy' of all types of media, which compete with each other for readers and ratings.

The relationship with the audience

Currently all television news organisations commission audience research. This tendency has increased since about 1990 due to a number of factors, such as changing technology, deregulation, new sources of demand, increased viewing and listening opportunities and audience fragmentation. These have all led to increasing competition in the broadcasting industry (Kent, 1994).

At ITN in particular, the maintenance of audience ratings is deemed to be crucial to the future security of the news business in the face of such broad and sweeping developments, because it is the audience which the company sells to the advertisers. Crucially, the BBC has had to enter into this commercial maelstrom due to the continuous debate about the validity of its licence fee. The initial argument here is why everyone should pay a licence fee for the BBC when it attracts a declining share of the audience. Its 1998 Programme Strategy Review used audience research to help the BBC to gain audience loyalty and to maintain or even improve its television news ratings in the contemporary competitive climate. However, it remains to be seen how these management-led research findings will be assimilated and interpreted by the journalists who produce and select the news. A major criticism which can be levelled at the BBC's new news policy is that there are no detailed plans about what the news programmes will contain or how they will be constituted. The findings from audience focus groups, commissioned and interpreted by BBC management, will be passed down for assimilation into the journalistic process and culture. The implication is that at the BBC, news will no longer be primarily determined by the importance of the news story, but rather by how the event or issue fits in with particular programme styles and audience profiles. When newsroom personnel at the BBC were discussing the logistics of covering the results of the local elections in May 1994, the conversation centred on the aim to present the figures so that they could be *understood* by the audience. In 1994 this was a relatively rare conversation at the BBC, because discussion of the audience has tended to assume until recently that it is generally more of a concept than a real force (Blumler, 1969). It is noticeable that the potential for audience involvement or interaction has been a neglected criterion. It appears that Madge's (1989) observation about the distant relationship between programme makers and their audience is now out of date in the competitive early 2000s. The activities of both the BBC and ITN in relationship to pleasing their audiences raise issues which directly relate to the nature of the public sphere, the interpretation of what constitutes the public interest and public opinion, as well as the relationship between television news and democracy.

This kind of research, upon which ITN in particular relies as a day-to-day indicator of the success of its programmes and as a determinant of its assessment of newsworthiness and public interest, is in fact a poorer indicator of the nature of the audience than that gained from focus groups. Audience ratings give a general indication of audience size and audience composition (in demographic terms). They do not indicate what audiences think or feel about programmes. ITN has long conducted more extensive research about its viewers and has already differentiated its programming, which is aimed at maintaining and building upon audiences as well as meeting specific contractual requirements from the ITV companies, Channels 4 and 5 and Planet-24 companies.

In contrast to the view of the audience held by the news organisation as a whole, as a statistically determined entity, journalists also share the common practice of envisaging their own audience. Whenever I asked any individual journalist how he or she saw his or her audience, the newsroom journalist, unlike the senior management, would never respond with a statistical analysis of the audience as being 'three million' or '4.6 per cent higher than the BBC's audience'. For many television news journalists the audience is much more organic and emotional (and probably inaccurate). The audience was variously described as follows: 'It's like my mother, you know, just got in from work, wants a cup of tea and her feet up, she doesn't want to watch anything too boring' (ITN correspondent, *5.40 p.m. News*); 'I always think of someone a bit like me, been to university, and doesn't want to be patronised, wants a bit more information' (ITN correspondent, *Channel 4 News*); and 'Well, I always think of my wife really, if I can find a story which will make her say "Oh really!" then I think it will be an interesting programme' (ITN editor, *5.40 p.m. News*).

Any analysis of the attempt by all news organisations to measure their audience ratings shows that these measurements do not have a high impact on the programme journalist's definition of the audience. What journalists have in common is that they all work to their own particular definition of the audience when selecting and producing television news stories. Nonetheless they are still able to adapt and change their audience visualisation to meet the requirements of different television news programmes. Therefore a migration from ITN's *5.40 p.m. News* to *Channel 4 News* would not necessarily be a problem for the journalist. In fact the journalist's personal and private view of the audience must, of course, conform to the remit of the programme, and the personalisation of journalistic activity (freedom to envisage the audience) is a mythical freedom. Journalists working on a programme have their own mythical relationship to the audience.

Gans (1980) argues that journalists (in the United States) are deliberately ignorant of the audience, and Schlesinger (1987:116) points to a 'missing link' between news producers and the audience. My own experience in all television newsrooms supports these views. Either broadcast journalists have little or no interest in their audience, or they create one stereotypical character whom they carry around in their heads wherever they go, adapting him or her to suit the particular programme they are working on. Similarly the audience may simply be judged in terms of which newspapers it reads. For example, the *5.40 p.m. News* programme editor at ITN aims his programme at people who read the quality popular newspapers, such as the *Daily Telegraph* at the top end of the spectrum and the *Daily Mail* and *Express* at the other. *News at Ten* aims its programme at the readers of *The Times*, the *Daily Telegraph* and the *Daily Mail*, while BBC1's *Nine O'Clock News* viewers are conceived of as *Financial Times* readers.

For journalists, a key news value is the idea of the relevance of a story to their particular audience. However, what constitutes relevance varies from newsroom to newsroom and is entirely relative to the priorities of the news organisation. Relevance is generally achieved through compromise between two main value judgements, namely what is important and what is interesting. News personnel usually refer to their news judgement by saying they select something that is either important or interesting to the audience. In practice both ITN and the BBC have to try to reconcile these two values in an attempt to marry the principle of public service broadcasting with the commercial imperative. News organisations select news according to a variety of guiding rules: 'Is the story interesting?', 'Is the story important?', 'Can something interesting be important?' and 'Can something important be made interesting?'

The BBC's news programmes and *Channel 4 News* have tended to aim for the value of importance, and try to make it interesting, although as argued earlier the focus on what is relevant may be changing news values. ITN's Channel 3 news programmes aim for stories which are interesting, arguing (perhaps defensively) that interesting stories can be important. *Calendar News*, *Big Breakfast News* and *GMTV News* aim for stories which interest and entertain the audience. Stories which are important will only be covered if they can be made interesting. Because of the differences in focus on what constitutes a relevant story for a particular audience, news programmes have different news values and different ideas about what serves the public interest. Problematically, if relevance becomes dominated by the priority to interest the audience through accessible news that is easy to understand, the depth and breadth of an issue can be compromised.

The impact of technology

It is notable that Burns (1969), Epstein (1973), Tuchman (1978) and Schlesinger (1987) all completed their observations of newsrooms prior to the evolution of electronic newsgathering and computer links to agency copy, analysing news production in terms of agency tape and teleprinters.[1] In the early 1980s, several important developments in technology helped to transform television news (Willis, 1990). The advent of satellite links facilitated the invention of live two-ways, where 'our own correspondent' could provide on-the-spot news from far off places. Electronic newsgathering (ENG) speeded up the whole process, changing the priorities of newsrooms and increasing the orientation towards the use of film. Television newsrooms were computerised. During the 1980s there was a large increase in news output, with the advent of twenty-four-hour competitors such as *Sky News*, the introduction of breakfast news programmes or programmes containing news, such as *GMTV News*, BBC's *Breakfast News* and Channel 4's *Big Breakfast News*, and minority audience news programmes such as *Channel 4 News*. This growth in news programming elevated the status of news in terms of resourcing and budgets towards a level only previously enjoyed by the current affairs programmes (Tunstall, 1993), as more news programmes began to compete for the same audience and aimed to provide a 'distinctive' news programme. At the BBC in particular, the merging of news and current affairs illustrated the increasing status of television news during John Birt's early period as deputy director-general and director-general. In the 1990s the proliferation of satellite and cable channels, the growth of the Internet, the merging of technologies and the potential for interactivity, the advent of Channel 5, digital broadcasting and twenty-four-hour rolling news programmes resulted in a massive growth in current and potential news and information supply for the audience.

At the same time, the investment in television news is being put under increasing pressure both at the BBC and at ITN. In the case of the former, the high investment of the early 1990s has now been stabilised and the News and Current Affairs Directorate has to compete more fairly in the internal BBC market (*Media Guides*, 1995–9). Such a development is of concern, as greater access to a high quantity of news output does not necessarily correlate with a more knowledgeable and informed audience. Too much live news which is raw and unedited and broadcast on twenty-four-hour rolling news channels, or edited down to short, fifteen-minute bulletins, may have a negative effect, if the former is too complicated or out of context and the latter simply becomes a set of repetitive rolling bulletins which sap resources from, and eventually replace, the mass audience news programmes. Only when senior broadcasting personnel recognise that the

---

[1] See Chapter 2 of Inglis (1990) for a discussion of the impact of technology, and MacGregor (1997).

image-and-information blizzard unleashed by technology requires analysis and should not simply be passed on, that news delivered at too fast a pace or very short, heavily edited pieces are not conducive to good audience understanding, can the television news medium provide information to enhance and enable audience participation in the public sphere. This is not currently a primary concern of most broadcasting institutions. In 1997 the BBC asked for audience feedback relating to its proposed digital channels and twenty-four-hour rolling news. The response clearly indicated to the BBC that there was concern that the rolling news programme would be repetitive and uninformative (BBC, 1997a), and there was little indication of a public demand for twenty-four-hour news. Despite audience apathy towards rolling news, the BBC has launched BBC *News-24* as part of its digital future, in direct competition with *Sky News.*

The BBC has to face a difficult decision with regard to its commitment to good-quality news delivered in a twenty-four-hour format, as development of rolling news allows less time for reflection and interpretation by journalists. Instead news is increasingly likely to be passed on in a live, raw and fairly unedited form. The signs are that this will be a future format for terrestrial television news providers, with short headline bulletins provided on most channels and dedicated, branded news channels (possibly eventually on a pay-per-view basis). As viewers increasingly become content browsers, it is likely the appointment news programmes will diminish as schedule features, and audiences will dip in and out of a variety of information sources (subject to their ability to access them).

There are also problems with reliance on technology, as instances of technological failure can have an effect on whether the story is even transmitted. Although improvements in technology can work positively to increase the possible range of news stories covered, to speed up the time it takes for an event to be reported to the public, and to facilitate live links to the place where the event is actually occurring, there is also a negative side to the equation. Situations can arise where a story is only partially, and perhaps misleadingly, covered because a satellite-link breakdown results in an event having to be missed or the informative nature of the transmission compromised. In the past, film of events often took several days to reach the news organisation, but this was an accepted part of news coverage. Today, a story often has to be covered immediately or the news organisation will have 'missed it'. The need for immediacy and speed of coverage, directly relating to improvements in the capabilities of new technologies, has superseded the inherent content or informational quality of the event or issue as a criterion of newsworthiness.

One can also argue that journalists are becoming too reliant on and unquestioning about the capabilities of new technology. Sometimes reporters and correspondents write a story without even leaving the building and are able to accompany this with film supplied either by a freelance camera operator, through the Eurovision network or via associate picture agencies, such as World-Wide Television News (WTN) and Reuters Television, which are similar to picture versions of the wires (see 'Reliance on news agencies' below). In part, the changing role of the journalist in Britain can be explained by the increased number of outlets some reports have to serve (despite organisational claims of programme differentiation). At the BBC, a report may be used by *Breakfast News*, and then updated and changed for the *One O'Clock News*, *Six O'Clock News* and *Nine O'Clock News* programmes, and at ITN for the *12.30 p.m. News*, *5.40 p.m. News* and *News at Ten*. At *Look North News*, journalists routinely have to produce reports which are bimedia, so that they can be used for both television and radio. The skills and time consumed attempting to meet such greedy demands of their work ensure that many journalists spend a good deal of their time in editing suites and in front of their computer terminals, becoming ever-more like MacGregor's (1997:211) 'battery hens', and increasing the divide between newsgathering and output. John Tusa noted in his 1994 James Cameron Memorial Lecture that 'it is, of course, a problem that has not crept up on us suddenly. Recently, a senior BBC correspondent said to me: "We're not correspondents any more. We're scarcely even reporters. We have become re-processors. There is no time for digging up the news"' (Tusa, 1994:4).

Another concern regarding technological developments was identified by a *Channel 4 News* editor, who believes that technology has had an unusual and often unnoticed effect on newsgathering which has, in turn, resulted in a faster turnover of news stories. He argues, and unfortunately it is difficult to prove, that a story is dropped a lot more quickly now than in the past. He comments that a few years ago, a news story would have been told one day and then analysed the next. In the late 1980s, the BBC began the precedent of trying to do both things in the same programme with their twin packs (story followed by analysis or backgrounder). *Channel 4 News* have now gone one stage further and try to analyse and tell the story in the same package, which results in the story becoming old news even more quickly. Usually stories which have been reported and analysed are dropped the next day, and so news is increasingly lacking in context and less useful in an informational sense. Indeed it would be entirely possible for the audience to miss significant events simply by missing one day's television news. Perhaps society is becoming more and more impatient by nature; television news may be becoming like convenience food, brightly packaged, quick, convenient and briefly satisfying, with no nutrition. The question to address is whether new technology is aiding the transference of information or knowledge, or whether it is converting the experience of news into Postman's (1989) nightmare.

A journalistic culture ensures that a certain set of shared practices, values and normative assumptions exist alongside a clear and identifiable set of skills and expectations within which journalists work. Environmental changes which affect journalistic practice (for better or for worse) are absorbed into the culture and converted to journalistic expertise. For example, technological development, which clearly causes concern for some journalists, is nonetheless quickly absorbed into the journalistic way of gathering and reporting the news. The relationship with the audience is similarly pragmatic. A journalistic culture can absorb the pressures to interest and entertain audiences and the aim to increase audience ratings. It is the pragmatic nature of journalistic culture which holds the key to the future value of the profession in its relationship with the public sphere. A pragmatic but discerning journalistic culture could resist some of the practices which reduce the informational quality of television news (such as increasing the tempo of the news, use of gimmicks, introduction of human interest stories to entertain the audience and so on), and reinvent itself through a pragmatic but considered negotiation of the changes forced upon journalism by technological development and the new commercialisation of the television news environment. However, when we go on to consider journalistic culture further, it is clear that many aspects of journalistic practice actually work against a positive relationship between journalism and the public sphere. For example, the relationship of journalists to the news agencies, the tendency to over-plan the news, and the adherence to the myth of editorial autonomy, which allows for control in the newsroom to be concentrated in few hands, all serve to reduce the opportunity for innovation or diversification of news values within a newsroom. This is further compounded by the constraints of costs, time and space and is perpetuated through a particular and exclusive journalistic newsroom language and the use of humour.

Reliance on news agencies

In all national television newsrooms one of the main sources of news is the national and international news agencies, or wires as they are commonly known. The sole domestic national news agency is the Press Association. (PA). International news is covered largely by two agencies, Reuters and Associated Press (AP), although the BBC also subscribes to Agence France-Presse (AFP) and United Press International (UPI). The news agency TASS was replaced by a very diminished Interfax service and ITAR (renamed ITAR-TASS in 1992), which neither the BBC nor ITN subscribes to. There are also separate wires covering economic and sports news. *Look North News*, for example, receives Reuters, PA, AP and a plethora of local wire services via Mercury, a local news agency. There are also keywords built into the system, so that the word 'Yorkshire', for example, can be used as a filter system. In this way the choice of newsworthy stories is predetermined by the news agencies and the filter system.

Each news agency has an extensive network of correspondents who aim to provide a comprehensive coverage for a subscription fee paid by the subscribing organisation. In the early 2000s such information is sent to every newsroom computer terminal, so in effect every single journalist is party to all the events which news agencies consider to be newsworthy. The copy taster in modern television newsrooms no longer occupies the same pivotal position, as all journalists are able to perform the task of sifting for newsworthy stories. Neither *Look North News* nor *Calendar News* had a designated copy taster in their newsrooms; the task of watching the wires was shared by all the staff.

Criticisms can be levelled at such a system of newsgathering. First, many of the reporters at news agencies are young and inexperienced, often moving on to work for television news organisations once they are adequately qualified. Secondly, news agencies which are effectively unaccountable are setting the agenda for news. Furthermore, the history of news agencies is instructive (see Schlesinger, 1987), and Smith (1991) argues that it is impossible to examine the global news agencies without considering their relation to capitalism. The news agencies are large commercial empires, built on the backs of colonial information systems, and the British news agency Reuters in particular was oriented towards promoting national interests in Britain's various colonies and promoting British interests world-wide (Lorimer, 1994; Read, 1992).

The news organisations willingly accept, and appear unquestioningly to pay for, the service, and most journalists defend the journalistic integrity of the agencies. In fact as one *Channel 4 News* producer pointed out, 'there is a mystical or even mythical quality about them. This is particularly so with the Press Association, which is revered throughout the industry as one of the best training-grounds for keen young journalists' (Producer, *Channel 4 News*, 25 June 1994).

In most television newsrooms the news personnel therefore can be removed from 'the sharp end' of the event but do not really contest the accuracy of the bulk of agency material. Obviously journalists check the different agency versions of the same story to ensure there are no major discrepancies, but they still have to rely on the agency perspective on that event. ITN in particular has to rely on international agency material more than the BBC, as it has fewer overseas bureaux.

Overseas news agency material (Eurovision and Asiavision) is available to members of the European Broadcasting Union (EBU). Both the BBC and ITN are members of this union and are entitled to ring in and request film of events occurring in different countries. There is a Eurovision and Asiavision conference six times per day,² plus a special relationship which exists between the BBC and ABC News in the United States and in 1994 between ITN and WTN. Such facilities enable journalists to acquire film of almost any major event in the world. Occasions when British film is requested are

---

² These are regularly scheduled news exchanges, each allocated twenty to thirty minutes of transmission time.

usually following major events such as Diana, Princess of Wales's death, large-scale accidents and disasters such as the plane crash at Lockerbie, or bomb explosions in Northern Ireland. It is interesting to note that the perception that other countries will get of British news is that it is full of violence, disaster or death.

Of key importance is the Eurovision news exchange system, which was started by the EBU in 1958. The Eurovision News Exchange (EVN) produces an enormous amount of daily news and information and has formed links with other television news agencies. It is the only news organisation which receives co-operation from countries at war with each other, and therefore plays a vital role in the free flow of global information.[3] Use of facilities such as the EVN overcomes some of the constraints of cost and logistics in relation to international stories, as an organisation's journalist does not have to be there to gather the story but can repackage it from pictures received via EVN. A criticism of gathering news information in this way is that a journalist who packages a story without being at the scene is obviously restricted in his or her knowledge and understanding of the event and the context in which it has taken place.

Newsroom constraints

Despite technological developments all newsrooms in news organisations are still constrained by cost, time and space. Schlesinger (1987:105) argues that journalists operate in a 'stop watch culture', the concept of which is an important part of a journalist's occupational ideology. Greater emphasis than ever is placed on the need for immediacy and speed, and the structuring of journalistic practice around this concept has resulted in a direct link between the journalist's time-perspective and the demands created by the nature of the work itself. The marrying of the routines of the newsday (Tuchman, 1978) and the creative ability of journalists as news producers has created a unique culture. Everything the journalists do has to be subordinated to the programme deadline, and so the notion of effective reporting includes a mixture of priorities, accuracy, impartiality and some creativity, as well as deadlines and time restrictions. As Schlesinger (1987:105) goes on to note, the journalists' relationship with time is 'a form of fetishism in which to be obsessional about time is to be professional in a way which newsmen have made peculiarly their own'. It is also a means through which journalists can, via a specific journalistic culture, provide themselves with a clear and identifiable set of expectations about their news product.

Some constraints on broadcast journalists are particularly pertinent to the reporting of complex news stories and clearly compromise the informational

---

[3] See Cohen *et al.* (1995) for an insight into the workings of the EVN information exchange system and its role in setting the editorial agenda.

quality of the story. Such constraints are related to the nature of television and the need to make a product which fits the form of the medium. The key problem is the amount of space allowed for each story in the running order. A story length of two minutes is not long enough to get meaning across (Simpson, 1994), and many stories are not even this long. The second problem arises from the objectivity norms within which journalists have to work. The requirement to have a range of voices often results in Labour, Conservative and Liberal Democrat spokespersons having a small statement in the news piece. This results in very short sound-bite pieces from the spokespersons and forces a correspondent to talk around what others have said. The correspondent cannot use this time to say what he or she would have liked to have said or to analyse or interpret events. The way correspondents try to get around this is to make a 'bite of sound' from a spokesperson which does not contradict what the journalist is saying, but this does not add depth or dimensions to a news story. A further constraint is the need to 'talk to the pictures'; that is, to ensure the journalist's words match the pictures shown. This practice does not always allow for the development of depth or context and restricts the amount of information a journalist can use in reporting a story. Often there is also a requirement from the editor for an adversarial aspect to the story. The programme editor may ask 'Where is the tension in this?', which means that the journalist has to find and develop a conflictual angle to the story.

It is in response to these particular professional criteria that journalists must learn to select, record and package their product in a way which practice and experience have taught them is the best possible one to cope with the constraints they must work within. The specific content of television news changes every day, but there is a tendency for programmes to use similar types of device and structure, such as presenters routinely introducing stories, live two-ways, spokespersons, film and graphics, to pass the message to the audience each day.

Routine utilisation of such devices can become farcical when the content does not fit. During the rail strikes in May and June 1994 the first two or three were covered by both the BBC and ITN news organisations, relating tales of commuter inconvenience, stranded passengers and so on. All the news programmes initially used similar techniques and formats to cover the stories, via live two-way links showing the novelty of stationary trains and empty stations, as well as showing alternative methods used by commuters to travel to work, and all the stages of the negotiations between Railtrack and RMT. Using pictures to convey a message is often easier than describing the scene using words. This technique can backfire if over-used, and by the time the television programmes were covering the seventh or eighth strike, these methods were quite inappropriate. As the nature of news content is usually so changeable, use of the same format procedures is not always so noticeable, and they can help to perpetuate the illusion of change and activity. However, when neither the content nor the format structures change, the repetitive and uninformative nature of television news is exposed due to repetition of the content. Most news stories are not similarly repeated and therefore content can seem to be important and relevant. In some cases it may be the newness of the story and the entertaining format devices that can be used to tell the story that make the story worth reporting, rather than any intrinsic importance to society.

Clearly news processes are subverted to the constraints of time and costs, and adhere to the rigid format structures and techniques of the news medium itself (they must be 'television-worthy'). They are also logistically constrained in terms of technological application. Therefore it is often the case that some news personnel appear to have less interest in the content or informational quality of the news itself than in the logistics of covering the story, or trying to ensure that an event can be covered successfully by the television medium. This adherence to the practical and the logistical aspects of television journalism can appear to be the key rationale of journalism, making it simply the product of the routinised organisation of the newsroom.

In contrast, the Output side of the operation often gives a greater impression of creativity and craft; the programme editor has a vision of the news programme, early in the newsday, which he or she does not want to be subverted to logistics and routinisation. Much of this – the conversations, the intellectual debate and the agonising over newsworthy priorities – is simply an illusion. At the end of the day programmes have to be logistically possible and are constrained by logistics. A contradictory phenomenon is exhibited by the programme editors. When the newsday begins, they are absorbed by the content and newsworthiness of the story; as the day progresses they become more involved with the subversion of that content to the format of the programme. Two or three hours before the transmission an editor is still talking to correspondents about the dimensions of the story, the spin-offs or links; however, the closer it gets to transmission time, the more obsessive an editor becomes about the programme format. The hybrid nature of a news editor's job also reflects the changing criteria of newsworthiness which occur during the newsday. For example, the closer it gets to transmission time, the more ingredients a story needs to make it newsworthy. These ingredients are exemplified by the news factors identified by Galtung and Ruge (1965), Tunstall (1971) and Bell (1991). Editors will routinely turn down stories offered to them by the copy taster or Newsgathering and Intake close to transmission, simply because there would not be time to cover them properly. Stories which would have been included in the news programme if they had happened two hours earlier are routinely ignored. For example, a story came on the wires about a plane crash in Japan to the BBC on 26 April 1994 at 1.15 p.m. (actually during transmission of the *One O'Clock News*). There was no information about deaths or casualties and so the editor for the day decided not to include it in the bulletin, as 'There might not be many dead.'

At the BBC in particular there are many good intentions to analyse issues or to go into something in more depth, but in reality this is often not possible due to time constraints or pressure of other work. Indeed, all the journalists in any newsroom appear to feel that the sudden or the unexpected (supposedly the bread and butter of news) can sometimes be a nuisance and inconvenient. One programme editor admitted that the nearer it gets to transmission time, the more he hopes nothing new happens. This is admitted at *Channel 4 News* more freely than in any other newsroom, as it is there that most planning ahead has to occur. In television newsrooms there are contradictory pressures; those of creativity, intelligence and the wish to be more analytical contrast with those of time, routine and costs. Negrine (1996) also points out that in reality there is a limited number of ways in which information for news stories can be collected. Most news is collected by all the news organisations in the same way: via shared press conferences, handouts, personal interview contacts, sifting through documents, talking to other reporters, press agencies and the wires. The shared experiences of news collection can lead to the 'me too' tendency identified by Bell (1991), with journalists from different organisations and programmes going for the same stories or story angles for fear of missing something that the opposition has got.

This adherence to a common set of journalistic activities leads to a shared set of journalistic experiences which underwrite a culture unique to journalism. Even news programmes like *Channel 4 News* and BBC's *Newsnight*, which deliberately try to break away from the 'me too' tendency, are still bound by the conventions and practices of journalism identified in this chapter. Indeed a programme such as ITN's *Channel 4 News*, which is more financially constrained than the more popular mainstream news programmes, and also aims to produce longer, more specialist items in its programme, has to adhere more strongly than the mainstream programmes to a planning ritual. This has the paradoxical effect of constraining its output.

Planning

An important part of journalistic culture is the planning process, and this is a key part of any newsroom routine. All newsrooms place great importance on this procedure. Schlesinger (1987) noted that there is a heavy reliance on a planning structure which provides a reliable agenda of stories at the start of any newsday (see also Epstein, 1973, and Golding and Elliott, 1979). In all cases newsroom practice is remarkably similar. In all newsrooms there is a weekly 'look-ahead', a planning meeting which is attended by some senior editorial staff, the programme editors, the Intake and Newsgathering editors from both the foreign and home desks, and some of the senior correspondents and producers. The numbers attending the meeting vary at different organisations, but this is a reflection only on the actual number of staff employed and not on differing attitudes to the importance of planning *per se*. At the meeting, the Intake or Newsgathering editors 'sell' new story ideas to the programme editors; this process is supervised by the head of news or equivalent, who interjects his or her own wishes at various points in the discussion. From this transaction, it is possible to ascertain that the journalists themselves feel that there is diversity in the range and type of news programmes produced by one organisation. This is illustrated by comments such as 'that's a *Six O'Clock News* story not a *One O'Clock News* story' (BBC editor for the day, *One O'Clock News*).

Once a rudimentary commitment to certain stories or forthcoming events has been established, Newsgathering and Intake can go ahead and continue to arrange for camera crews, to book lines and to allocate journalists. These confirmed stories are then put into the appropriate day's prospects. One problem with this degree of planning ahead is that sometimes, on-the-day events can supersede the coverage already planned, which can be expensive. The *Channel 4 News* format dictates that it, like *Newsnight*, has to plan carefully and well in advance, as it must fill five-minute story slots. At *Channel 4 News* there is an obvious inflexibility built into the programme structure, and therefore, due to format and cost constraints, the programme editors cannot really afford to drop a pre-planned story unless it can be run the next day.

Each national newsroom has a group of planners (or in the regional newsrooms, often just one person). They occupy the weekly forward planning desk in the Intake or Newsgathering section of the operation and are usually situated the furthest away from the news output desks, signifying their distance from on-the-day news. Potential stories enter the newsroom in a variety of ways. Many come in via press releases from Government and Opposition ministries, the police, universities, quangos, pressure groups and other large-scale institutions. The increase in public relations exercises by such organisations in the 1980s and 1990s resulted in a vast amount of literature and sometimes video footage. Most of these routine press releases contain information relating to future events, and these are entered into the computer in date order. When the date comes along, it is usually the case that the routines of the planning mechanism have ensured that there is a camera crew and a correspondent allocated to the event. Many such events, which Boorstin (1964) termed 'pseudo-events', are staged specifically for the media. Because of the tendency for all the media to use the same techniques of newsgathering and planning, most of the news media will attend. Homogeneity in journalistic culture means that most mainstream news programmes are afraid to go out on a limb and ignore a government press conference in favour of a piece on East Timor. The Press Association also gives advance notice of forthcoming events, and the planners scan the wires for such information. All television newsrooms routinely receive court lists and information from the specialist correspondents, which have not gone on general release. Finally there is the odd telephone call tipping the newsroom off about an event which will occur.

On the day before the event, the daily forward planning desk will look at the events available the next day and, in liaison with the Intake and News-gathering desk and programme editor, and on the basis of commitments made at the weekly look-ahead meeting, will start to arrange for the appropriate crews and equipment to cover the story. When the prospects appear at the beginning of the newsday, the list of the day's events are also accompanied by brief details about the arrangements for the day.

The prospects generally contain about ten or twelve possible leads to follow during the day. Some journalists are already at work on the stories which have been planned and advertised in advance. The clear and identifiable set of practices and expectations in a newsroom is reflected in the communality of the planning procedure in all television newsrooms, and is very indicative of the nature of the television news product itself. Journalistic culture has resulted in a developed set of expectations that the newsworthiness of a story or event does not depend on the unexpected or the sudden, but can be anticipated and designed well in advanced. However, once the event itself is happening the journalistic priority then becomes immediacy. Immediacy, or recency (Bell, 1991), means that the best news is something which has only just happened. The importance of immediacy has always been a shared priority of journalistic culture, but has been restricted by technological constraints. Today it is possible to convey a story as it happens. Twenty-four-hour news coverage by news organisations such as CNN leaves the cameras rolling so the audience can watch events as they occur and develop. Technological process has augmented the importance of immediacy as a criterion of newsworthiness; 'immediate' can now often mean instantaneous coverage, instead of coverage which gets the news to the audience as soon as possible. Within the context of such high levels of competition, technological proficiency and journalistic sophistication, there is an obvious requirement for excellent planning and control to ensure that all the disparate parts of the newsgathering and news planning operation are geared up to cover the forthcoming story as efficiently and effectively as the competitors.

Extra reliance on planning and preparation may affect what can be considered to be newsworthy by the news organisation. Generally resources are committed to events which are known of in advance. Because journalists rely increasingly on the wires for information about the world, then it follows that the rest of the news stories competing for a place on the programme must exhibit more newsworthiness-enhancing factors than if planning did not take precedence and all journalists were out searching for stories. This is particularly noticeable on *Channel 4 News* and BBC2's *Newsnight*, where a large commitment is made to pre-planned stories at the expense of covering on-the-day occurrences well, or sometimes not covering them at all.

Unpredictability (Galtung and Ruge, 1965) is not a vital element of the news, due to the rigid format structures of news programmes and the progression of the planning process. There is no question that the editorial staff at *Channel 4 News* in particular, and to a large extent at ITN's Channel 3, recognise that many of the stories they cover are diary stories, although editors at the BBC still talk in terms of the *ad hoc* nature of the newsgathering process. This is because extra resources available at the BBC have allowed editors to have stories prepared in advance and in reserve and to drop three or four of them during a news bulletin in favour of newer or more important stories. At ITN, due to the greater financial constraints within which the news operation is conducted, it is much rarer for stories to be dropped. Indeed, when Intake at ITN has over-committed resources to a story which is not actually particularly newsworthy, the newsdesk will then try to oversell it to the programme editors to try to justify the expenditure. One programme editor likened this to the technique of 'ankle tapping' in a football match; the news editors try to psyche the programme editors into believing the story is newsworthy and cannot be missed out of the programme. Technological improvements in all newsrooms, and cost constraints at ITN in particular, have augmented the need for pre-planning. This has to be reconciled with making sure the coverage is as fast and extensive as its competitors's news.

The myth of editorial autonomy

A shared journalistic culture is related to constraints, rules and logistics, but also relies upon the myth of editorial autonomy and the masking of hierarchical control. At the BBC, in both London and Leeds, the euphemism of 'guidance' is used to refer to policy decisions by managerial staff regarding the content of television news output (Schlesinger, 1987). At ITN and *Calendar News*, such euphemisms were deemed less necessary and most policy decisions were communicated down to newsroom staff via bulletins or meetings. The different cultures can to some extent be accounted for by the sheer size of the organisation. At ITN and YTV's *Calendar News* the senior management are much physically closer to the news production and selection process on a day-to-day basis. Therefore they can intervene or 'see' problems and communicate them to the staff rather informally. Furthermore, the strong commercial imperative which dominates at *Calendar News* and ITN make them much more like any corporate body which operates a simple line-management system. The BBC in contrast attempts to appear to be more democratic, with horizontal lines of communication. In practice, however, the BBC actually uses hierarchical practices which it seems to feel the need to mask.

In common with Schlesinger (1987), I found that in general there exists a particular journalistic culture whereby news personnel (at both ITN and the BBC, and to a lesser extent at the regional newsrooms) do not consider themselves to be under such control. Programme editors in particular appear to see their freedom from daily constraints as intrinsic to their role as the creators of a news programme and the arbiters of the newsworthy. The younger, less experienced editors for the day acquiesce more willingly to the obvious increase in supervision and control imposed on them by senior news editors, when they are editing the programme.

For example, at the BBC the editor, TV News Programmes, spends more time at the Output desk when a younger, less experienced editor is in charge. At ITN, *News at Ten* is generally edited by two senior, seasoned editors working in rotation. When a younger editor is editor for the day, the head of News and his or her deputy are in much closer contact with the programme's progress on that day than is usual. One young editor commented to me before we went into the 6.10 p.m. meeting, where the structure of the programme is finalised, that he did not expect it to remain the same, whereas the other editors 'knew more clearly what the programme should look like'. Such meetings are always attended by the head of ITN Programmes, his or her deputy and the presenter, and on this occasion they duly switched two or three of the young editor's stories around, and also issued one or two firm instructions about the inclusion of a piece of film.

All the senior programme editors, however, have a different explanation of editorial control. As they have learnt what is appropriate and acceptable, it seems that they have more autonomy and control, when in fact they have simply begun to subscribe to the corporate view. The journalistic culture of television newsrooms denies management control of newsworthiness, centring it instead on the programme editor. According to several programme editors, there is a mechanism of control which operates to ensure that non-newsworthy pieces which are simply 'hobby horses' of the senior editorial staff do not feature high in the programme's agenda, or do not get on at all. Conversely, senior editorial staff may over-rule programme editors, and insist that a news item be moved higher up the running order or added into the programme.

Younger journalists who resist editorial directives can acquire labels that damage their careers by mishandling stories. At both ITN and the BBC there are several cases of journalists who are classed as 'unpromotable', or are on some kind of probation. Editors gave me examples of correspondents they had to watch, telling me that 'that correspondent can never be relied upon to return a piece the right length', or 'that one never manages to get a decent interview, we always have to redo it' (BBC editor for the day, News and Current Affairs), or 'I've got to watch her because she always goes over the top about women's rights' (ITN programme editor). The programme editor will also request certain journalists for certain stories, for example 'don't send Sally on that, she'll cock it up – I want John' (ITN programme editor, names changed), or will caution journalists as he or she assigns stories to them: 'don't do another Benson and Hedges on me' (ITN programme editor).

The shorthand linguistic code used by the programme editor is incredibly specific, although to an observer it is sometimes nearly unintelligible. Obviously a journalist who has made a mistake must work on probation, proving that he or she can master an editorial brief and fit into and co-operate within a particular journalistic culture in order to gain or regain the programme editor's trust. All programme editors supervise the untrustworthy or inexperienced journalists far more closely than the reliable ones, who are often left more to their own devices. At the BBC in particular the very senior specialist correspondents would not expect to have a young, fresh-faced editor for the day watching over them.

Real control over the news product in the television newsroom therefore is concentrated in few hands. Although all news personnel and journalists are working towards a common goal, many just work on their allocated parts of the news programme. Senior editors and programme editors have the most control, and only they have an overview of the whole programme. Although the presenters need to see the shape of the programme, they do not become involved in the editorial process and may only disagree or comment on small aspects of its overall structure or content. Editorial staff ensure that control of production of the final news product is devolved only into the hands of responsible correspondents and producers, who will act as controllers of the disparate sections of the newsroom. Therefore, although a cameraman, particularly an experienced one, will have a much better idea of the best way of filming an event, he or she will still be working subject to a correspondent's directions and specifications. Similarly a video-tape editor's skills are vital to the editing process, but he or she will work in accordance with the wishes of the producer and the correspondent who are writing the story. Any dissent has to be reconciled within the context of the correspondent's overview of the whole story. Any issues which cannot be reconciled are always then referred back to the editor.

A common expectation of journalists, and one in which journalistic culture is deeply grounded, is that all activities in the newsroom are inferior to the primary one of making news. Therefore those people who have the most control of this process, namely the editors, producers and correspondents, are all able to demand compliance from the other newsroom personnel, such as video-tape editors, camera operators, graphics engineers and production staff. These demands always increase and intensify the closer the programme gets to transmission time, and once in the gallery, the programme editor has supreme control of all the newsroom personnel, who will react immediately to his or her every demand. At this point there is no dissent whatsoever.

In contrast to Schlesinger (1987), I did not find evidence of dissenting journalists whiling their days away filing or working in the archives. This is probably because since 1977 there has been enormous technological change and a good many of the clerical and routine jobs have been replaced by computer systems. Furthermore, the reduction in staff, at ITN in particular, ensures that no one can get away with doing very little or not being allocated stories as a punishment. Exile in a television newsroom today might be to the forward planning desk, Newsgathering or an early morning programme, but it would still involve the journalist working directly in the news production process.

Editorial control is further reinforced by the numerous meetings which structure every newsday. Higher-level policy meetings occur in every news organisation and are attended by the senior editorial staff. At these meetings, policy issues such as the manner in which the organisation will handle Northern Ireland, elections or forthcoming leadership elections will be discussed and a formula agreed. The formula then becomes part of the common currency of the newsroom until it is a taken-for-granted response and underpins the culture of the newsroom and news practice. At both the BBC and ITN there is acknowledgement that the organisations are not impartial about acts of terrorism or racism, and that there are certain procedures to be followed when reporting elections. Sometimes such decisions or the opinions of senior editorial staff are passed down to the newsroom journalists in a positive manner. At the BBC, the staff were told that the violence policy of the BBC had been adhered to and the journalists got the 'thumbs-up' from above. More negatively, they were told that there was concern expressed by senior management about a left-wing bias in a piece by a senior correspondent in South Africa. Although it is evident that such procedures are actually policy directives which will shape and set precedents for all subsequent reporting on those or related issues, most news personnel subscribe to the editorial ideology of autonomy, refusing to see beyond the programme editor for any real mediation of control over the news product. The culture of editorial autonomy is therefore perpetuated.

As news personnel do not attend the policy meetings chaired by the very senior news personnel, such as the managing director News and Current Affairs at the BBC or the editor-in-chief at ITN, they are not aware of the extent to which higher decisions are passed down to the programme editors. When the programme editor returns back to his or her programme and holds the next meeting with the newsroom staff, the editor does not claim that he or she is following a particular line because he or she has just been told to do so. In general the only time the programme editor will admit to being told what to do is when he or she has been instructed to do something which contradicts the journalistic ethos in the newsroom. In such cases an editor will claim 'we've got to do a story on Arafat today because the editor-in-chief has got a bee in his bonnet about it' (ITN programme editor). In this way, by openly illustrating the more perverse examples of senior editorial control in a pejorative manner, he or she is often able to intimate that control over his or her actions, by senior editorial policy on a day-to-day basis, is weak and sometimes ill informed.

The programme editor may accumulate myths about his or her newsworthy preferences, whereupon it can follow that the staff may try to second-guess an editor's choices.[4] At *Channel 4 News* a story was circulated that Liz Forgan, former editor of Channel 4 programmes, had a hatred of sports news, royalty and crime news. However, the perpetrator of this so-called myth was the contractor at Channel 4, who did not want the news programme to move down-market by covering these potentially light or serious human interest and crime stories in a trivial manner.

Often comments about senior editorial and editorial staff made by journalists tend to overplay the romantic notion of editorial idiosyncrasy, which nevertheless is credited with being the sole reason a story has got onto the running order in the first place. In reality the programme editor, or indeed the senior editors, can really influence only the choice of one or two news stories which would not otherwise have been chosen. In the case of the senior editors this is viewed as being a 'bee in their bonnet', and often such stories are regarded by journalists as not being particularly newsworthy. Programme editors actually have devices for burying such stories in their news programme and actually have allocated slots or positions which they use for them. Programme editors' choices of unusual stories, again in reality, are restricted to one or two lesser stories which they may pick out from the wires or from the papers. These are generally viewed by the journalists working on the programme as being newsworthy 'because the editor says they are', whereas senior editorial choices are often derided by the programme editor for not being newsworthy. In effect, the notion of newsworthiness here is actually being determined by newsroom politics and the fact that the programme editor will prefer to be the arbiter of what is newsworthy, rather than senior editorial staff, who no longer get their hands dirty in the newsroom itself. Therefore the journalistic culture of the newsroom tends to support the programme editor's choices above those of the senior editor, and it becomes a newsroom mythology that newsworthiness really is 'what my editor says it is'. Thus mythologies abound about how journalists watching a news programme from home can tell that 'Paul edited it because it had a story about a dog in it', or that 'story number three came from "the suits"' (ITN correspondent, *5.40 p.m. News*).

The structured nature of the news organisation ensures that the real power is located at the top of the hierarchical pyramid. For example, the editor-in-chief at ITN told me quite unequivocally that he directly intervened in the coverage of Rwanda in order to increase the impact of the story. Furthermore, such a visible medium as television news ensures that the senior staff can tune in at any time to watch their company's product, and journalists know that the 'top brass' might be watching at any time. Whilst this

---

[4] This in fact happened in a much larger and important way to John Birt. The mythology of Birtism pervaded newsrooms in 1987, before he became director-general of the BBC, and the BBC news staff tried to put into practice his theoretical version of good news coverage.

probably does encourage conformity there is no doubt that the journalists working on a particular programme believe they are working to the programme editor's vision.

Editorial control is present in every television newsroom. Journalists in the main conform to this control, and dissent is rarely expressed in any way which could be damaging to their careers. Editorial control at the BBC, ITN and YTV is pushed down the system via structural procedures and conformities, producing a journalistic orthodoxy which news personnel simply regard as being the true nature of journalism itself. Therefore although the journalists' zone of operation must be defined to a large extent by the particular structures and practices of the organisation they work for, there is also a general sense in which the mediation of control via the editorial system, its hidden power and the subscription to the ideology of editorial autonomy is a common feature of any television newsroom, and underpins journalistic culture.

Newsroom language

Homogeneity in journalistic culture is grounded in the editorial and journalistic values which are communicated via a specific journalistic language. A common feature of all television newsrooms is the use of journalistic jargon and code. Not only are there a great many technical terms for newsroom practice, rules and operations, there are also many shorthand ways of conveying information amongst themselves in the most efficient manner. Because of the nature and structure of the television newsday, and its inevitable rush at the end, journalists need to be able to communicate complex newsroom values to each other quickly and effectively. Thirty minutes before the broadcast, the editor is often holding two or three conversations at once, relaying information and absorbing it at an accelerated rate, punctuated by a constant stream of telephone calls which become shorter and shorter.

This need for a rapid communication system has resulted in a newsroom language which can be almost unintelligible to a visitor. Vast amounts of facts and information are conveyed in short terse phrases, such as 'you'll have to oov it, twenty seconds' (BBC editor for the day, *Six O'Clock News*), which means 'Change the existing piece which contains film and a reporter's voice-over to pictures only and the presenter will talk over the film on air. The film must be reduced in size to fill twenty seconds of airtime.' When these terms are linked together into a stream they require translation. For example, a briefing by a programme editor ran as follows:

Intake editor: If it slips a bit it could be very sick couldn't it.
Programme editor: It's going to be terrible ... it's going to be shit.
Intake editor: It's all right if we've got links there, if the worse comes to worst and the judgement is at twelve forty-five.

> *Programme editor:* No, it's twelve o'clock it says here. From 12 o'clock and you know that British judges always give the punch line at the end.
> *Intake editor:* Yeah, but it'll be OK they like to go for lunch. (ITN programme editor and Intake editor, *12.30 p.m. News*).

On the basis of this discussion, which lasted twelve seconds, the court case was included in the news programme as a newsworthy story. One of the major criteria which ITN's *12.30 p.m. News* and BBC's *One O'Clock News* have to use to determine the newsworthiness of a story is whether the event happens in their time. The rush to fill these programmes with adequately prepared news stories is one of the most tense periods in any television newsroom, because the editors have a great deal of difficulty getting enough information through on time. Discussions with other staff are, by the nature of the time constraints, even more brief than on other news programmes where there is a much longer time to prepare.

Often there are short ironic exchanges between journalists about the shortfalls in their practice, such as this: 'The art of television news is to simplify', 'Surely – you mean to trivialise and simplify?' Journalists sometimes deliberately use symbolic images which are clichéd, but will also make a joke or an ironic comment about what they have done. In other words they admit the artifice to colleagues. For example, after an aircrash the camera crew will look for a damaged doll on the ground; similarly after a house fire there is often a lingering shot of a burnt toy symbolising the tragedy (ITN cameraman). When *Channel 4 News* covered the Amsterdam plane crash in October 1992, the news editor admitted that the camera crew looked for a damaged push-bike so that they could get a shot of the broken wheel spinning round in the wind. Such pictorial symbols of disasters can be made very poignant, particularly when accompanied by music or a strong narrative. John Birt referred disparagingly to this type of news making being based upon the 'movie model' of news, where the instinct is to make the film first and write the words to suit the pictures (Birt and Jay, 1975b). It is precisely these visual clichés which can be so easily parodied, in programmes such as Channel 4's *Drop the Dead Donkey*, whose unethical journalist Damien often plants a symbolic artefact in a camera shot to increase the impact of the story.

Journalists are often humorous about the news itself. For example, Prince Charles's attack on political correctness and his support for smacking children led to many comments about his hypocrisy in trying to advise the rest of us. One editor came across and joked that she wanted to find a trendy woman expert who says you can breast feed until you are 50 to reply to Charles. When Walter Burns, the news editor in Howard Hawks's screen adaptation of *The Front Page*, said 'Forget the Nicaraguan earthquake, I don't care if there are a hundred thousand dead', he was articulating McLurg's Law. Philip Schlesinger (1987) also came across this law when he was observing at the BBC. It was expressed to him as 'one European is worth twenty-eight Chinese, or perhaps two Welsh miners worth one thousand

Pakistanis' (p. 117). This law relates to Galtung and Ruge's (1965) news factor regarding 'cultural proximity', according to which a story is more newsworthy and has greater impact if it relates to people from one's own country.
For example, twenty-two dead British at Waco in Texas made the story
newsworthy for British journalists. It is treated as a joke, however, by journalists themselves, as they are all aware of their obvious bias in this area.
Often they will say 'there are not enough dead' (an ITN correspondent, *News
at Ten*), or as I had it explained to me in colloquial terms at the BBC, 'one
dead in London is worth seven dead in Sheffield' (a BBC bulletins producer).

Sarcasm, cynicism and irony are common currency in any newsroom
situation. This is probably due to a variety of common features to be found
in all television newsrooms, such as high pressure, and a concentration of
intelligent and articulate people. The seemingly callous nature of some of
their comments does not reflect their real feelings in relation to death and
destruction, but is similar to the type of gallows humour exhibited by the
medical profession. This is a strategy of coping with situations which are
sometimes harrowing and at best nerve-racking. Emotions can be hidden by
humour, and the culture of journalism demands that people do not give in
to time-consuming and inconvenient feeling.

Broadcasting language and humour used during the transmission itself are
much more constrained, and broadcasters are careful not to offend the public, who do not understand and are not made aware of journalists' informal
modes of communication. Journalists make every effort not to offend the
audience by being sexist or racist. At the BBC it was noticeable that there
was much more discussion about politically correct issues, and more debate
than at ITN about whether or not scripts should be changed to make them
more suitable. The BBC has provided all its national and regional journalists
with a *Style Guide* which opens with the reminder that 'staff should seek
innovation and originality, transcending "clichéd thinking"' (BBC, 1993d:2).
This, coupled with the *Producers' Guidelines*, attempts to ensure that the BBC
speaks with one politically correct voice. In contrast the journalists at ITN
and at *Calendar News* are not provided with such a prescriptive set of instructions and guidelines, and different news programmes adopt their own particular styles and rules. For example, a producer of ITN's *12.30 p.m. News*
asked the editor 'do we like the "House of Horrors" phrase?' about a piece he
was writing referring to the house of mass murderer Frederick West. The editor replied 'no, we don't but the 5.40 do' (ITN programme editor, *12.30 p.m.
News*).

And finally, humorous stories do become news stories, particularly when
they are unusual enough to interest people. Light human interest stories are
included in many news programmes, but they are most common in the
regional programmes and children's programmes. ITN's *News at Ten*'s
famous 'and finally' piece is used as a mechanism to end the programme on
a high note, and is seen by some more 'serious' journalists and commenta-

tors as evidence that the programme is going down market and pandering to commercial values. However, even the BBC's *Nine O'Clock News* has been known to transmit the odd light story. This slight change of practice at the BBC is seen by some journalists as an example of the resistance to Birtist philosophy and the over-concentration on worthy stories. In 1994 Jay Blumler argued that the BBC was responding more to audience wishes than ever before and that this was manifest in the inclusion of more domestic stories and human interest stories.[5] In 1998, following the BBC's Programme Strategy Review, there was little doubt about this.

The similarities exhibited by different news programmes and news organisations in news production can be clearly seen through the routine utilisation of similar format devices, such as: presenters who introduce stories and interview guests and spokespersons; the use of live two-ways to highlight the fact that an event is actually happening, has just happened or will happen; the use of spokespersons as a method of ensuring impartiality; the reliance on film to illustrate a storyline; the use of graphics as an aid to explanation and so on. It can also be seen in instances where all news programmes and news organisations routinely recognise the intrinsic newsworthiness of the same stories.

A journalistic culture is produced by and produces a set of consistent formulas, practices, normative judgements and explicit values. A journalistic mythology is passed down to successive generations of journalists. It is transmitted and sustained via: training; shared experiences; shared distance from an understanding of the audience; shared reliance on technology and electronic information sources; shared understanding and acceptance of logistical constraints such as costs, time and space; the need for planning; shared misunderstanding of the origins of control, via agreement on the myth of editorial autonomy; and a shared journalistic language. The significance of the existence of a particular culture, which in this case is journalistic, is that the production of a homogeneous set of skills and practices ensures a professional standard and quality. However, there is a problem inherent in a journalistic culture which constrains itself through practice to adopt specific readings of events and issues. The key difference between journalism and other skills-based professions is that the former contributes directly to the knowledge-base of society, and therefore has to ensure that it provides a diverse range of information, in order to contribute to the pluralistic nature of Britain in the 2000s.

Agreement on normative values and practices is secured by a common newsroom culture, which is deepened and compounded by a common agreement on the value of objectivity as a principle of television journalism. It is to this key element, which underpins journalistic conceptions of newsworthiness and newsroom culture and practice, that we now turn.

[5] Personal communication from Emeritus Professor Blumler in April 1994, prior to my newsroom visit to the BBC.

6

Journalistic objectivity:
ideal and practical

All television news production is grounded in a shared adherence to and understanding of the need for objectivity as a professional ideology for television news reporting. The assumption that objectivity is vital for news coverage is based on regulatory requirements and has implication for news processes, news content and the relationship of television news producers to their audience. It also relates directly to the degree of trust that audiences place in news reporting, in the belief that television news is not partisan or biased in content. For journalists, objectivity in news is a professional ideal. Many journalists recognise that objective reporting is a goal which cannot be fully attained (McQuail, 1992) but nonetheless, the ideal of objective practice is a key component of journalistic culture, which is underwritten by acquisition of particular skills. McQuail (1992) argues that objective practice for journalists is both a skill and a virtue, and Tuchman (1978) argues that it is aspired to via routinisation of practice.

The routinisation of objectivity has attracted the interest of many critics, who argue that the objective reporting of events in the world is impossible and that journalistic aspirations towards objectivity in news reporting are undesirable, since it has an adverse effect on the final output. Golding and Elliott (1979) usefully point to three possible views of objectivity and impartiality in relationship to journalism: first, the professional view that it is possible to be objective and impartial and that this can be achieved through the acquisition of certain skills and values; secondly, that the idea of objectivity is problematic and unattainable, but that impartiality is desirable and possible; and thirdly, that neither objectivity or impartiality is possible in journalism, and they are simply labels applied by journalists to rules which govern their working practices. It is to an elaboration of those three positions that I now turn.

The journalistic belief in objectivity and impartiality

Within their different television news organisations, and working to different pressures and versions of the public interest, journalists must ensure that they are producing a product which will be *judged* to be impartial and objective news. Therefore for television journalists, the practice of objective reporting is central to their task and is a professional ideal. An enquiry by Boyer (1981) produced a set of statements about the meaning of objectivity derived from a study of what journalists themselves say about objectivity. According to Boyer, journalists believe that they look for balance and even-handedness in presenting different sides of an issue; they attempt accuracy and realism in their reporting; they present all the main relevant points; they aim to separate facts from opinion, but treat opinion as relevant; they try to minimise the influence of the writer's own attitude, opinion or involvement and avoid slant, rancour or devious purpose (see also McQuail, 1992:184–5). This is advantageous for journalists because it provides a set of guidelines which they can follow when selecting and producing news. The responsibility for the content of the news can be left with the sources, allowing journalists to be relatively free from having to justify or defend the content of their stories. Instead, journalists can concentrate on the structure and construction of their piece, which is put together like a jigsaw puzzle, using a variety of different pieces of information from different sources. By devolving the responsibility for the substance of stories to sources, some journalists can avoid the need to acquire expert knowledge and detailed information about events and can therefore move easily from one story type to another, as required.

The belief in the possibility of objective and impartial news underpins a shared journalistic culture (see Chapter 5). There are similar rules and practices, rituals and routines in all television newsrooms, which result in similar format and production processes. Certain journalistic traditions are common in all newsrooms. The significance of this is that it results in an acceptance of certain 'official' explanations or formulas for telling a story to which all journalists adhere. The use of 'official' spokespersons is defended by journalists as a way of producing objective coverage of events. Adoption of routine practices results in particular selection norms which determine why stories are reported or ignored. These norms primarily reflect expediency, news values and logistical constraints on journalistic practice. Generally the journalistic attempt to be objective arises *within* the stories and is not necessarily a primary imperative in the selection procedure (although journalists are constrained by law from selecting material which is biased in favour of a particular viewpoint). Clearly there are a few occasions when journalists do select stories in order to achieve balance in coverage, most often when political parties are covered during the periods before and during an election. Sometimes the BBC may reject a story on the grounds that it has a south-east of England bias. Applying objectivity norms to selection criteria actually distorts news values, pushing newsworthy stories out of the news agenda. Clearly news selection is related to a broader range of imperatives than objectivity requirements. Journalists articulate their impulse for news selection or rejection of stories in the following broad-based ways:

Reasons journalists give for why stories become news

- 'It's a quiet newsday.' The story has only got onto the running order because not much else is happening (producer, BBC's *Six O'Clock News*, 12 May 1994).
- 'It interests or involves a lot of people' or 'The audience can identify with the event because it shows the problems of day-to-day living' (programme editor, ITN's *5.40 p.m. News*, 15 June 1994). An exemplar of this was the inclusion of a story about a policeman hitting a 15-year-old boy who was misbehaving; the policeman was suspended, but received a good deal of public support. This story was covered extensively by the tabloid news-papers and picked up some television news programmes because, 'It makes people say "oh really"' (programme editor, ITN's *5.40 p.m. News*, 16 June 1994), or 'It's got the "Hey Maud" factor' (editor for the day, BBC1's *Six O'Clock News*, 12 May 1994), or 'It's got some nice human stuff in it' (correspondent, BBC's *Look North News*, 29 July 1994).
- 'It's worthy.' It is a story which ought to be done because it is important, but it may be, and often is, boring (producer, BBC1's *One O'Clock News*, 27 April 1994).
- 'It is something different', or 'It's new', 'It moves the story on.' For example, a new development such as the mass exodus of refugees in Rwanda moved the story on from coverage of bloodshed and massacre, providing new pictures and a new storyline (programme editor, BBC1's *Nine O'Clock News*, 5 May 1994).
- 'We've got great pictures.' This confirms the visual imperative of the television medium (see Tunstall, 1971).
- 'It's the sheer scale of the thing' (see Galtung and Ruge, 1965).
- 'It's on the front page of the papers.' All programme editors and news personnel check the papers everyday. However, for the programme editor of ITN's *5.40 p.m. News*, the fact that a foreign story had made it to the front page of the newspapers encouraged him also to cover the story.
- It fulfils a particular programme need. For example, there is often a search for the perfect 'and finally' story or a 'good story after the break', or 'We need a better second story' or 'We need something different' (programme editor, ITN's *News at Ten*, 20 June 1994).
- 'It's a first', 'It's got Brits in it', 'Everyone else is there', 'It balances the programme', 'It's a death plus' (i.e. it is more than just an 'ordinary' death or an ordinary event) (programme editor, ITN's *5.40 p.m. News*, 14 June 1994).

• 'It is in the diary.' Coverage of the story has been planned and resources committed to it (programme editor, *Channel 4 News*, 23 June 1994).

Reasons a variety of journalists gave for why stories do not become news[1]

• 'We've already done that.'
• 'It's not our kind of story.'
• 'It's too expensive.'
• 'It's too late, my programme is full.'
• 'It's too tacky, too down-market.'
• 'It's boring.'
• 'It's yesterday's news.'
• 'We've not got any pics.'
• 'It doesn't happen in our time.'
• 'It doesn't move the story on.'
• 'We've not got cameras there.'
• 'Not enough dead.'
• 'Too samey.'
• 'It can wait.' This story could be told any time, and does not have a particular 'peg' at the moment.
• 'Everyone's packages have come in over-long so something will have to go.' This occurs when correspondents disobey the programme editor and squeeze a few extra seconds by making their package longer than the allocated time. If several correspondents do this on the same day it can result in a piece being dropped.
• 'It would take too much telling.' The story is too complicated for the medium and for the time allocated to it.

The common practice which allows journalists to identify what is and is not a good story reduces the possibility of investigative journalism and enables objectivity norms to be applied within news stories. This restricts the contribution television can make to the diversity of opinions because, by setting a common-sense framework, journalistic habit and imposed constraints ensure that a matrix is developed within which discussions and decisions are contained and restrained.

The practical application of objectivity norms within selected stories is formulaic. It is most commonly applied via devices such as the routine use of facts and figures; two spokespersons; live pictures to show that something is happening; use of previous storylines to set a precedent or storyline to follow and so on. Such practice underpins and perpetuates a common journalistic culture, where the practical application of objectivity falls short of the ideal.

[1] These comments were collected over several months' observation in a variety of newsrooms and I have not attributed them to particular journalists, as they were often repeated.

The regulation of impartiality

The ideal of objectivity is only implicit in the regulatory framework, within which the television news broadcasters must operate in their role of serving the public interest by producing news which is impartial. The concept of impartiality is clearly distinct from objectivity but is a guiding principle of British broadcast journalism (McNair, 1994). Impartiality implies a disinterested relationship to news content, in which the journalist does not attempt to shape material in favour of a particular opinion or viewpoint. Objectivity clearly has broader demands than this.

The word 'objectivity' is rarely used by regulators, but is substituted by words such as 'impartiality', 'accuracy', 'balance' and 'fairness'. The BBC is careful to ensure that it meets the requirements set down in the annexe to the licence and agreement in 1964, which states that the BBC accepts a duty 'to provide a properly balanced service which displays a wide range of subject matter ... [and] to treat controversial subjects with due impartiality ... both in the Corporation's news services and in the more general field of programmes dealing with matters of public policy' (BBC, 1993c:21). The *Producers' Guidelines* (a handbook of some 275 pages) is circulated to correspondents, producers, programme makers, editors and managerial staff at the BBC. This book is referred to on a daily basis and the BBC's position on objectivity in news reporting is very clear. 'Programme makers should be at their most scrupulous in factual areas ... Reporting should be dispassionate ... [good reporting] should offer viewers and listeners an intelligent and informed account that enables them to form a view. A reporter may express a professional judgement but not a personal opinion' (p. 21).

The BBC is forbidden in Clause 13(7) of the licence and agreement from broadcasting its own opinions on current affairs and matters of public policy. The BBC also stresses that it is important to ensure impartiality occurs over time, so it is not necessary that all sides have an opportunity to speak in a single programme. Broadcasting during elections is specifically governed by Section 93 of the Representation of the People Act 1983 (referred to in the newsroom as 'the RPA'), although there is no legal requirement that all candidates be given exactly equal treatment. Fringe candidates are not accorded parity.

The news programming of the ITV system is also regulated in terms of serving the public interest impartially. The Broadcasting Act 1990 requires that 'any news given (in whatever form) in its programmes is presented with due accuracy and impartiality; that due impartiality is preserved on the part of the person providing the service as respects matters of political or industrial controversy or relating to current public policy' (Broadcasting Act, 1990:6(1)6). The requirement for ITN to provide news which is accurate and impartial is controlled by law and regulated by the ITC, as it was by the IBA and the ITA before it.

The requirement for both the BBC and ITN to produce impartial and objective news is a legal one, a part of the constitution of the two systems laid down by government from their inception. Those who accuse journalists of hi-jacking the concept in order to become more professional, or somehow to avoid making a personal judgement, forget that journalists or organisations which break the law are likely to be heavily penalised. The BBC has to guard against penalties such as the removal of senior staff or governors by a government, and needs to ensure that governments renew its charter and the licence and agreement. ITN needs to try to ensure that it continues to be the sole, or at least the main, provider of television news to the independent television companies. The ITC, in its review of ITN's performance, concluded that 'ITN has provided a well-resourced, authoritative and attractive news service, meeting the requirements of the Broadcasting Act 1990 for high quality' (ITC News Release, 21 December 1995), one of the key requirements being the provision of an impartial news service.

The ITC planned to conduct a further review of ITN's performance in 1998, illustrating how the pressures on ITN are different from those of BBC news. Although both have versions of the public interest in their ideas of objectivity and impartiality and in their regulatory guidelines, ITN has the additional problem of having also to satisfy the ITV companies and not just the ITC. These companies can in principle choose alternative types and suppliers of news programming besides ITN as long as they meet the ITC guidelines and ensure profitability for the ITV companies. ITN is therefore much more vulnerable than BBC news in this respect.

The problems of objectivity and impartiality

The professional claim, and the regulatory requirements which imply, that objectivity in reporting is possible and desirable is of concern to sociologists. Indeed much of the sociology of journalism has, from the outset, been concerned with 'establishing that [news] information was produced, selected, organised, structured, and (in consequence) biased' (Collins, 1990:20).

Most sociological research begins from the assumption that the media, and therefore news and journalism, are human constructions shaped by the social world from which they emerge (Berkowitz, 1997). As I showed in Chapter 5, a particular and specific journalistic culture exists in all newsrooms, which produces a set of formulas, practices and normative judgements and values. The journalistic norms and shared experiences which are passed down to successive generations of journalists ensure that news is not, nor can it be, a mere reporting of the world 'out there' but is value-laden. Central to the sociology of journalism is the argument that these values support the status quo, and therefore help the powerful vested interests of the establishment. Indeed, this problematic is not simply a British concern. Michael Parenti comments that 'objectivity means that reporters should avoid becoming politically active, and should keep their distance from their subject, while commentators, editors, and owners socialise, dine and vacation with the political, military, and corporate leaders whose views and policies they are supposed to be objective about' (Parenti, 1993:53).

However, these three positions fail to address the most critical objections to objectivity. First, objectivity is impossible to attain because the unavoidable process of news selection must also result in subjective judgement by the journalists. The journalists themselves may be unaware they are making normative judgements (White, 1950) and few critics believe there is a conspiracy at work in the television newsroom, but news by its nature is value-laden and therefore cannot be objective. Secondly, omissions are always made in news reports as a result of the process of editing and selection, and such omissions may themselves make implicit assumptions and judgements about the events being reported. Thirdly, the news is produced in the context of numerous powerful internal and external pressures and powerful and efficient sources, which will have an effect on the final product (Gans, 1980).

Whilst objectivity is seen by some as being impossible, it is seen by others as being undesirable. Critics such as Glasser (1984) view the practices which journalists adopt in their attempt to report in an objective manner as unwelcome. Glasser refers to objectivity in journalism as an ideology which is a type of bias (McQuail, 1992). Journalistic belief in objectivity forms and underwrites journalistic action. According to Glasser (1984) these beliefs promote bias against the watchdog role of the media in favour of the status quo, due to efforts to report the facts and remain value-neutral, and also act against a journalist taking responsibility for independent thinking. And yet a fact is clearly different from a subjective opinion or value and therefore one should, in principle, be able to check and verify facts (indeed journalists make this a principle of their professional training). Research into the factualness (and therefore by implication the objectivity) of news reports has been approached in various ways, all of which are beset with problems of their own. For example, it has proven difficult to obtain a set of reliable facts against which to check media facts (Blankenberg, 1970). Other sources of facts, those sources which set themselves up as being factually correct, such as news agencies, have proved to be selective, open to human error and not immune from bias (McQuail, 1992). By checking with persons or organisations which are the subjects or sources of news, Bell (1991) has shown that whilst factual errors are usually trivial, claims of misrepresentation or out-of-context reporting of comments are common. In contrast, the audience, when asked, seems to place a high value on the accuracy of television news reporting (Goodwin and Whannel, 1990; Gunter and Winstone, 1993).

Glasser (1992) believes that the use of particular media formats influences journalists in their selection and use of sources. Journalists tend to use 'reliable sources' which in practice usually means prominent members of society (Altheide, 1985; Ericson *et al.*, 1991; Schlesinger and Tumber, 1994) who tend to reinforce, not challenge, the status quo. The practice of objective news reporting results in a bias against independent thinking. As journalists are expected to remain value-neutral and impartial, there is no longer a need for them to have a critical perspective. There is a bias against the journalist assuming responsibility for what is reported. According to Glasser (1992) the ideology of objectivity implies that news is somehow 'out there' ready simply to be reported. It is somehow independent of the reporter, who will not be held responsible for it. Accordingly, aspiring to objectivity and claiming that it is possible to achieve it are misleading, as objectivity cannot be delivered. Crucially the so-called objective story is likely to contain hidden messages which favour one account more than others, for example those who finance the news (Shoemaker and Mayfield, 1987), or it may work in the interests of established power (McQuail, 1992).

The concern is that the use of objectivity as a practical guide to news selection, production and presentation is likely to favour the more wealthy and better-organised interests in society. These views are more likely to gain access to the television medium, and therefore contribute in the official public sphere, than those of under-resourced and less privileged groups. Diversity in television news is directly restricted by the attempt to practise objective reporting. Such reporting tends to exclude strong beliefs and partisan views, or implicitly devalues such news. Taken to its most critical extreme, the attempt to practise objective reporting can be seen to serve the interests of the establishment actively, reinforcing the status quo and protecting the interests of the power elite (Gans, 1980).

Observation of journalists at work in the newsroom has shed some light on the criteria they employ in their selection of news stories, and this has gone some way towards explaining some of the biases which are automatically built into the news product. Hetherington (1989) found that journalists consciously or unconsciously base their choice and treatment of news on two criteria: first, the political, social, economic and human importance of the event; and secondly, whether it will interest, excite and entertain their audience. For Shoemaker and Mayfield (1987) and Shoemaker and Reese (1996) the micro factors of working routines and socialisation of journalists in the newsroom, as well as the political, social and institutional forces that act upon the newsroom, namely the external hegemonic influences on news, prevent news content from being objective.

Generally, British television news selection processes reflect the ebbs and flows of events to a limited extent. This results in uneven coverage of world regions (Wallis and Baran, 1990) and patchy and uneven representation of minority views. This bias in news is seen to be unwitting (Golding and Elliott, 1979). But despite the problems related to the attainment of objectivity, journalists adhere to the idea that it is better to attempt to be objective (and fail) than to be partisan in any way at all, and they justify such a position by saying (in what many believe to be an enlightened view) that they 'do their best'. Indeed, many journalists realise themselves that objectivity is simply a professional ideology, a normative assumption which cannot in reality be attained. The journalist Britt Hume (cited in Parenti, 1993) urged that news-people should not try to be objective, they should try to be honest (which might be considered by some to be equivalent to being objective). Instead of reporting the approved version of events and issues journalists should try to find out if the source is actually telling the truth, otherwise what is passed off for objectivity is a mindless acceptance of other people's views and not the truth. Problematically, honesty and truth are as open to social construction as is objectivity. Such an attempt at finding the 'truth' is actually what the police and legal processes such as interrogations, cross-examination in court and so on attempt, in order to present different sides of an argument for a jury to decide what is true. This is not an easy task to take on and it means that a journalist who wishes to pursue the 'truth' has to be an investigator, importantly involved in interpretation and assessment of events on behalf of the audience, to help its understanding and comprehension.

Many of the criticisms of objectivity in journalism are generally under-pinned by the assumption that objectivity is always relative. As news pro-duction and viewing occur in socio-cultural settings, then these define and limit what is fair and reasonable. In other words, ideas of what should be reported in what way vary from society to society and from issue to issue. The assaults on objectivity (as a professional journalistic ideology) come from those who believe that social reality is humanly produced and humanly maintained, that is, reality is a social construction (Carey, 1989). This type of critique is problematic because, although we might agree that all social reality is socially constructed, this does not mean that we logically cannot assume objective reports are possible about it. Also, reports are human com-munications and as such have to be put into language. They are necessar-ily and unavoidably linguistic constructions. Again, this does not mean that logically objective reports about reality are impossible, rather it suggests the opposite. We can accept that social reality is socially constructed and that news reports about social reality are linguistically constructed. We can also accept that news reports about social reality are socially organised via organ-isations like ITN or the BBC etc., but again this does not mean that, logically, objectivity is impossible. Indeed the objections to objectivity are weak and rely upon an assertion that judgements are grounded in the conditions within which they are made, that is, socially constructed reality or organ-ised reality. Neither of these in and of themselves says much about judge-ment, logic or mathematics (or indeed honest reporting).

A different and interesting approach to the problem of objectivity is given by Judith Lichtenburg (1991). She examines the assault on objectivity made by sociologists and other critics, and argues that we cannot simply abandon objectivity and that those critics of objectivity do not actually do so them-selves. Although they appear to reject objectivity they are covertly relying upon it. She argues that although it is not realistic to believe that anyone can be objective we still need to assume that objectivity as an ideal is both possible and valuable. However, she, like the critics of objectivity, concludes that, 'paradoxically, the aspiration to objectivity can contain biases of its own, by advantaging established sources or by encouraging an artificial arithmetic balance between views, and tempting reporters to maintain the appearance of neutrality even in the face of overwhelming "non-neutral" evidence' (Lichtenburg, 1991:229–30).

It is therefore useful to unravel the seven basic suppositions and propositions relating to the above concerns about the journalistic practice of objective reporting.

1   Objectivity is an ambiguous concept. It is seen by some as an ideal which cannot be attained, and as an ideological prop for vested interests in society. The regulatory requirement for journalists to work to a criterion of objectivity and impartiality, which is advocated on the grounds of public interest, is linked to the political system and therefore is established by the validating system. Yet the aim of attaining some kind of objectivity in their reporting is seen by all television journalists as a goal or a moral imperative which they must strive for in order to make both themselves, and their profession, reach higher standards and to ensure that they retain their position within the confines of a governmentally determined role for broadcast journalists.

2   In essence both critics and some journalists agree that objectivity is an ideal and is unattainable.

3   The problems of trying to attain objectivity in journalistic reporting lie in the nature of journalistic practice and the formulas adopted in the newsroom. Journalists adhere to certain formulas to ensure that a news story appears as, and can be read as, being as objective as possible. One way to achieve this is to fill news reports with facts and figures (Tuchman, 1978). These and good pictures, which show that something is actually happening or has happened, can be used to make a 'neutral' presentation of events. The same effect can be achieved by using the live two-way device, where a journalist is placed outside the building where a meeting is taking place in order to stress that the event is really occurring. Such actuality shots also go towards ensuring a story is seen to be newsworthy, but are unlikely to add anything useful to the information received by the viewer. The use of expert sources which favour certain opinions above others presents a problem, as it is likely to favour the interests of established power or, even worse, actively serve those interests.

4   The attempt to provide balance in news reporting does not necessarily further journalistic aspirations to achieve an objective news report. It is possible for broadcasters to ensure that coverage of an election cam-

paign, for example, is balanced in terms of airtime and still fail to be objective in their coverage.

5   If the nature of broadcast journalism prevents it from being objective or impartial, but it does not instead seek to challenge undemocratic practices, we have to ask what its role is in a democratic society. It is of note that so-called gurus of this type of 'bias against understanding', such as John Birt, will criticise challenging or overbearing interviewers 'who sneer disdainfully at their interviewees' (Birt, 1995:2). Birt appears to be contradicting himself, because the criticism of interviewers and journalists who confront and challenge politicians is a criticism of challenging journalism. If all journalists can do is to provide anodyne, unchallenging information, which is virtually spoon-fed to them by politicians, or sensational entertainment to retain the audience, this has a negative impact upon the role of television news and the ability of journalists to interpret information in a meaningful and useful way for the audience.

6   Despite the intentions television journalists have of achieving objective writing and political correctness, their mission is thwarted by the frame of 'natural' images from which television news is selected and produced. This frame is created via the use of metaphors and myths in the news which we all understand, creating a common-sense language with which many of us tend to agree. When a metaphor is used, a word is applied to an object or action to which it is not literally applicable, for example an owl becomes wise, or New York the Big Apple (Fiske and Hartley, 1990). Often metaphors exist without always being recognised as such. Mumby and Spitzack (1985) made a study of the language of television news in six political stories on three United States networks, and found a total of 165 metaphors. Using the metaphor of drama, for example, makes sense of, 'politics as a "stage" upon which talented individuals "perform" as stars' (Fiske, 1987:291). A myth is a legend or fable which is created and in turn creates 'reality'. The mythic quality of television news is, like metaphor and common sense, grounded in news language. The news language carries with it cultural meanings rather than just representational ones. For example, the mythology surrounding a fictional hero was applied to Oliver North during the Irangate crisis in the United States. Similarly, the mythology of a villain was applied to Colonel Gadafy ('mad dog', 'tyrant', 'deranged ruler': Fowler, 1991:115), to Saddam Hussein (Chomsky, 1989) and to the Branch Davidian leader David Koresh in 1993.

     Common-sense explanations of the world are based on individualistic or naturalistic assumptions. Often an event can be understood simply through individual behaviour, or common-sense world views can be very societally determinist and can reference social forces in certain ways; for example, through comments such as 'You can't stop progress.' A naturalistic explanation would assume that certain things are 'natural' reasons for behaviour, such as that it is 'natural' for people to fall in love, get married and raise a family. Common-sense assumptions have long been embedded in television news; for example, the importance of the family unit, the sovereignty of the royal family (although this has been shaken by the actions of its younger members and to an unprecedented extent by the death and funeral of Princess Diana in Aug./Sep. 1997), the importance and authority of elites (via the use of expert sources and stories about famous people doing ordinary things), the role of women, explanations of poverty, the reasons for industrial conflict and so on.

7   Although any attempt to be objective implies the (impossible) feasibility of somehow removing values and stereotypes from news content, journalists working in television news do go to great lengths to ensure that they cannot be accused of being biased. It is the compromise position which journalists take up between playing an active part in society by providing interpretation of complex issues on the one hand, and the attempt at an 'objective' reporting of information from a variety of sources on the other, which is problematical. This leads to an accusation that the attempt at objectivity in broadcast journalism fails to serve the public interest, reduces plurality of news information and compromises the depth and breadth of the information transmitted. Sometimes news reporting needs to be partial as it reflects the basic values of the population. Of course it is difficult for the media to be impartial about evil, horrific crime, abuses of state power and terrorism, and normally they do not attempt to be so.

Overall these seven basic suppositions and propositions display the problem of applying the practices of objective reporting in situations where a more investigative or partisan method of reporting should be used but is not. The ending and aftermath of the Waco siege in Texas is a practical illustration of some of the pitfalls of adopting the formulas of objective reporting exemplified in the use of expert sources, live two-ways, political spokespersons, live reporting and so on, whilst not being able to treat a story impartially because of prior common-sense judgements made by journalists and particular spokespersons about the nature of the story.

David Koresh and his new religious movement, the Branch Davidians, did not get any coverage by the British media until 28 February 1993, when the Alcohol, Tobacco and Firearms Agency (ATF) made an attempt to storm their compound at Mount Carmel, Waco, Texas. Four American agents were killed and fifteen were wounded, six Davidian members died and the so-called Waco siege began. The rationale for the attack by the ATF appears to be twofold. First, there were allegations of child abuse by David Koresh, made by an ex-member of the Branch Davidians who left the compound. Secondly, Koresh and several of his followers were known to be buying a large quantity of firearms. Since the raid by the ATF several critics and academics have questioned the need for it to have used such force to serve a warrant. Indeed it is still not clear why the ATF, which as yet has presented no concrete evidence that the Branch Davidians were guilty of anything, attacked the compound at Mount Carmel on 28 February 1993.

The first televised coverage of the ATF attacking the compound at Mount Carmel was shown on British television on 1 March 1993 by several mainstream news programmes. Waco was now 'on the news agenda'. CNN and other United States networks had their reporters in position the day before.

Fifty-one days after the raid by the ATF, on 19 April 1993, the Federal Bureau of Investigation (FBI), which had been staking out the compound since March 1993, began bombarding the Mount Carmel compound with 'non-pyrotechnic' tear gas,[2] allegedly in an attempt to flush the children out of the compound and end the siege (Moorman, 1994:81). Tanks began punching holes in the walls of the compound and gas canisters were pushed inside the building. However, a fire or fires were started inside the compound and within two or three minutes it had become an inferno. Television cameras were well placed to capture the events on film.

The fire(s) at the compound started at about 6.27 p.m. GMT on 19 April 1993, following a six-hour bombardment by the FBI tanks. At the end of the BBC's *One O'Clock News*, the presenter added that there were 'developments at Waco' but did not elaborate what those might be. The end of BBC1's *Six O'Clock News* caught the fire starting, but it was *Channel 4 News* at seven o'clock which was the first to cover the story at any length, accompanied by film of the burning compound. All the other news programmes followed with the story later that evening and continued to cover it in some detail for the next two days.

During the reporting of the events in Waco, Texas, certain common-sense assumptions were adopted by all the press and broadcasting organisations, illustrating the symbiotic relationship between the two and the reliance on the same sources for information. Analysis of the news coverage also illustrates a willingness to follow the authorities' interpretation of the events (via use of two or three FBI spokespersons and members of an anti-cult organisation). The story coverage by British television news showed a lack of interpretation or analysis of the event, and only 'official' explanations of David Koresh's intentions and behaviour were broadcast. When reporting the Waco disaster, the British media simply acted as witnesses to an American media event and reported the official line.

---

[2] Moorman (1994:81) argues that the 'non-pyrotechnic' tear gas was actually CS gas. The US government, along with 120 other nations, signed an agreement at the Paris Chemical Weapons Convention that they would not use CS gas on other nations.

British journalists agree that the Waco story was newsworthy, because 'it had Brits in it', 'good visuals', 'good human interest' and 'a lot of dead'.[3] The newsworthiness of the Waco story was enhanced through the possession of certain characteristics which combined to make the story highly significant to all news organisations, including BSkyB and CNN. As Tunstall (1971) indicated, the possession of film increases the prominence given to a story; indeed the visual imperatives of television are so strong that the need for film, or at least still pictures, dominates. The events leading up to the ending of the Waco siege were captured live. They also occurred at a time when they could be accommodated by the newsday. *Channel 4 News* in particular was well placed to be the first to tell the story (see the news factors of periodicity, identified by Galtung and Ruge, 1965, and recency, identified by Bell, 1991). The story was predictable because the FBI had alerted news organisations that a media event was about to happen, ensuring that the news media were on hand to film it. As the logistics of the filming operation had already been taken care of, live links to correspondents and reporters could be established without difficulty. All the news organisations in Britain used this facility to emphasise the liveness of the events in Waco. These events were negative (Galtung and Ruge, 1965) and easy to record (Bell, 1991), which enhanced the story's newsworthiness.

News items of an extremely complex, ambiguous or abstract nature cannot easily fit the format of television news. However, Postman (1989) argues that the more dramatic the news is, the more likely it is to pass Galtung and Ruge's thresholds. The Waco story contained elements of a docu-drama, with the polarisation of the actors into the authorities and the cultists, or good versus evil (Jones and Baker, 1994). Finally, the story contained an element of cultural proximity (see Galtung and Ruge, 1965) because British people were members of the Branch Davidians. All the British television news media were able to bring in a human interest angle relating to the deaths of British victims and the effects on their families. This was perceived by all the television news media as a very important dimension of newsworthiness in this instance.

Despite the use of the formulas and practices of objective reporting, the commitment to the fair and accurate reporting of the event was abandoned almost immediately through the use of speculation, official lines of explanation (from the FBI, the United States government, anti-cult organisations and medical experts) and the adoption of the pejorative value-label of cult. The cultural differences between the United States and Britain meant that the events in Waco were so far removed from everyday life in Britain that they seemed to be almost fictional. Also, there was no problem with the story because the political fallout, if any, would occur in the United States and not in Britain, so it was possible to speculate superficially whether the attack by

[3] Based on newsroom conversations in April–June 1994.

tanks on the Branch Davidian headquarters had been bungled by the FBI, or was instigated by the behaviour of those inside the compound. The people inside the building were consistently described by the media as extremist cult members or even criminals, and there was a strong sense immediately that the media were fixing the blame for the events on these people.

The early adoption of the word 'cult' to describe the Davidians allowed both the media and the authorities to pursue the rather simplistic but attractive explanation of Koresh being power-mad and brainwashing his followers. There was no attempt to explain Koresh's beliefs via statements from biblical scholars. According to some scholars the term 'cult' is virtually meaningless (Goldberg, 1994). It has become a label that is simply applied to religious groups that are regarded as marginal, radical or dangerous. As soon as a cult gains credibility by numbers, such as those of Jehovah's Witnesses and Seventh Day Adventists, the label tends to drop away. As the term is so clearly pejorative, it follows that any group so labelled will be assumed to exhibit the worst imagined behaviour, such as brainwashing, child abuse, polygamy, violence and so on. By supplying a label for a group and not an explanation, the organisation and its followers can be successfully ostracised by the media and the authorities (Barkun, 1994) and all pretence at objective reporting is abandoned.

Dayan and Katz (1992) show that any kind of media event celebrates what are generally establishment initiatives, and that these are unquestionably hegemonic. The media event staged by the FBI on 19 April 1993 was no exception, and the common-sense frame of interpretation and conditions for reporting were well established and continually passed on to the media by the authorities.

The types of expert chosen by the media and the authorities to advise and provide information had an important impact on the content and tone of the media reports and upon the attitude and actions of the FBI and ATF. Many experts drawn on by the media to explain the events were part of the anti-cult tendency in the United States, comprising a mixture of deprogrammers, ex-cult members and disillusioned relatives of cult members. The deprogrammers kidnap members of new religious movements and attempt to force them to renounce their association (Lewis, 1994). The type of advice and analysis provided by such experts was often supplemented by medical experts, who tended to describe Koresh as exhibiting psychotic tendencies. In the United States the Cult Awareness Network (CAN) has consolidated a powerful access network to the media, ensuring that it has become institutionalised and credible as a source of authoritative information. As Schlesinger and Tumber (1994) show in the area of crime reporting, it is vital for organisations or individuals, in the battle for access to the media, to be able to make a large commitment and investment in order to build up good media relations. Because media reporting of cults tends to focus on them only when they are newsworthy, it follows that the media are attracted to reporting only cult stories about scandals, atrocities, failures, negative or sensational behaviour, or any other outrageous or dramatic aspects of such movements. Therefore journalists, unlike academic scholars, do not routinely analyse such organisations to learn more about them.

At no stage were biblical or theological scholars quoted in the mainstream media, even though they would have been able to offer a detailed explanation or interpretation of Koresh's beliefs. For example, it was not acknowledged by the media that Koresh had taken his name from a messiah, King Cyrus (Isaiah 45). The Greek translation of this Hebrew word is Christos, from which the name Christ is derived. This ancient king Cyrus was called Christ. The media endlessly reported that Koresh believed he was Jesus Christ, when in fact he believed he was one of the many messiahs who have consistently appeared throughout the Bible with specific tasks to follow (Tabor, 1994). Koresh believed his task was to solve the mystery of the Seven Seals and was writing at the time of his death (see Tabor and Gallagher, 1995, for a copy and analysis of the text written by David Koresh, printed directly from a computer disk which was saved by a survivor of the fire). The FBI, however, held press briefings at which they consistently claimed that Koresh was a high-school dropout, implying that he was not capable of writing a book.

Following the simple and unbalanced storyline that Koresh and his followers were extremist 'religious nuts', it was easy for the FBI and therefore the media to imply that these people were to blame for the events that claimed their lives (indeed it was automatically assumed by all the broadcast media that the fire in the compound was a mass suicide plan). Although the deaths of the children were mentioned several times, the implication was that the mothers were to blame for not letting their children escape when the FBI had invited them to do so. This was furthered by the universal reporting of Clinton's statement, in which he officially and publicly put his stamp of approval on using military weapons and tactics against United States civilians in the case of religious differences, denying that the tactics were too strong or inappropriate. 'I was surprised at calls for the resignation of the Attorney-General because some religious fanatics murdered themselves' (President Clinton quoted on all British television news programmes, 20 April 1993).

As Koresh was reported as being an extremist, the violence he had shown whilst defending the compound from the ATF, and his alleged violence against the children, were reported in the context of extremism. As Schlesinger notes, '"extremist" violence, therefore, becomes the object of moral repugnance, whereas the legitimate violence of the security forces is handled within a framework which emphasises its regrettable necessity' (Schlesinger, 1991:205).

Events and issues relating to the events at Waco might be defined as being centred on the freedom to worship, human rights abuse and abuse of military power, but were reported in terms of legitimate (if bungled) authority, madness and restoration of order. David Koresh and his followers were reported as extremists who used violence against themselves (in the form of an assumed mass suicide, although there was no proof of this at the time) and against others, and therefore were legitimately controlled via the use of state violence. In part, these news angles came from a precedent already set by the news media for the reporting of cult activities. As one journalist said, 'the first thing you do is look for something else that has happened like it' (a correspondent, BBC1's *Nine O'Clock News*).

The press and the broadcast media immediately drew parallels with the Jonestown Massacre. In 1978 the Reverend Jim Jones had set up the Jones People's Temple in the Jonestown commune in the jungles of Guyana. Upon his instruction more than nine hundred people committed suicide by drinking poison; those who did not were shot. As soon as the fire began at the Waco compound, FBI agents were reported as saying, 'oh my God they're killing themselves' (film of FBI agent Bob Ricks speaking, shown on ITN's *12.30 p.m. News*, 20 April 1993). David Koresh was consistently presented as a clone of Jim Jones by the American authorities and all the news media, and yet we actually still know very little about Koresh (Palmer, 1994).

Despite the specific and partial angles which the television news programmes adopted in relation to Koresh's perceived activities, the news story was reported using the practical application of objectivity norms. The devices employed to ascertain 'impartial' coverage were interviews with a variety of spokespersons, who gave political, medical or anti-cult perspectives, and the endless reporting and updating of the numbers of dead and injured British members of the Branch Davidians. This gave the illusion of an impartial approach through the distancing of the news organisation from the actual events and the reporting of facts rather than opinion. The use of experts who had experience of cults actually skewed the reporting further against the Branch Davidians. The use of live footage of the scene showed the audience what was happening, but left it confused as to the cause of the fire.

But I have shown that in fact the reporting of the ending of the Waco siege was advocative in style. Despite the critical and judgemental line which was taken, television news journalists did not in consequence draw upon the normative support of the values of freedom and diversity. This type of reporting normally sits uncomfortably with the professional ideals of objectivity in practice (McQuail, 1992). The reporting of the events in Waco clearly did not. The adoption of a speculative, stereotypical, partisan and human interest approach towards reporting of the events, set within an objective frame of reporting, led to particularly uninformative and limited coverage of Waco. Human interest news was used to tell the stories about the British people killed in the fire. Elements of drama, myth and personalisation were used, focusing on emotion and the senses. These aspects of news reporting strain against neutrality and adherence to fact and served to sensationalise and further mystify the Branch Davidians' activities in Waco.

In this case the adoption of the presupposed norms of objective reporting led to poor information quality and to an unquestioning adoption of certain lines of explanation. To be more informative, the television news media needed to adopt a more critical and discerning approach, with less reliance upon journalistic precedence (i.e. the adoption of a narrative structure and explanation from apparently similar events in the past to 'explain' a current situation), upon explanations by authorities (such as the ATF, the FBI and the United Nations), and upon the use of live film without interpretation or investigation.

To promote diversity of information from a variety of sources, the basic but important principle of pursuing an investigative (even openly partisan) approach to television journalism should produce the variety of pluralistic public interest journalism which is needed to nourish the public sphere and protect democratic process and citizenship rights. The practices and values underpinning the practical application of objectivity in reporting can lead to an information deficit. Without the basic tool of information, citizens are unable to act competently in the public sphere, are unable to be discerning about institutions of authority, and cannot contribute to, or argue against, the political, economic or social processes which affect their everyday life.

Chapters 5 and 6 have shown that similarity in journalistic practice is grounded in a shared journalistic culture. A journalistic mystique underpins much of the structural and formal processes of journalism which can be found in every television newsroom. Journalists do not appear to view their roles as being bureaucratic and formulaic in nature unless they are working in the newsgathering or planning part of the newsroom process. Some of those working on the Output process of the news product will admit that a high percentage of what constitutes news is already pre-planned, but all talk in terms of the *ad hoc* nature of the news process and are committed to ensuring that their news product adheres to the legal requirements of objective reporting.

Clearly, television journalism is constrained as an information source, and we have seen how this is further compromised by the use of particular practices in the name of objective reporting. New influences and developments in journalism, such as multi-skilling, desk-editing, job compression and a greater emphasis on reporting live events as they unfold, do not (as far as journalists are concerned) disrupt the production of objective and impartial news. Given the problems inherent in the adoption of so-called objective reporting and the constraints this places on the informational quality of news programmes, these contemporary developments have important implications for the public sphere and the relation of television news to a democracy. This is particularly the case if they result in further deterioration in the quality of television news information. The evolution of a diversity of audiovisual forms (investigative, objective and partisan types of news and information) which contain different types of news information and explanation is needed more than ever.

Although journalism is underpinned by a shared journalistic culture and by a common agreement on the value of objectivity as a principle of television journalism, different terrestrial television news programmes have diversified to produce different types of television news. Terrestrial television news has adopted a variety of formats and logos which give the appearance of a diversity of news values. It is whether there is diversity in content (not style) of news programming which is of concern. It is to this we now turn through an analysis of the different conceptions of newsworthiness and news values of different terrestrial television news programmes.

7

TV news values:
diversity within unity

Television news values are clearly related to the shared culture and common-sense values which shape journalistic practice. Journalistic practices, which involve conventions of choosing, selecting and producing the news, occur through ritual, precedent and habit. As I have shown, these processes are assumed by journalists to be desirable and help them become more 'scientific' or objective in their reporting. This impetus towards professionalism and the need to be objective help to alleviate television journalists' concerns that they are changing the status or importance of whatever they choose to cover simply by the decision to choose it, or how it is presented.

The routinisation and conventions of journalism underpin television news values and establish the framework of public interest within which all television journalists work. This framework informs the value of the contribution television journalism makes to the public sphere and shapes the relationship journalism has to democratic processes. In Chapter 1, I showed that television journalism is constrained by the medium itself and that it is trying to compete with entertainment and drama genres, resulting in a variety of television news sub-genres. This does not necessarily mean that terrestrial television news is failing to inform citizens *per se*. To assert that television news is falling short of meeting criteria which would improve its relationship to democratic process is to invite the question of what is a reasonable role and standard to expect from it in the first place.

An influential attempt to theorise the media's role in society is the liberal press theory (McQuail, 1994). This theory is routinely used for setting a standard against which both the press and television journalism can be and have been measured. The functions expected of journalism produce a set of values which provide a version of what journalism *should* be about. Prescriptive functions, such as binding society together, giving leadership to the public, helping to establish the public sphere, providing for the exchange of ideas between leaders and masses, meeting needs for information, providing a means for group expression, providing society with a mirror of itself, being

157

an instrument of change, acting as the conscience of society, and acting in the public interest, have generally been accepted as an *a priori* role for the media in general and journalism in particular.

However, Keane (1991) views the early modern ideal of the liberty of the press as being seriously flawed and requiring a radical rethink in order for a new conception of the public service model of communications to be developed. Such a model would then expose those power structures which are currently invisible and describe how a plurality of tastes and opinions could be expressed and represented through true diversity of content and output, thereby enabling us to understand the way in which journalistic procedures could empower a plurality of citizens. This model of diversity would expose the free-market rhetoric of freedom of choice as excluding diversity of access to and representation of voices by the media. Keane unfortunately does not make any specific suggestions relating to the cost, the policies, the political strategy or the legislative structures which would be needed to apply his model of the ideal public service broadcasting environment.

In general, journalism has routinely been scrutinised, theorised, assessed, judged and regulated in relation to its shortfalls and departures from the liberal press model. But other responsibilities of journalism should be addressed. Walter Lippmann's (1922) view of journalism as the domain of the expert elite was modified a little in his later work. Nonetheless Lippmann's view that citizens need expert accounts of complicated issues, and that those accounts should be provided by the journalists themselves, sets up a prescription for what constitutes journalism and also gives journalists freedom to determine what constitutes newsworthiness. Such an assertion implies passivity on the part of the citizen and does not require journalists to involve people in the process of democratic decision-making (Fallows, 1996). Fallows argues that the public is not seriously engaged with politicians or politics in the United States simply because of the way politics is portrayed by journalists. Journalists, according to Fallows, talk at people rather than with or to them. Such a procedure does not hold the viewer's attention for long because it does not involve the viewer in solving or considering a shared problem or event. Journalism tends to ignore the connections which exist between issues even though the public are aware of them. Complex, inter-related events in public life are thus often presented as single events.

Taking issues and turning them into single events is the essence of much of journalism. However, it has long been recognised that this can be misleading. Hall *et al.* (1978) studied the reporting of mugging in the news and showed that the news, by taking the issue out of context and simplifying it to a series of one-off events, gave the impression that mugging was happening continually and that no one was safe. The BBC, following John Birt's abhorrence of the 'bias against understanding', has long attempted to try to explain issues, resulting in the twin pack described earlier. Many of the BBC's reports are dealt with in this way. In contrast ITN may simply report two separate stories on the same theme. This illustrates important differences in styles and content of news reporting.

For example, on 22 April 1993, the government released its employment figures, revealing that unemployment had actually fallen. This occurred before lunch, in time for ITN's *12.30 p.m. News* to use it as their lead. ITN divided the reporting of the story into three categories. The first was a straight report of the fall in unemployment figures for the second month in a row, accompanied by film and seven seconds of graphics. The second was a totally different human interest story about some unemployed people setting up their own labour exchange, and the third was a live link to Gillian Shephard, who said how marvellous the drop in unemployment was for everyone concerned. BBC1's *One O'Clock News*, on the other hand, also reported the drop in unemployment as a straight story, but followed it up, not with a twin pack in this case, but with a studio discussion via a television link. It set up a live link between Shadow Employment Secretary Gillian Shephard, the Employment Secretary and a Liberal Democratic spokesperson. There then followed a much more lively debate during which Gillian Shephard's confident assertions were challenged and links were made back to the first piece. Finally, the presenter and the economics correspondent had a studio discussion.

ITN's report of the event was less challenging or informative than that of the BBC. The latter attempted to engender debate and to link the issues and reasons for the drop in unemployment. ITN in contrast simply reported the three pieces individually, gave the Employment Secretary a chance to make her points, and then told a human interest story about how some people were coping with unemployment.

Television news journalism often tries to find a yes–no solution to complex issues about which citizens are ill informed or ambivalent. The tendency for journalists to find experts who are either strongly for or against an issue (usually in the name of objectivity) does not necessarily reflect the public's view and therefore may fail to engage or inform them (Fallows, 1996). Nonetheless, this professional practice of journalism, which is grounded in a shared culture, common-sense values and ingrained habits, empowers journalists to define what is newsworthy.

Joshua Halberstam (1992) identifies three theories of newsworthiness. The first analyses news as a speech act, whereby any report of a current event is considered to be newsworthy by virtue of being published. Newsworthiness is created and not discovered through its act of publication. It follows then that news is whatever the editor or the journalist says it is. The second theory analyses newsworthiness according to the degree of importance or significance of the event or item in question. In the third theory, newsworthiness is analysed in terms of people's interests. Halberstam, in part, supports the third theory, arguing that the concept of newsworthiness is linked to the satisfaction of actual human interests.

These three theories are especially useful, since they offer explanations of the concept of newsworthiness pertinent to particular news programmes and illustrate the different notions of public interest journalism operating in different television newsrooms. I shall now go on to show how each of the three theories is applicable to different news programmes, illustrating the different priorities programmes have in their own relationship to newsworthiness.

The first theory, where the editor is the custodian of news values and the public interest, is a recurring subject in television newsrooms and is often cited by journalists themselves as an explanation of newsworthiness. This theme is more pertinent to an explanation of journalistic mythology and bureaucratic arrangement than to a holistic account of the constituent features of newsworthiness.

The second theory tries to reconcile the need to attract and retain audience interest with the notion of importance and significance. At the BBC such notions are closely aligned to its vision of what is in the public interest. Serving the public by providing them with information which is enlightening and informational has its roots in the origins of the BBC and John Reith's attitude to the needs of the public (McIntyre, 1993). As stories which are important cannot always be interesting, journalists working for news programmes which seek to report worthy stories (such as the BBC's *Nine O'Clock News*, in its role as a journal of record) argue that to be able to make an important news story interesting is an endorsement of their ability as a journalist. Other journalists working for rival news companies would argue that such news stories are boring. The audience, it is noted, does not have a voice in this discussion, but does have the ability thankfully to switch off, and in the multi-media environment is becoming more empowered in this respect. However, the BBC's newly competitive stance may result in it increasingly changing its definition of newsworthiness away from one which prioritises importance to one which aims to interest the public. The BBC's *Six O'Clock News* has for several years differentiated itself from the other BBC1 news programmes by slightly modifying its interpretation of both newsworthiness and the public interest. It has done this by broadcasting more domestic stories and interesting news stories rather than the more worthy stories provided by the *Nine O'Clock News* and *Newsnight* (see Figure 1, p. 35 for an illustration of how news programmes are constituted from different news sub-genres).

The need to attain and retain audience figures is of particular importance to commercial news programming, and the pressure to interest the audience remains paramount. ITN's Channel 3 news programmes are more likely to broadcast news stories which will interest and even entertain the news audience, illustrating the clear but narrowing differences in perception between the BBC and ITN's Channel 3 news providers about what is in the public interest.

Halberstam's third theory is particularly relevant to the definition of television news at ITN's Channel 3; *Big Breakfast News*, YTV's regional news magazine *Calendar News*, and *GMTV News*. News here is defined in terms of people's interest, and related very strongly to what will engage the audience and keep it entertained.

Programmes such as the BBC's *One O'Clock News*, *Children's Newsround*, the regional news programme *Look North News* and the *Six O'Clock News* fall between the themes of news as importance and news as interest. As I have already argued, however, the BBC's 1998 Programme Strategy Review recommended that the *Six O'Clock News* should move further towards a definition of relevance as being what interests the audience. BBC2's *Newsnight*, BBC1's *Nine O'Clock News* and ITN's *Channel 4 News* are more likely to pursue stories of importance and significance, as defined by them (although, of course, this is not meant to imply that journalists working on programmes such as the *Nine O'Clock News* have no interest in retaining an audience).

Although the application of Halberstam's three theories of newsworthiness show clearly that different news programmes relate to the different features that constitute newsworthiness, this differentiation is not reflected in research. A good deal of research (see for example the edited work by Berkowitz, 1997) has concentrated instead upon the values and messages in television news, with television news content, production and effects seen to be related to a product of a uniform structure, format and process. This research ignores the possibility of there being a diversity of definitions of the constituent features of television newsworthiness, depending upon which news programme and which news organisation are being analysed. Indeed it ignores the concept of genre differentiation; and yet, despite the adherence of journalists to a common set of values and assumptions, it is still clear that different conceptions of newsworthiness and what is in the public interest relate very strongly to different news programmes, different news organisations, and wider influences relating to the increasing commercialisation of broadcast television news.

To consider what constitutes news in British terrestrial weekday television news in the 2000s it is necessary to take a multi-organisational and multi-programme approach. Newsroom priorities can be assessed via the analysis of a production culture existing in different newsrooms. Adoption of a multi-organisational, multi-programme perspective on the content of television news (see Chapter 1) allows us to see clearly how programme and organisational commitment to domestic and international news coverage differs between news channels. National news was defined as stories which were purely British news or about British citizens. For example, a murder in West Yorkshire was classed as domestic news, and the murder of a British citizen in the United States was classified as a national story.

International news was defined as stories which were purely news from overseas. For example, the murder of an American citizen in the United States was classed as international news. When an international news story originated in a foreign country but the sign-off was from London (illustrating that the material had been fed to and edited by ITN in London), the story was still classified as an international news story.

Table 3 shows how in April 1993 BBC2 and Channel 4 devoted over 50 per cent of their airtime to international news, followed by 43.4 per cent by BBC1 and 35.1 per cent by ITV. A high percentage of ITV's news stories fall into the category of domestic news, but Channel 4 also broadcasts a large number of stories falling into the domestic news category, because the channel has two news programmes which are very different. The *Big Breakfast* programme is aimed at children and teenagers, provides short news bulletins within an entertainment programme, and concentrates on domestic news. *Channel 4 News* at 7 o'clock in contrast is a serious, high-quality news programme and tends to broadcast fewer, but longer, international stories than the other channels.

Table 3   *Commitment by terrestrial channels to international news, April 1993*

Channel	National news (percentage of airtime)	International news (percentage of airtime)
BBC1	56.6	43.4
BBC2	44.2	55.8
ITV	64.9	35.1
Channel 4	43.2	56.8
All	56.4	43.6

Table 4 shows that in April 1993 BBC2's *Newsnight*, *Channel 4 News*, BBC1's *One O'Clock News* and *Nine O'Clock News* and ITN's *News at Ten* all devoted more than 50 per cent of programme time to international news. Programmes aimed at younger viewers are clearly more committed to national news stories (for example BBC1's *Children's Newsround* at 74.3 per cent and Channel 4's *Big Breakfast News* at 71.0 per cent). ITN's *12.30 p.m. News* and *5.40 p.m. News* also reveal a high commitment to national news stories (67.8 per cent and 63.8 per cent respectively). Interestingly, BBC1's *Six O'Clock News*, in spite of claims by the editor, during an interview in June 1994, of a commitment to increase domestic news to try to appeal to the audience, has a quite low figure of only 53.6 per cent national news, although this is higher than the national news output of the other mainstream BBC1 news programmes. This may be an indication that the BBC in April 1993 was adhering to some extent to its mission to be a journal of record through its commitment to covering world affairs. It could also be explained by the unusually dramatic international events occurring during the week analysed, which was affected by the ending and aftermath of the Waco siege in Texas. Barnett and Gaber's (1993) analysis of a week the same

Table 4   *Commitment by terrestrial news programmes to international news,*
            April 1993

Programme	National news (percentage of airtime)	International news (percentage of airtime)
BBC1's *Breakfast News*	53.1	46.9
GMTV News	55.6	44.4
Channel 4's *Big Breakfast News*	71.0	29.0
ITN's *12.30 p.m. News*	67.8	32.2
BBC1's *One O'Clock News*	47.3	52.7
BBC1's *Children's Newsround*	74.3	35.7
ITN's *5.40 p.m. News*	63.8	36.2
YTV's *Calendar News*	100.0	0.0
BBC1's *Six O'Clock News*	53.6	46.4
BBC1's *Look North*	99.8	0.2
Channel 4 News	37.7	62.3
BBC1's *Nine O'Clock News*	45.9	54.1
ITN's *News at Ten*	49.0	51.0
BBC2's *Newsnight*	44.0	56.0
Total: all programmes	56.4	43.6

year showed that ITN's *5.40 p.m. News* and BBC1's *Six O'Clock News* devoted 11 and 22 per cent of their programme coverage to international news respectively. Any future reduction in commitment to international news indicates a real decline in the information quality and diversity of television news and would contradict the BBC's claim that it is 'taking very seriously the desire to see more international reporting' (BBC, 1997a). In April 1993, the *BBC's Nine O'Clock News* devoted 54.1 per cent of its programme to international news and the *Six O'Clock News* devoted 46.4 per cent. The BBC's policy to domesticate the *Six O'Clock News* further, and to ensure that 50 per cent of the *Nine O'Clock News* is comprised of international stories, could reduce the amount of international news shown by the BBC even when big international news stories occur.

A method of assessing information quality of television news is by measuring the length of news stories (see Tables 5 and 6). Table 6 shows that in April 1993 BBC2's *Newsnight* produced the longest news stories, followed by *Channel 4 News*. The BBC overall produced the longest news stories, most above the two-minute bench-mark. None of ITN's news programmes are above the two-minute bench-mark (see Simpson, 1994).[1] The average lengths of news stories broadcast by ITN on both Channel 3 and Channel 4 are shorter than those on BBC1 and BBC2. This confirms findings

---

[1] John Simpson, foreign correspondent at the BBC, argues that a news story must be longer than two minutes in order to avoid the criticism of being down-market.

Table 5   *Average story length by terrestrial television channels, April 1993*

Channel	Average story length (mins)
BBC1	1.8
BBC2	5.2
ITV	1.3
Channel 4	1.0

Table 6   *Average story length by terrestrial television news programmes, April 1993*

Programme	Average story length (mins)
BBC1's *Breakfast News*	1.2
GMTV News	0.5
Channel 4's *Big Breakfast News*	0.2
ITN's *12.30 p.m. News*	2.0
BBC1's *One O'Clock News*	2.2
BBC1's *Children's Newsround*	1.5
ITN's *5.40 p.m. News*	1.5
YTV's *Calendar News*	1.4
BBC1's *Six O'Clock News*	2.2
BBC1's *Look North*	1.5
Channel 4 News	2.6
BBC1's *Nine O'Clock News*	2.1
ITN's *News at Ten*	1.4
BBC2's *Newsnight*	5.2

by Barnett and Gaber (1993), but also fuels the debate about programmes or channels going down-market. If such criticism has validity then it might seem surprising to find that BBC1's average length of news story is only one minute and forty-eight seconds, given John Birt's commitment to alleviate the so-called bias against understanding (Birt and Jay, 1975a, 1975b, 1976a, 1976b; BBC, 1992, 1993c, 1993e, 1994a). However, the average length of programme figure for BBC1 is reduced by BBC1's *Breakfast News*, *Children's Newsround* and *Look North News*, and not by the more mainstream news programmes such as the *One O'Clock*, *Six O'Clock* or *Nine O'Clock News*. The low average figure for BBC1's *Breakfast News* results from the large number of bulletin-like updates of the day's main news stories. As these make up the bulk of the programme they have been included. Other very brief items appearing in most programmes, such as newswraps, newsbelt summaries and short regional television news bulletins, have been excluded from the average story-length measure because they would falsely reduce the overall figure.

Table 7 shows that, in a comparison of the mainstream news programmes between 1993 and 1996, there has been an overall reduction in the amount of time devoted to news stories by all the mainstream news programmes with the exception of ITN's *News at Ten*. With longer stories, the BBC provides more information and analysis than ITN. When ITN produces longer stories they are often made up of interviews with little information content (Harrison, 1995; Catlow, 1997) and live two-ways (Harrison, 1995). Although the drop in story length between 1993 and 1996 is quite low, it is of some concern if it results in less information being transmitted or indicates a long-term trend. ITN's *12.30 p.m. News* shows a marked lessening in story length due to the reduction in the programme length from thirty-five minutes in 1993 to twenty-five minutes in 1997. The programme dropped a 'talking point' slot at the end of the news. The increase in ITN's *News at Ten*'s average story length figure from 1.4 minutes to 1.6 minutes may be a reaction to those who criticised the programme for going down-market. Of concern is that the majority of mainstream terrestrial television news programmes are offering slightly reduced story lengths and less international news than in 1993.

Table 7   *Average story length by mainstream terrestrial television programmes, April 1993 and December 1996*

	Average story length (mins)	
Programme	1993	1996[a]
ITN's *12.30 p.m. News*	2.0	1.6
BBC1's *One O'Clock News*	2.2	2.1
ITN's *5.40 p.m. News*	1.5	1.3
BBC1's *Six O'Clock News*	2.2	2.0
BBC1's *Nine O'Clock News*	2.1	2.0
ITN's *News at Ten*	1.4	1.6

[a] Catlow, 1997

Table 8 shows that if we examine the content of television news, different terrestrial channels have different commitments to news stories, providing some informational diversity over the four channels. ITV provides more human interest, court stories and stories about acts of violence and control of violence than the BBC or Channel 4.

We can also consider terrestrial television news programme content 1993–6 via several broad programme typologies. There are several different types of news programme produced each day, and this analysis covers BBC1's *Breakfast News*, *One O'Clock News*, *Children's Newsround*, *Six O'Clock News*, *Nine O'Clock News* and *Newsnight*. ITN produces programmes for Channel 3: *12.30 p.m. News*, *5.40 p.m. News* and *News at Ten*. ITN also produces programmes for Channel 4 (*Channel 4 News*) and for Planet-24 (*Big Breakfast News*). Good Morning Television produces *GMTV News*. Yorkshire

Table 8   *Diversity of domestic news content by terrestrial television channels,*
          April 1993

Content category	BBC1	BBC2	ITV	Channel 4
	Percentage occurrence of story type over one week's output			
Domestic				
Political – general	4.0	2.2	1.6	5.2
Government policies	0.8	–	0.7	0.8
Politicians – personal	0.1	–	0.4	0.4
Politicians abroad	1.6	4.3	1.1	2.4
Local government	0.7	–	–	0.4
Economics and government	2.1	6.5	2.4	2.0
City news	4.6	8.7	2.9	1.2
Industrial news	11.6	10.9	10.2	10.9
Education and government	0.5	2.2	0.5	0.8
Education and schools	0.6	4.3	0.9	1.2
Violence/control of violence	6.4	2.2	9.1	2.4
Court inquests	9.3	2.2	10.5	7.3
Human interest (light)	3.3	–	5.1	7.7
Human interest (serious)	5.1	2.2	13.3	7.7
Community action	3.2	2.2	4.4	1.6
Sport	7.4	–	5.3	7.3
Royalty	–	–	–	2.0
British Forces	0.4	–	0.9	0.8
Health and government	–	–	0.2	–
Medical discoveries	–	–	0.4	0.4
Health reports	–	–	0.4	–
Help lines	0.9	–	0.9	–
Environmental disaster	0.2	–	–	–
Conservation	0.9	–	0.9	1.6
Scientific discoveries	–	–	–	–
Disasters and accidents	3.9	–	–	0.8
Religion	1.2	2.2	–	0.8
Other	0.4	–	–	–
International				
European politics	2.2	4.3	1.1	1.6
World politics	3.4	10.9	3.1	5.6
Economy	4.3	–	1.1	1.2
Business affairs	0.7	–	–	–
Law	0.7	–	0.2	1.6
Disputes	4.0	10.9	0.9	3.2
Violence	12.9	21.7	13.5	15.7
Human interest (light)	–	–	–	1.6
Human interest (serious)	0.6	–	1.3	2.0
Health	0.6	–	–	0.4
Environment	0.9	–	–	0.8
Science	0.5	2.2	–	–
Disasters	0.1	–	–	–
Sport	–	–	–	0.4

Note: See Appendix I for categories.

Tyne-Tees Television produces *Calendar News* and BBC North produces *Look North News*. These news programmes have several important differences: they are broadcast at different times of the day; they are targeted at different audiences; and they are produced by different media organisations or different sub-departments with different aims, goals, perspectives, personnel and budgets. Each programme has a different remit. *Big Breakfast News*, for example, is a brief update of news stories in the context of an entertainment programme, as is *GMTV News*, whereas *Newsnight* and *Channel 4 News* seek to provide much more information and analysis.

Breakfast news programmes

The BBC's *Breakfast News* is not agenda-setting in the same way as its Radio 4 *Today* programme. The news which is broadcast is rolling news, and the programme is not considered to be as important as the organisation's mainstream news programmes by the journalists or the organisation. Many of the news stories are 'left over' from the day before or mark forthcoming events in the day. Unlike the other BBC news programmes, *Breakfast News* is padded with other activities, such as an analysis of the daily papers, the weather, travel information, local news and a public phone-in, and permits more general chat than the mainstream bulletins. The set was redesigned in 1997, providing a softer feel, and further differentiates BBC *Breakfast News* from the *One*, *Six* and *Nine O'Clock News*. The news bulletins provided by GMTV and Channel 4's *Big Breakfast* are small parts of the overall programme and provide a brief but repetitive round-up of the news. This is sandwiched between entertaining non-news items in the main programmes.

Table 9 clearly shows the commitment of BBC1's *Breakfast News* to national and international stories about the economy. This is in large part due to *Business Breakfast News*, which in 1993 was shown from 6 o'clock to 7 o'clock every morning. This concentrated mainly on business news at home and abroad. Often these stories were used again during the day by the BBC's other news programmes.

GMTV News deals with a much smaller range of content categories than BBC1's *Breakfast News*, covering the international violence dimension provided by the ending and the aftermath of the Waco siege in Texas to a similar extent to the other news programmes. *GMTV News* shows a much stronger commitment than the BBC's *Breakfast News* to human interest stories and to stories about control and acts of violence. The concentration on the serious side of human tragedy was apparent when the programme covered, in more depth than any other, the victims and the families involved in the events following the end of the Waco siege. It also covered unique stories, such as 'Briton in Saudi sentenced to 120 lashes' (*GMTV News*), as well as headlining stories such as 'police in London combing the area to try to find a woman and two young children after Samaritan's call' (*GMTV News*).

Table 9   *Diversity of domestic news content by terrestrial weekday breakfast news programmes, April 1993*

	Percentage occurrence of story type over one week's output		
Content Category	*BBC1's* **Breakfast News**	*ITV's* **GMTV News**	*Channel 4's* **Big Breakfast News**
Domestic			
Political – general	4.6	1.0	6.1
Government policies	1.0	–	0.6
Politicians – personal	0.2	–	0.6
Politicians abroad	1.5	–	1.7
Local government	0.3	–	–
Economics and government	1.7	2.3	0.6
City news	6.3	3.7	–
Industrial news	11.7	10.7	10.1
Education and government	–	–	0.6
Education and schools	0.7	–	1.7
Violence/control of violence	7.0	12.3	1.7
Court inquests	9.3	9.3	17.3
Human interest (light)	2.2	4.0	10.6
Human interest (serious)	4.9	18.0	19.5
Community action	3.4	4.7	2.2
Sport	8.5	4.7	9.5
Royalty	–	–	2.8
British Forces	–	–	1.1
Health and government	–	–	–
Medical discoveries	–	–	0.6
Health reports	–	–	–
Help lines	0.8	–	–
Environmental disaster	–	–	–
Conservation	0.2	1.3	2.2
Scientific discoveries	–	–	–
Disasters and accidents	4.8	3.3	1.1
Religion	0.8	–	0.6
Other	0.5	6.3	–
International			
European politics	2.5	1.3	0.6
World politics	2.4	3.7	3.9
Economy	5.4	–	0.6
Business affairs	1.0	–	–
Law	0.8	–	0.6
Disputes	3.9	0.3	2.2
Violence	11.4	12.7	15.1
Human interest (light)	–	–	2.2
Human interest (serious)	0.8	0.3	2.8
Health	0.2	–	–
Environment	0.7	–	0.6
Science	0.3	–	–
Disasters	–	–	–
Sport	–	–	0.6

Note: See Appendix I for categories.

Channel 4's *Big Breakfast News* emphasises the human interest aspects of the news, concentrating on both the light-hearted – 'old policemen are retiring to the Costa Del Sol', 'what a fringe says about a man' – and the more serious – 'has Dennis Thatcher got cancer?' It also covers the highest percentage of royalty stories, often covering those ignored by the other news programme. As with all news programmes during the week studied, *Big Breakfast News* also concentrated on the international violence dimension of the ending and aftermath of the Waco siege in Texas.

Lunchtime news programmes

ITN's *12.30 p.m. News* and BBC1's *One O'Clock News* are broadcast to an older audience, whose composition the BBC and ITN know less about than they do of the audience watching their other news programmes. Furthermore, the programmes are much greater victims of time constraints than the other news programmes broadcast later in the day. It is often a scramble to get the programmes on air at all. Often the programme editors have to take almost any story which is on offer just to fill the programme, but their programme can set the tone for the rest of the day.

Table 10 shows that ITN's *12.30 p.m. News*, with the exception of the high international violence coverage, has a fairly even spread of coverage over a variety of content categories, although there is some concentration on stories falling into the serious human interest category. In contrast, BBC1's *One O'Clock News* concentrates more heavily on industrial news, often using the storylines identified by BBC1's *Business Breakfast News*.

Early evening news programmes

ITN's *5.40 p.m. News* has a very distinct character and style and favours popularist news values. The programme is very successful in terms of audience appreciation. It lasts for only fifteen minutes and is distinguished by its constant use of the live two-way and human interest stories. The programme editor accounts for this by saying that the programme's remit is to *interest* the audience.

BBC1's *Six O'Clock News* grew out of the ending of *Nationwide* and the failure of its current affairs successor *Sixty Minutes* in the mid-1980s. Therefore it originally sought to be a link between news and current affairs, with a 'news plus analysis' remit. In a sense it was Birtist before Birt. However, in the early 1990s this programme began to move towards a more domestic news agenda and included some human interest and lighter pieces aimed at interesting the audience. (In 1994 the programme editor was more committed to audience research than the other BBC programme editors and found that political news was boring to viewers.) The *Six O'Clock News* is more likely to reject a news story on the grounds that it is boring, and in the

Table 10   *Diversity of domestic news content by terrestrial weekday lunchtime news programmes, April 1993*

	Percentage occurrence of story type over one week's output	
Content category	ITN's 12.30 p.m. News	BBC1's One O'clock News
Domestic		
Political – general	4.5	3.6
Government policies	3.0	–
Politicians – personal	–	–
Politicians abroad	4.5	3.6
Local government	–	1.8
Economics and government	1.5	1.8
City news	7.6	3.6
Industrial news	7.6	10.9
Education and government	3.0	1.8
Education and schools	3.0	–
Violence/control of violence	4.5	3.6
Court inquests	7.6	5.5
Human interest (light)	–	–
Human interest (serious)	9.1	5.5
Community action	1.5	1.8
Sport	1.5	–
Royalty	–	–
British Forces	1.5	1.8
Health and government	–	–
Medical discoveries	1.5	–
Health reports	1.5	–
Help lines	1.5	1.8
Environmental disaster	–	–
Conservation	–	1.8
Scientific discoveries	3.0	–
Disasters and accidents	–	–
Religion	3.0	3.6
Other	–	–
International		
European politics	–	1.8
World politics	1.5	9.1
Economy	3.0	3.6
Business affairs	–	–
Law	–	–
Disputes	4.5	7.3
Violence	16.7	21.8
Human interest (light)	–	–
Human interest (serious)	3.0	–
Health	–	1.8
Environment	–	1.8
Science	–	–
Disasters	–	–
Sport	–	–

Note: See Appendix I for categories.

1990s had a slightly different approach towards serving the public interest and what was newsworthy from the *One and Nine O'Clock News* programmes.

Table 11 shows that ITN's *5.40 p.m. News* has a relatively low concentration of human interest-type stories. Although this is surprising, given the programme's remit to interest the audience, the highest proportion of stories fall into the court inquests and international violence categories. This data is interesting, as observation on the *5.40 p.m. News* desk at ITN revealed the editor's commitment to human interest stories and a genuine preference for the domestic news story rather than the international one. I assume therefore that the high number of stories falling into the international violence category during the week studied shows that the ending of the Waco siege story in particular (which accounts for most of the international violence coverage by this programme) contained sensational dramatic ingredients, which made it unquestionably newsworthy for the *5.40 p.m. News*.

BBC1's *Six O'Clock News* content coverage is very like that of its *One O'Clock News* (Table 10), with slightly less commitment to international news, especially in relation to politics and the economy.

Late evening news programmes

The BBC's *Nine O'Clock News* and ITN's *News at Ten* are both flagship programmes and are both described by journalists as being journals of record, although some BBC journalists express doubts about ITN's *News at Ten* deserving such a title. Both programmes have better resources than the other news programmes shown during the day and both attempt to show something different from what has already been broadcast. One of the most striking differences between the two is the programme editor's awareness of the audience. At *News at Ten*, the attempts to retain the audience's interest has been turned into a science, with audience ratings analysed every five minutes during the programme. In contrast to the recent attitude of the BBC to the audience, in 1994 the *Nine O'Clock News* editor did not believe that it was 'useful or healthy to try to simply give the audience what it thinks it wants' (BBC editor, *Nine O'Clock News*). This evidence of a rather paternalistic attitude to the purposes of broadcasting highlights the dramatic change the BBC has made since 1994 in relation to its view of the audience.

Table 12 shows that the *News at Ten* programme has a tendency to move away from the *5.40 p.m. News* court and inquest reporting, towards a slightly increased coverage of international news. *News at Ten* is deliberately constructed to be different from the *5.40 p.m. News* (ITN editor, *News at Ten*). However, there was also, during the week studied, an increase in the amount of international violence covered; in fact a quarter of all news broadcast during that week was devoted to international violence. In part this was due to increased footage of the Bosnian atrocities being shown on the later programme, but there was also a tendency by *News at Ten* to dwell more on

Table 11   *Diversity of domestic news content by terrestrial weekday early evening news programmes, April 1993*

Content category	Percentage occurrence of story type over one week's output	
	ITN's 5.40 p.m. News	BBC1's Six O'Clock News
Domestic		
Political – general	2.2	3.4
Government policies	2.2	–
Politicians – personal	2.2	–
Politicians abroad	2.2	1.7
Local government	–	1.7
Economics and government	4.4	5.1
City news	–	–
Industrial news	8.9	15.3
Education and government	–	3.4
Education and schools	4.4	–
Violence/control of violence	2.2	5.1
Court inquests	15.6	6.8
Human interest (light)	2.2	–
Human interest (serious)	6.7	1.7
Community action	–	–
Sport	6.7	1.7
Royalty	–	–
British Forces	2.2	1.7
Health and government	–	–
Medical discoveries	2.2	–
Health reports	–	–
Help lines	4.4	1.7
Environmental disaster	–	1.7
Conservation	–	1.7
Scientific discoveries	–	–
Disasters and accidents	–	–
Religion	2.2	3.4
Other	–	-
International		
European politics	–	1.7
World politics	2.2	10.2
Economy	2.2	–
Business affairs	–	–
Law	–	–
Disputes	–	5.1
Violence	20.0	20.0
Human interest (light)	–	–
Human interest (serious)	4.4	–
Health	–	1.7
Environment	–	1.7
Science	–	1.7
Disasters	–	–
Sport	–	–

Note: See Appendix I for categories.

Table 12 *Diversity of domestic news content by terrestrial weekday late evening news programmes, April 1993*

Content category	Percentage occurrence of story type over one week's output	
	BBC1's Nine O'Clock News	ITN's News at Ten
Domestic		
Political – General	4.7	3.1
Government policies	1.6	1.6
Politicians – personal	–	1.6
Politicians abroad	3.1	1.6
Local government	1.6	–
Economics and government	6.3	4.7
City news	–	–
Industrial news	15.6	7.8
Education and government	1.6	1.6
Education and schools	1.6	1.6
Violence/control of violence	3.1	3.1
Court inquests	4.7	7.8
Human interest (light)	–	–
Human interest (serious)	1.6	6.3
Community action	–	–
Sport	3.1	4.7
Royalty	–	–
British Forces	1.6	4.7
Health and government	–	–
Medical discoveries	–	–
Health reports	–	–
Help lines	–	1.6
Environmental disaster	–	–
Conservation	–	1.6
Scientific discoveries	–	–
Disasters and accidents	–	–
Religion	1.6	1.6
Other	–	–
International		
European politics	3.1	3.1
World politics	6.3	6.3
Economy	4.7	4.7
Business affairs	–	–
Law	1.6	1.6
Disputes	6.3	1.6
Violence	23.4	25.0
Human interest (light)	–	–
Human interest (serious)	–	3.1
Health	1.6	–
Environment	1.6	–
Science	–	–
Disasters	–	–
Sport	–	–

Note: See Appendix I for categories.

the violent nature of the day's events. During the week studied, there was little room for the lighter 'and finally' piece. This too is relatively unrepresentative as the news was dominated by the events at Waco, Texas, for two days. Again it is interesting to note under what circumstances a programme will drop part of its traditional and established format: the dramatic ending of the Waco siege obviously contained the right ingredients to motivate such a change, and yet, as I argued in Chapter 6, all television coverage was particularly uninformative.

Of interest are the similarities of coverage in terms of content categories between *Channel 4 News* (see Table 13 over), and the BBC's *Nine O'Clock News* (see Table 12). It is possible that this may, in part be explained by the similar aims of the two programmes to be a journal of record (editor, *Nine O'Clock News*, May 1994; editor, *Channel 4 News*, June 1994), but it could also be partially explained by the fact that the BBC's current *Nine O'Clock News* editor used to edit *Channel 4 News*. If the spread of news categories shared by *Channel 4 News* and the *Nine O'Clock News* is indeed the mark of a journal of record, then these two programmes are good bench-marks against which to assess this particular criterion of newsworthiness, but it also indicates how an editor can be chosen for his or her views or editing style.

Minority audience news programmes

BBC1's *Children's Newsround*, *Channel 4 News* and BBC2's *Newsnight* attempt to set their own agenda far more than the other terrestrial television news programmes. *Channel 4 News*, however, is more constrained than *Newsnight* in doing this because it is broadcast during the newsday and therefore has to reflect some of the main news stories being broadcast by the other news programmes. Often *Channel 4 News*'s newsbelt stories are simply written from the wires, using film acquired from Channel 3. The lower status accorded to many of the mainstream news stories of the day is compounded by *Channel 4 News*'s in-depth attention to stories which are not currently on the national news agenda. Coverage of such unusual stories can be rather hit and miss. Occasionally *Channel 4 News* may set the news agenda by discovering a newsworthy story, but in general some of its coverage is regarded by the rest of the broadcast media as not particularly newsworthy. Other journalists sometimes criticise *Channel 4 News* for staying with one story for too long and going 'past its newsworthy sell-by date'.

Table 13 shows that BBC1's *Children's Newsround* has a much smaller range of content categories because, as outlined earlier, it sets its own agenda each day. The programme often picks up on only one or two of the main news stories of the day. The intense concentration on stories of a light human interest nature and sport reflects some of the optimism of *Children's Newsround*, which is often a good news programme. It also casts the

Table 13   *Diversity of domestic news content by terrestrial weekday minority*
audience news programmes, April 1993

	Percentage occurrence of story type over one week's output		
Content category	BBC1's Children's Newsround	ITN's Channel 4 News	BBC2's Newsnight
Domestic			
Political – General	–	2.9	2.2
Government policies	–	1.4	–
Politicians – personal	–	–	–
Politicians abroad	–	4.3	4.3
Local government	–	1.4	–
Economics and government	–	5.8	6.5
City news	–	4.3	8.7
Industrial news	–	13.0	10.9
Education and government	–	1.4	2.2
Education and schools	–	–	4.3
Violence/control of violence	–	4.3	2.2
Court inquests	–	7.2	2.2
Human interest (light)	37.5	–	–
Human interest (serious)	4.2	2.9	2.2
Community action	–	–	2.2
Sport	16.7	1.4	–
Royalty	–	–	–
British Forces	–	–	–
Health and government	–	–	–
Medical discoveries	–	–	–
Health reports	–	–	–
Help lines	4.2	–	–
Environmental disaster	–	–	–
Conservation	12.5	–	–
Scientific discoveries	–	–	–
Disasters and accidents	–	–	–
Religion	–	1.4	2.2
Other	–	–	–
International			
European politics	–	4.3	4.3
World politics	–	10.1	10.9
Economy	–	2.9	–
Business affairs	–	–	–
Law	–	4.3	0.6
Disputes	–	5.8	10.9
Violence	8.3	17.4	21.7
Human interest (light)	–	–	–
Human interest (serious)	–	–	–
Health	4.2	1.4	–
Environment	8.3	1.4	–
Science	–	–	2.2
Disasters	4.2	–	–
Sport	–	–	–

Note: See Appendix I for categories.

ordinary person in a more favourable light than the other mainstream news programmes, which often only cover the ordinary person when he or she becomes a victim or an eye-witness to a disaster. Children therefore hear about 'the first woman to walk to the North Pole', 'children learn to look out for fire in the Hazard Alley Project in Milton Keynes', 'the world's luckiest tortoise' or the 'Shakespeare play to be put on for the first time for hundreds of years at the New Globe Theatre'. This alternative type of news is an indication of how news agendas could be different if there was not a tendency to concentrate on the more pessimistic nature of world events. However, as BBC news presenter Martyn Lewis found to his cost, to try to tell seasoned journalists that it would be better to try to look for good-news stories is asking them to reconceptualise the constituent features of newsworthiness.[2]

It appears that in the main good news and trivia are key news values in children's news. However, the programme also contains worthy stories (such as a piece on the rain forest) and mainstream serious news stories, if they are deemed to be sufficiently important (such as the death of Diana, Princess of Wales). In contrast, much serious news is perceived as being for adults, and programmes which seek to include too many good-news stories, such as those in ITN's *News at Ten*'s 'and finally' slot, may be accused of going down-market. High-quality, up-market news is perceived as a serious concept, and for some critics good news or news which is entertainingly or sensationally presented moves too far away from that principle.

BBC2's *Newsnight*, in common with the other BBC news programmes, has a commitment to economic news and may, for example, devote twelve minutes to a story about government borrowing on a day when no other news programme reports it. In the case of international stories, *Newsnight* usually pieces together a set of events without seeking to report each one as a separate news story. In contrast, ITN usually reports different aspects of events in different story packages. *Newsnight*'s method of reporting events provides much more information about and context for a situation, as it does not seek to simplify it by denying the audience knowledge of the complexity of the issues. This is something that the mainstream news programmes usually cannot reconcile, so the individual news stories which are finally transmitted are often lacking in context. However, in common with all the other news programmes, *Newsnight* dwelt on the international violence dimension of the events in Waco and, unusually for a programme committed to analysis, did not follow up the original violent story with any analysis of the background or the causes, but reported the violent event in isolation.

---

[2] In the mid-1990s Martyn Lewis, a well-known BBC presenter, went on record as supporting the deliberate reporting of good-news stories. This suggestion was met with derision by some journalists who view this practice as trivialising news.

Regional news programmes

BBC1's *Look North News* is controlled rigorously by Television Centre in London, and the programme still adheres quite strongly to a Birtist philosophy of news analysis. Journalists spend time trying to work out an interesting issue behind the latest local crime story. In contrast YTV's *Calendar News* is a news magazine programme, filled with a variety of stories, many being light and having some human interest. The programme has a hybrid format of serious hard news delivered straight in a local opt-out, followed by lighter stories from the studio. What is deemed to be newsworthy at *Calendar News* depends entirely on which part of the programme it is aimed at.

Table 14 shows that the regional news programmes *Calendar News* and *Look North News* both have a propensity towards coverage of court inquests, control and acts of violence, and sport. The major difference between the two programmes lies in the tendency for *Calendar News* to cover more light-weight human interest stories, such as 'the policeman who keeps winning quizzes', 'farmer who makes pig models', 'the oldest bowling green in the UK, opened today by the Mayor of Chesterfield', and the 'sixty-sixth flower show in Harrogate'. This can be compared with the much more serious type of human interest story on BBC's *Look North News*: 'solvent abuser victim's funeral, father has made an emotional appeal and the vicar has warned other children', 'gift of life, two Yorkshire boys who died after a fire last week gave their organs to a baby', or 'community in mourning, funeral today of two young children killed in a house fire'. The tone of the two programmes is markedly different. *Look North News*'s presentational style is much more like the BBC's national news programmes; the presenters sit behind a desk and talk direct to the camera. *Calendar News* on the other hand has variously been presented from the newsroom (where the presenters sit on couches next to potted plants), from a studio, or from opt-outs (small, five-minute bulletins presented from specific parts of the region). The last are presented formally, and the contrast between a light news story presented in the studio and the harder local news read out in a traditional style can sometimes jar. The hybrid nature of the *Calendar News* set is also reflected in its news content categories.

Differences in reporting the news

In 1993 the BBC, ITN, GMTV and Yorkshire Tyne-Tees Television news programmes produced news which exhibited some differences in news content. It follows that they also had different organisational criteria which influenced output and selection, illustrating the divergent television newsroom epistemologies. These differences can be exemplified by the coverage of a massacre in Bosnia which was reported from a variety of perspectives on the same day, Friday 23 April 1993. BBC1's *Breakfast News* reported that the members of the self-proclaimed Serb Parliament were to meet regarding the latest Vance–Owen peace plan, with the likely response of non-acceptance. *GMTV*

Table 14   *Diversity of news content by terrestrial weekday regional news
            programmes, April 1993*

Content category	Percentage occurrence of story type over one week's output	
	ITV's Calendar News	*BBC1's* Look North News
Domestic		
Political – General	–	–
Government policies	–	–
Politicians – personal	–	–
Politicians abroad	1.3	–
Local government	–	1.6
Economics and government	–	–
City news	–	–
Industrial news	13.3	7.8
Education and government	–	–
Education and schools	–	–
Violence/control of violence	9.3	10.9
Court inquests	17.3	23.4
Human interest (light)	20.0	9.4
Human interest (serious)	8.0	14.1
Community action	12.0	9.4
Sport	10.7	9.4
Royalty	–	–
British Forces	–	–
Health and government	1.3	–
Medical discoveries	–	–
Health reports	1.3	–
Help lines	1.3	–
Environmental disaster	–	1.6
Conservation	–	3.1
Scientific discoveries	–	–
Disasters and accidents	4.0	7.8
Religion	–	–
Other	–	1.6

News did not bother to cover the story at all, preferring to concentrate on
the police search in London for a caller to the Samaritans who seemed
unable to communicate, leaving a distressed child on the telephone trying to
explain where she lived. *GMTV News* treated this story as an emergency,
giving out telephone numbers and updates throughout the morning and
involving the audience with the drama as much as possible. Channel 4's *Big
Breakfast News* led on the Samaritan's story, but also reported that 'British
troops have admitted there is little they can do about the Bosnian blood-bath
in Vitez'. ITN's *12.30 p.m. News* was far more dramatic about the so-called
blood-bath, reporting that 'in Bosnia, scenes of horror met British troops

when confronted with a Muslim village destroyed by the Croats' and 'in Bosnia, sickening evidence of the murder of Muslim citizens by Croat forces has been uncovered by British forces', with the added caution that 'you will find the pictures in this report particularly disturbing'. The focus of the report was initially to show images of the violence by the Croats, but then to go on to concentrate upon the plight of the British Forces in Bosnia, and their feelings about the atrocity. BBC1's *One O'Clock News* also concentrated on reporting the violence and showing film of burnt houses, and, like ITN, focused in upon the curled, burnt hand of a corpse on the staircase. In both cases the film was carefully edited to ensure that the audience did not see more than a fleeting glimpse of the burnt body. Martin Bell of the BBC demonstrated the organisation's mission to protect the audience from the reality of the situation when he said, 'what happened here can frankly not be shown in any detail – there is a roomful of charred bodies and they died in the greatest of agony' (BBC1's *One O'Clock News*).

In contrast, ITN's *12.30 p.m. News* showed the room in which the people had died. The viewer could see only what appeared to be charred wood and rags, but nonetheless the audience were shown an image of the atrocity which the BBC would not allow it to see. The BBC in its lunchtime report also went on to develop the story, moving away from the dramatic scenes in the Bosnian village and the distress of the British Forces, which it did not dwell upon, to show film of the Bosnian Parliament meeting the day before. The BBC report speculated whether the peace plans, which were dismissed out of hand the previous day, could be revived in view of the Croat atrocities. The story was then developed further, to Tuzla, where Kate Adie reported on a team of ambassadors from the United Nations who were apparently on their way to investigate reports that food supplies were not reaching the village. There was no film of the ambassadors, but plenty of shots of hungry and miserable-looking villagers in Tuzla.

BBC1's *Children's Newsround* chose to ignore the events in Bosnia and led with a story about a world health campaign to fight tuberculosis. ITN's *5.40 p.m. News* opened with a dramatic lead. The presenter greeted the teatime audience with the following words: 'Hello. They were given no mercy, men, women, children, burned alive in their homes. British Forces came upon the massacre, proof that atrocities are being committed by all sides. Some of the pictures in this report are particularly disturbing' (ITN's *5.40 p.m. News*, 23 April 1993).

ITN stressed the dramatic, the human tragedy, the plight of the British Forces and the horrific violence. The programme also inserted this 'teaser', 'Paul Davies's *full* report will be on *News at Ten*', so those viewers interested in the macabre events could watch more of them in full later in the evening. In a sense human tragedy and horror were promoted as a hook for the next programme.

BBC1's *Six O'Clock News* reported the story in the same style as the *One*

O'Clock News, but included a new piece about Lord Owen arriving in Belgrade for further talks. *Channel 4 News's* film of the Bosnian village was very similar to that shown by the BBC and ITN earlier in the day. However, it had not been as heavily edited as the film for the mainstream programmes and the audience was allowed a more lingering look at the human remains in the village cellar, accompanied by the shot of the burnt hand used by the other programmes. The accompanying narrative was not particularly sensationalist in content or style, but simply allowed the audience to see more of the situation than the BBC or the peak-time ITN programmes. Both these mainstream early evening programmes would have had to be very careful not to show anything too horrific to a mass audience of children and adults. In contrast *Channel 4 News* is watched by a smaller audience and has more freedom to be challenging. A foreign affairs correspondent in London went on to report on the continuing diplomatic wrangling over the Bosnian conflict via a live link to the Foreign Affairs Committee spokesman.

Even past the 9 o'clock watershed, the BBC was still showing the film of Martin Bell telling the audience that he could not possibly let it see the results of what had occurred, followed by the same report used for the *Six O'Clock News*, of Lord Owen arriving in Belgrade. The only new addition to the report was a small oov (out of vision) report that President Clinton said he would decide on a tougher policy towards the Serbs in the next few days (which was a tenuous link to the story about *Croat* atrocities). ITN's *News at Ten*, however, took advantage of the post-watershed slot and treated the audience to the promised full report, accompanied by lingering shots of the bodies in the cellar and a variety of shots of the burnt hand (and arm) on the stairs. ITN introduced this news report with the caution that 'we must warn you that our report by Paul Davies contains pictures of those burnt bodies. They are deeply disturbing images which illustrate the horror of the Bosnian War' (ITN's *News at Ten*, 23 April 1993).

Newsnight did not linger on the bodies in the cellar, preferring to move away from what was now the mainstream news story of the day, towards a unique package. This was supplied by Jeremy Paxman in Tuzla, claiming that the village epitomised the complexity of the Bosnian War.

Clearly the dimensions of the news stories emphasised by each news programme indicate the types of news priority those programmes have. ITN's *12.30 p.m.* and *5.40 p.m. News* reported the violence as it had occurred and concentrated on the human suffering and impact of the atrocities, using the macabre and extreme nature of those events in a dramatic way to draw viewers to the *News at Ten* programme. In contrast the BBC chose to protect its audience from the horror of the situation by acting as a censor, allowing the audience to catch a small glimmer of the horror, by showing a burnt hand, but assuming that for reasons of taste and decency, BBC viewers would not want to see anything further. There is a no-blood policy at the BBC, so viewers are similarly not allowed to see shots of bloodstains on pavements or walls, let alone on the victim. However, both the BBC and ITN mainstream news on BBC1 and Channel 3 told what was ostensibly the same story, therefore providing similar information.

By ignoring the massacre and concentrating upon stories about international health, international environment, international disasters and accidents and human interest, BBC1's *Children's Newsround* illustrated its remit to be different from the mainstream news. Similarly the two minority audience programmes, *Channel 4 News* and *Newsnight*, showed a different approach in coverage. Both covered the massacre and atrocities in a rather matter-of-fact way, moving quickly onto different dimensions of the Bosnian issue.

News programmes provide some differences in their range of information; consequently different programmes make different contributions to a citizen's knowledge and ultimately to his or her potential for competence in the public sphere. However, the diversity in newsroom epistemologies (which are grounded in organisational culture and history) is most strongly noticeable in the minority or specialist programmes such as *Children's Newsround*, *Newsnight* and *Channel 4 News*.[3] An important value of television news is that diversity of news values exists despite the existence of a shared journalistic culture and a common adherence to the practical application of objectivity. I have shown that differences in news values also apply to television channels; for example, BBC2 and Channel 4 both have a higher commitment to international news output than BBC1 or ITN on Channel 3. Furthermore, I have shown that sometimes different news programmes have different interpretations of the news value potential of the same event and extract different stories or storylines from that event.

Where similarities exist between television news programmes, they tend to be based on reporting international news events such as the ending of the siege in Waco. Here television news programmes will take a similar media line. The main point remains, namely that different news programmes still have *different* levels of commitment to explanation of complex issues, with programmes such as the *Big Breakfast News*, *GMTV News*, and ITN's *12.30 p.m.* and *5.40 p.m. News* telling the story straight, without elaboration or diversification. By contrast *Newsnight*, *Channel 4 News* and BBC1's *Nine O'Clock News* in particular are less inclined to offer such simplistic explanations for an event, preferring to explore other issues relating to the occurrence. Both *Newsnight* and *Children's Newsround* tend to follow a different news agenda from the other news programmes, and *Channel 4 News* tends to report international news in fewer but longer sequences than domestic news.

[3] Although an analysis was not made of S4C's news coverage during this week, its remit to produce news for Wales and Welsh speakers would similarly provide a variety of news stories.

The politicisation of the news

What emerges as an issue of major concern is any further movements of mainstream mass audience news programmes on ITV and BBC1 towards over-politicisation of issues (telling all stories from a political angle or personalising political stories to make them more interesting to the audience), prioritising interesting and entertaining the audience over and above informing it, at the expense of in-depth coverage of politics and economics, partial and inaccurate coverage of international events and further reduction in the length of news stories. A comparison between the output of the mainstream

Table 15   *Domestic and international news content of BBC mainstream news programmes, April 1993 and December 1996*

	Percentage occurrence of story type over one week's output					
	BBC1's		BBC1's		BBC1's	
Content	One O'Clock News		Six O'Clock News		Nine O'Clock News	
	1993	*1996ᵃ*	*1993*	*1996ᵃ*	*1993*	*1996ᵃ*
Domestic						
Politics	12.6	25.9	15.3	28.4	18.9	32.3
Economics, industrial and city news	14.5	5.2	15.3	4.5	6.3	3.1
Health	–	6.9	–	6.0	–	6.2
Court inquests	5.5	19.0	6.8	20.9	4.7	12.3
Violence/control of violence	3.6	5.2	5.1	6.0	3.1	7.7
Human interest	7.3	3.4	1.7	8.9	1.6	4.6
Sport	–	1.7	1.7	4.5	3.1	1.5
Royalty	–	5.2	–	1.5	–	1.5
Environment	1.8	5.2	3.4	1.5	–	–
Scientific discoveries	–	5.2	–	1.5	–	–
Disasters and accidents	–	–	–	–	–	–
Religion	3.6	1.7	4.3	–	1.6	–
Transport	–	1.7	–	1.5	–	1.5
Other	3.6	–	3.4	1.5	1.6	–
International						
Politics	10.9	5.2	11.9	7.5	9.4	16.9
Economy and business affairs	3.6	–	–	–	4.7	–
Law	21.8	1.7	–	–	1.6	1.5
Disputes and violence	7.3	5.2	25.1	3.0	29.7	6.2
Human interest	–	–	–	1.5	–	4.6
Health	1.8	–	1.7	–	1.6	–
Other	1.8	1.7	3.4	1.5	1.6	1.5

Table 16   *Domestic and international news content of ITN mainstream news programmes, April 1993 and December 1996*

| Content | *Percentage occurrence of story type over one week's output* | | | | | |
| | ITN's 12.30 p.m. News | | ITN's 5.40 p.m. News | | ITN's News at Ten | |
	1993	1996[a]	1993	1996[a]	1993	1996[a]
Domestic						
Politics	16.5	22.8	13.2	24.4	14.2	29.4
Economics, industrial and city news	15.2	14.0	8.9	6.7	7.8	4.4
Health	3.0	8.8	2.2	8.9	–	7.4
Court inquests	7.6	14.0	15.6	22.2	7.8	28.9
Violence/control of violence	4.5	7.0	15.6	6.7	3.1	5.9
Human interest	12.1	10.5	8.9	15.6	6.3	13.2
Sport	1.5	3.5	6.7	8.9	4.7	8.8
Royalty	–	1.8	–	4.4	–	1.5
Environment	–	1.8	–	–	1.6	–
Scientific discoveries	3.0	3.5	–	–	–	1.5
Disasters and accidents	–	1.8	–	–	–	–
Religion	3.0	–	2.2	–	1.6	–
Transport	–	1.8	–	2.2	–	–
Other	4.5	–	2.2	2.2	7.9	–
International						
Politics	1.5	3.5	2.2	2.2	9.4	5.9
Economy and business affairs	3.0	–	2.2	–	4.7	–
Law	–	1.8	–	–	1.6	–
Disputes and violence	21.2	–	20.0	2.2	26.6	2.9
Human interest	3.0	3.5	4.4	2.2	3.1	–
Health	–	–	–	–	–	–
Other	–	–	–	–	.	–

[a] Catlow, 1997

Note: See Appendix I for categories.

news programmes on ITV and the BBC in 1993 and 1996[4] (Tables 15 and 16), if accurate, shows that some of the concerns may be well founded. The increase in political coverage by all the mainstream news programmes appears superficially to be a positive activity. But these changes in newsroom priorities affect television news's relationship to a liberal democracy. The

[4] I have included this work by Louise Catlow, an MA student at the University of Sheffield, out of interest. As far as I am aware Catlow's is the only analysis which is similar enough to my own to bear comparison.

excavation and analysis of the unaccountable areas of public life is important to help citizens to understand and perhaps even control events which affect them. By exposing injustice and corruption and challenging official lines of argument, journalism helps the public to make a judgement about the validity and authority of political institutions and the relationship Britain has to the rest of the world. However, this has to be done in a certain way, as there is a danger that a public which is continuously exposed to information about politicians who are shown to be scheming endlessly, or which is over-exposed to politicised stories *per se*, will cease to take an interest in the political news coverage, or even in the political process itself (Fallows, 1996). A balance obviously has to be struck between the presentation of important issues to the public and the temptation to politicise them. This increase in political stories may simply reflect the increased investment by both ITN and the BBC in their political units based at Millbank. It is likely that this increased coverage of politics is a reflection not of the increased scrutiny of political life but of increased coverage of political activities *per se*, at the expense of coverage of other issues. We have seen that coverage of international events may be declining and that international politics, especially European politics, is thinly covered. Coverage of national economic stories has fallen and stories about health, poverty, homelessness, the elderly and so on are poorly covered by the mainstream media. The tables also show an increase in the coverage of human interest stories by the BBC's *Six* and *Nine O'Clock News* programmes and by ITN's *5.40 p.m. News* and *News at Ten*, as well as an overall increase in the coverage of court stories and stories about violence and the control of violence. The news agenda appears to be coalescing around issues of politics and politicisation of many aspects of public life, and around stories about human interest, violence and the consequences of violence.

This chapter has shown, using empirical data from content analyses, that despite the adherence of journalists to a shared journalistic culture and the common acceptance of the value of practical objectivity via the adoption and application of objectivity norms, diversity of news values does exist in different television newsrooms, and that this diversity provides a range of television news stories. Problematically, the value of this diversity is compromised by a formulaic approach to international news coverage, use of similar sources, over-politicisation of news events and a reduction in news story lengths. Public service broadcasters must guard against the urge to provide easily digestible news at the expense of its nutritional content if they are to continue to provide a viable alternative to the commercial news forms which are developing. The key to concern about information diversity is that journalism is intimately bound up with citizenship rights and has a social responsibility to attempt to engage and empower its viewers and readers. One particularly important role is the representation of the various minority publics which are emerging due to fragmentation and diversification of

British society. The diversification of the television news genre (to become more like the newspaper industry, in the sense that there are now many different types of news programme) should reflect the fragmentary nature of the audience and readership. However, it is unlikely that market-driven television and newspaper diversity can either adequately and accurately represent the diverse range of viewers which currently exist in British society, or provide adequate and equitable access to those viewers. The exclusion of some citizens from access to information is not new. Neither is the existence of official and unofficial realms of communication. What is new is the potential scale for exclusion. Deterioration of existing information sources, coupled with economic exclusion from alternative sources of information, is a recipe for disaster.

Fortunately in the early 2000s, a diverse range of free-at-source news programming still exists (although it is under great pressure). The next chapter provides a closer cultural analysis of the differences between the news output of the commercial and public service broadcasters, to consider more closely the range of news diversity in British terrestrial television news.

8

TV news and different
cultural norms

Commercialisation of television news and competition between the variety of news providers is seen by some to lead to homogenisation of information content. Conversely, Chapters 5, 6 and 7 have shown that whilst terrestrial television newsrooms operate according to similar cultures and values there is still some variety of information content provided. The tendency towards diversity of content coverage is driven, and will be further driven, by the market-oriented rush towards providing niche news products. Each terrestrial news organisation, in common with global news providers such as Bloomberg, CNN and BSkyB, is trying to find ways of acquiring a share of an assumed (and from their point of view lucrative) market for news and information. We are witnessing a deliberate diversification of the television news genre in response to the macro pressures caused by the globalisation of news and information supply and demand, the new commercialisation of television news and technological developments.

Television news is being challenged by forces which lead to a focus on the chase for audience ratings. This inexorably leads to the idea (increasingly acted upon) that a tip towards entertainment or interesting the viewer will lead to an increase in audience share. The current trend in British terrestrial television news is towards attracting audiences through a popularisation of the news product and the changing priorities news providers such as the BBC have in providing more relevant news. This is manifest in the reduction in coverage of international news, shorter news stories, and increase in human interest news and news about violence or the consequences of violence (see Chapter 7). Evidence from the United States is not comforting in this respect; the panicky attempt to hold on to or gain American audiences has resulted in a decline in standards and definitions of news. There is an increased need for news organisations to become efficient and cost-effective. Reforms at ITN and the Birtist regime at the BBC are centred on the aim to produce news more efficiently, through reforming the processes of news production, at the expense of content.

Hume (1996) argues that the increased use of tabloid formats, which place the emphasis on drama, violence, celebrity gossip, sex, scandal, sleaze and so on, can only boost ratings in the short term. The trend in the United States towards the increasing 'tabloidisation' of television news formats has actually proved to be counter-productive in the long term, with audiences becoming increasingly distanced from the news, due to a reduction in trust and customer loyalty.

The temptation for all television news programmes in Britain to go down-market, and consequently to offer similar popularist news content, is great given the pressures they face. The main focus of the 1998 Programme Strategy Review at the BBC was to attract and retain a younger audience. To do so, the organisation has had to concentrate more on what the mass audience wants to see in television news. On the face of it, this appears to be in keeping with public service broadcasting sentiments about quality, diversity and increased access. The reality may prove to be more about an increase in ratings and the creation of a two-tier news, via adjustments of BBC news values. This emanates from a changing interpretation of what constitutes the public interest for different programmes and different audiences. If the BBC ceases to set a standard for terrestrial television news output by failing to provide a diverse range of news stories, the informational quality of public service television news may be damaged. To remain of high quality, information diversity has to be broad-based, include diversity of representation of minorities, and allow diversity of access (where esoteric, in-depth or wide-ranging news programmes are not placed in inaccessible parts of the schedule, or restricted to low-access channels such as BBC *News-24*) as well as providing diversity of choice. As Schiller (1996) argued, if useful information becomes increasingly privatised or commercialised, then the possibility of a rational, information-rich society becomes increasingly unrealistic.

These concerns are valid even at a time when governments are making more information available via electronic initiatives such as Government On-Line, Direct Access Government, Open Government (*www.open.gov.uk*), updated Government Information Services (GIS), electronic city halls, public access terminals and electronic benefits systems using smart cards. Crucially, it is unclear at this stage whether such information will open up the possibilities of more rational, two-way communication and interaction between citizen and policy maker. It is likely that citizens are generally better informed about many issues in the 1990s and early 2000s than in the 1960s (although there is also the danger of information overload). Citizens have more freedom in the 1990s and early 2000s than at other periods in history, because alternative groups and public spheres are developing. But conversely, it is also possible that citizens may have more knowledge but less and less chance actually to use that knowledge as active political citizens, due to the decrease in accessibility and accountability of public figures and public institutions. Ironically, direct access can also mean more remote access – government without a human face. It is too soon to condemn initiatives which are about open government. It is not too soon to warn about the consequences of a badly handled medium. Social responsibility remains the key issue.

Terrestrial television news organisations have a social responsibility to continue to provide useful information to the citizen about state activity. An even more important role for the television medium is to be seen as acting as both interpreter and interrogator on behalf of the citizen. However, the increasing use of entertainment formats, live two-ways, and political interviews conducted by presenters rather than political correspondents, reduces the quality of the information which emerges from the television news programme. Brian Wenham's comment on how the BBC's scheduling has changed illustrates this point perfectly:

> It is odd that, having fought so long to get access to Parliament, broadcasters make such patchy use of it ... so not knowing quite what to do, they duck. They did so majestically a year back. Robin Cook was in mid-flight in the debate on the Scott Report. It was clear to anyone paying attention that this was one of the great post-war Parliamentary occasions. Cook had reached point three out of five. The telly lost its nerve. 'There we leave Robin Cook, for *Ready, Steady Cook*.' It was a very low moment. (Wenham, *Evening Standard*, 19 February 1997:51)

Even if citizens do not choose to watch in large numbers, it is important that such information and interpretation still exist as an alternative and as a general right to a diverse range of knowledge about the world. I have shown that a range of television news agendas and values does still exist. It is these I shall now examine more critically. For the purpose of the discussion here, I shall continue with Halberstam's (1992) theories of newsworthiness as 'interest' and as 'importance', since the distinctions between these two concepts are pertinent to a comparison between the different philosophies to be found in different news organisations and in different notions of what is in the public interest.

The various epistemological influences at work in various television newsrooms and news organisations result in some different priorities for each news programme. Such influences affect the criteria of news selection and production. News can be broadly determined, therefore, as 'importance', 'importance plus some interest', 'interest plus some importance' or 'interest and entertainment'. BBC journalists have tended to talk about news in terms of 'importance'. In 1987 and 1988, in response to the Birtian views on news, a recruitment drive occurred which recruited individuals to be custodians of the BBC vision; those people have since recruited others and the culture of the BBC has changed. What is interesting is that:

> Not everyone agrees with each other; there is still some dissent, thank goodness. What this has meant for newsworthiness at the BBC is that importance and

significance are stressed as news values and the interesting but not significant is played down. For example the 'BBC's consensus' on this would involve me knocking a trivial human interest story off the programme editor's running order if I thought it was not suitable. This happens about six times a year. (BBC senior editor)

At ITN Channel 3 journalists tend to talk in terms of what is 'interesting' or notable: 'We try to find stories which will interest the audience. I mean they have just got in from work, want to put their feet up. They don't want to be bored to death. That's not to say we don't cover big stories which the BBC go for, but we do try to make them interesting too' (ITN producer). The main priority for ITN is to be noticed: 'We aim to be distinctive, to stand out from the crowd and to be talked about' (senior ITN editor). Generally the priorities of ITN's Channel 3 programmes are to be accessible to a wide range of people, to be lively and interesting and to cover a broad news agenda. Unlike the BBC, until its 1998 Programme Strategy Review, ITN has long had a policy of ensuring that the audience 'gets to know the correspondents' by repeatedly using the same ones.

Another senior figure at ITN finds it more difficult to define news than the journalists in the newsroom because he believes that ITN's output is now so diverse that there is not one single news philosophy at work: 'If pushed I would have to say that ITN's news philosophy is accessibility, which comes across in our writing style, a sense of humour and a sense of adventure.' At Channel 4 journalists talk in terms of a mixture of what is both interesting and important to them as providers of a very different type of news and highlight their aim of marrying the two concepts together: 'We try to put the narrative and the analysis together, because sometimes the background is actually not very interesting because it's simply historical. We are not educationalists but we're there to give people the information with which they can form their own judgement' (programme editor).

One problem with asking journalists about what they see their remit to be, or the priority of their news organisation, is that it is not entirely clear what they mean by the words 'important' or 'interesting'. It is therefore useful here to continue to develop the themes visited earlier in this book and to have a closer look at the understanding of the terms in different television newsrooms, in order to analyse how they relate to what is considered to be newsworthy at ITN and the BBC.

Importance is associated with ideas such as consequence, significance, weight, gravity, seriousness or solemnity. I have shown that BBC journalists' news values and what constitutes newsworthiness at the BBC are shaped by these ideas. Interest, on the other hand, is associated with words such as 'attention' and 'notice'. Here the core feature of the idea is not so much the serious nature of the event or issue but rather the amount of attention it attracts. The essential differences between the two highlight the distinction in values at the BBC and ITN and in different television newsrooms.

There are problems with importance in relation to newsworthiness. As Halberstam (1992) notes, there are difficulties in deciding at what point a story or an event becomes important enough to warrant its telling, and he questions whether an important event should be told regardless of the actual public interest in the consequences. For example, if importance is taken as the most significant news value it follows that the discovery of an event showing that the planet will be destroyed in billions of years must be newsworthy because it is of such human significance. But realistically, the consequences of this particular event for ourselves and our future relatives are not particularly significant, and so the story is not newsworthy other than in having some scientific quirkiness. It follows that what is important must be qualified to include the proviso that the event must be important to us *today or in the foreseeable future*.

Furthermore, it might be argued that stories such as an obscure decision by the House of Lords, or a breakthrough in a particular mathematical calculation, should be reported because such information must be important to someone. Such information would be incredibly boring to everyone else and so would not be deemed to be newsworthy. A further qualification then of the journalistic understanding of importance is that the event must be important *to a large number of people*.

If newsworthiness is analysed purely in terms of what is interesting, one finds again that there are certain problems with this. Assuming that anything that occurs in the world might be of interest to someone, then it is obviously not possible to include all such events in the news just because they are interesting. The journalistic understanding of what is interesting, as of what is important, *must apply to a large number of people*.

We encounter a problem if we try to rationalise either important or interesting events purely in terms of numbers. It is easy to argue that because lots of people are interested in stories about skateboarding ducks or the royal family then these should be included in the news every night. This approach would pander to the wants of the people. *Audience choice would lead news selection*. If, however, journalists were to argue that the state of the economy or religious services are important to many people and therefore should be included in the news every night, this would distort news values. This would result in a paternalistic approach to news provision by giving the audience what it was perceived to need. *Audience choice would be restricted*.

Therefore a compromise between what is important and what is interesting often underpins newsworthiness and occurs in most newsrooms. Of significance is the nature of this compromise. At the BBC a trade-off has taken place between what the organisation deems to be important and what is seen to be interesting. This is primarily motivated by the journalists themselves as would-be viewers, and by the consensus of values which has been built up via the recruitment practices of the BBC since the late 1980s. BBC journalists steer themselves away from becoming too boring by being ironic about their role and analysing their own boredom threshold in relation to the news stories they are covering. Complaints about stories which are simply worthy and not newsworthy proliferate in the newsroom. The journalists at the BBC know that senior news management dislikes '"media-created" or hyped-up stories, which are like sand devils which are caused by a storm which whips up lots of sand: it looks impressive, it blows in everyone's faces and then suddenly it is gone' (managing director of News and Current Affairs, 25 June 1994).

To some extent the compromise to which I refer was played out in the early 1990s, when news programmes contained fewer stories told in more depth via the use of the so-called twin pack. BBC television news output between 1987 and 1992 had a different format structure, until the programme editors began to ensure that a more diverse range of stories was offered, resulting in a greater number of news stories per bulletin (although this ability to diversify the news content of different programmes was temporarily put under threat by Birt's attempts to introduce super-editors at the BBC in September 1997). In the 1998 Programme Strategy Review, diversification of BBC news programmes was of paramount importance. Many journalists at the BBC believe that the method of analysing news events used by the BBC in the late 1980s was boring and unpopular with the audience, 'who were turning off from the *Nine O'Clock News* in particular in droves' (BBC editor, *Nine O'Clock News*).

Television news journalists at the BBC made pragmatic and gradual adjustments throughout the early to mid-1990s, back to more familiar and popular methods of reporting and selecting the news. As a BBC correspondent confided:

> There is a contradiction between *Extending Choice*, which was 'dropped' as soon as it was publicly launched, and the reality of Yentob's programme schedules, which became fact with programmes like *999* and more *EastEnders*. At the same time the drastic changes made in news have made a pragmatic shift back towards a slightly more populist approach, particularly the *Six*. Birt does identify the problem himself – he knows it is very unlikely that a programme can be distinctive, different and popular.

The BBC has already shown itself to be capable of pragmatic change and of resisting threats to its culture.

At ITN *GMTV News* and *Calendar News*, a different type of compromise is taking place, between the desire to be so interesting that the audience is entertained into watching the news programme from start to finish, and journalistic news values relating to the significance of certain events to the regional or national citizen. The method which is often used in such cases is one which makes the important event interesting; thus stories are personalised, in the tradition of Pulitzer (Weaver, 1994), by being told in relation to the effect of an event or issue on an ordinary person. For example, disasters are often retold by an eyewitness, or the human interest aspects of stories are drawn out and emphasised, or, as John Birt complained, stories about the budget are told in relation to pints of beer.

Sometimes organisations appear to break free from the stereotypes described above. For example, the *Nine O'Clock News* at the BBC does cover human interest stories, and *News at Ten* routinely covered important votes live in the House of Commons (although it has not been able to do this since being moved to a different time in the schedule).

In summary, the news philosophy of the BBC was clearly indicated by Tony Hall, the managing director of News and Current Affairs, who argued that public service broadcasting values are paramount to ensure diversity and range of coverage of issues and events. John Birt's review in the BBC's 1995–6 annual Report and Accounts focused on these priorities: 'wherever possible, we sought to put events into context, to interpret the significance of extraordinary developments and expose complex underlying issues' (BBC, 1996c:30).[1] This view has been incorporated by the managing director of News and Current Affairs into his analysis of what constitutes good news practice:

> We have to continue to change news at the BBC. We don't want any Ameri-can-style features, but we do want to broaden the agenda. There are still a lot of areas in the world which are not being covered. We need to get journalists to consider these more untraditional news values. To do so we need to get jour-nalists out of the newsroom more and away from the newsroom culture. We need more specialist correspondents who can 'create' stories and analyse them.
> (managing director of BBC News and Current Affairs, 25 June 1994)

The news philosophy at ITN concentrates on production of a diverse range of news products. In this case the concept of diversity is linked not to public service broadcasting but to diversity of choice provided by the television news market. According to a senior ITN editor, 'News is all about diversity at ITN. We produce a wide range of news programmes. Also the notion of news-worthiness is changing even further with innovations such as the IBM desk-top. Soon we will all be able to select news, which means that individuals and companies will decide what is newsworthy.'

ITN's approach to news was criticised by the BBC's managing director of News and Current Affairs: 'ITN journalism can give the illusion of getting to the nub of things but not to the fact' (25 June 1994). An ITN correspondent who commented on the ability of ITN to produce a wide range of programmes indicated that 'because ITN is so flexible in terms of its news output, I'm not sure any longer what the central core values of ITN news are any more'. An ITN programme editor went further, to say that, 'ITN is either a bespoke tailor or a cheap tart – it will produce whatever is required for the customer.'

---

[1] And yet the BBC is having to face up to the problem that although it may believe it should introduce more serious, worthy, foreign news into its programmes, its own research has shown that many viewers will not be interested.

At the BBC, news production is couched in terms of controlling the news production process. This involves training journalists to understand a particular BBC version of what constitutes newsworthiness. In the past this has involved providing a diverse range of news stories within each of its mass audience news programmes shown on BBC1, and providing more specialist news for BBC2. As already indicated, this approach was to be changed in 1998–9 with programmes becoming more targeted at specific audiences. The BBC is diversifying its mainstream, mass news programmes into a variety of different television news genre (see Figure 1 in Chapter 1). At ITN, journalists work to contractual demands and supply what contractors require in a news and information market. It is apparent that despite the BBC's traditional mission to serve and to occupy the high ground in terms of news values such as solemnity, significance and importance, it has now adopted new values of accessibility and relevance. This affects and changes the BBC's news values, which relate to the new types of diversity and variety of news programming outlined in broad terms in 1998 in the organisation's Programme Strategy Review.

An early example of the problems the BBC has faced in trying to reconcile its need to provide accurate and reliable news with its need to beat the competition occurred in May 1994. John Smith had died of a heart attack the day before and all national news outlets had covered the story. At the morning conference on 13 May 1994, it was noted that *Sky News* had been the first to break the news of his death, followed by ITN and then by the BBC. A senior BBC figure was unapologetic about this, as he argued that they had quite properly waited for the source of the information to be verified, and the three minutes which were lost to the competition during this time were actually immaterial in relation to the historical significance of what had occurred. Another senior editor disagreed. He argued instead that, in the newly competitive climate, it was really important that the BBC should not have lost viewers. He feared that it was quite possible that being late with the news might have lost them viewers who saw the announcement on another channel first. Both *Sky News* and ITN have previously made mistakes by rushing to get the news on the air first. The view at the BBC was that it would never be forgiven for any errors, as they would cause 'a stain to its culture'. Such unprecedented risk-taking now has to be reconciled with the culture and ethos of the organisation in the face of the increasingly competitive external environment within which it operates. Following the death of Diana, Princess of Wales, the BBC is having to reflect upon its own practices in response to public opinion. It has reviewed its proposed coverage of the death and funeral of the queen mother in the hope that it can make it more relevant to the viewers.

For the BBC in particular, it is apparent that the introduction of such intense competition has challenged its existing news culture in two ways. First, by forcing the organisation to try to get on the air more quickly, it causes a problem for BBC journalists by challenging their sense of news value, as well as the informational quality of a news story. Speculation is not encouraged at the BBC and has been alien to its news culture, so the organisation is caught between the need to be competitive and the need to be accurate. Secondly, lowering the newsworthiness threshold of what might make an acceptable news flash by commercial news providers, such as *Sky News* and ITN, may result in many more news events (which are less newsworthy) being treated with the sense of urgency and excitement traditionally reserved for very big ones. This could mean that the BBC will have to reconsider its policy towards what is sufficiently newsworthy to warrant a news flash and to reassess its own perception of newsworthiness, importance, what constitutes useful information and what serves the public interest.

At the BBC, newsworthiness has traditionally operated according to the principles of worthiness, analysis, broadening the news agenda and diversification (of representation and choice). It now has to reconcile these principles with beating the competition from Channels 3, 4 and 5 produced by ITN, *Sky News* and CNN, which provide greater consumer choice of programming. At ITN's Channel 3 and Channel 5, at *GMTV News*, *Big Breakfast News* and *Calendar News*, newsworthiness is ostensibly driven by the need to interest, entertain, build and maintain the audience. For these types of programme the move towards diversification of the news product is therefore driven not by public service values but by demands made upon it by its contractors. At ITN's *Channel 4 News*, BBC1's *Children's Newsround* and BBC2's *Newsnight*, such pressures are less obvious, as these programmes serve minority audiences. At *Channel 4 News* in particular there are strong budget constraints and strong contractual obligations which shape its news values.

Television news programmes most clearly illustrate their different news values and public interest principles in relation to particular categories of news story. What follows is an analysis of the different priorities and values exhibited by the current range of terrestrial television news programmes on Channels 1–4.[2]

Parliamentary politics

In many ways ITN's *5.40 p.m. News*, BBC's *Six O'Clock News*, *GMTV News*, *Big Breakfast News* and *Children's Newsround* reflect the attitude articulated by the *Sun* newspaper when television cameras first began broadcasting the House of Commons: 'Commons TV Voted Big Yawn!' (Hetherington and Weaver, 1992:170).

Those working for the BBC's *Six O'Clock News* do not like to cover political stories, as audience research has shown that it is likely to lose viewers,

---

[2] At the time of data collection, Channel 5 did not exist.

and the BBC is becoming increasingly concerned about ratings. If the *Six O'Clock News* has to cover a political story the editor prefers one of his general correspondents to do it rather than the Westminster Office, as the latter does 'lots of boring interviews with boring politicians' (BBC1 programme editor). This trend towards a lighter tone in the coverage of politics has resulted in an increasing number of political interviews being done by the presenter or a general correspondent. The scrutiny of politicians and their policies is therefore being diminished in an attempt to keep the audience interested.

Similarly, editors of ITN's *5.40 p.m. News* will only show a politics story if, as mentioned in Chapter 1, it 'involves a good punch-up at PMQs [Prime Minister's Questions]'. This attitude to coverage of politics is echoed at *Calendar News*, but not by the lunchtime news bulletins at ITN or at the BBC, which sometimes have to take items simply because they are ready in time and others are not.

Election results, on the other hand, seem to give the opportunity for lots of technological wizardry. This is most extreme at the BBC, where attention to the graphics results in a very stylised presentation. The results are usually still fairly complicated and difficult to understand. ITN's attempt to explain the election results in graphics form is less complicated and does not rely on the use of a person and graphics interacting. There is variable usage of graphics across the different television news programmes. BBC1's *Nine O'Clock News* and BBC2's *Newsnight* use more graphics as a matter of course than the *One O'Clock News* and *Six O'Clock News*. ITN's *News at Ten* also relies on graphics more heavily than the *5.40 p.m. News*, which tends to avoid them or only uses them for simplification purposes. This accords with the journalists' own perceptions regarding political stories: 'the *5.40 p.m.* will take anything as long as it is one minute ten seconds, and *News at Ten* will take anything as long as it has a graphic in it!' (ITN producer).

In addition, PMQ is routinely recorded by all national television newsrooms. This is increasingly a heavily staged, rather theatrical affair and the media generally only stay in the gallery for about twenty minutes. The programme editors of the national news programmes automatically build in a slot for a piece from PMQs just in case anything interesting is said or happens, and often this will supplement an existing political story. In all cases, the prime minister is filmed leaving Number Ten each week, just in case the correspondent who is covering the story needs to have the film available. Often the audience will notice a lack of continuity in the clothes the Prime Minister is wearing if the broadcasters attempt to use a piece of archive film of him or her leaving Number Ten and marry it up with the PMQ film.

The economy

Covering economic stories on television news is problematical, as there are difficulties in 'selling' economic stories to the programme editors. Also, the practice of journalism itself constrains the ways in which complex stories about the economy can be told. The economics correspondent at the BBC tries to sell programme editors the idea that money is the second most important thing in their lives (after sex). To try to make economic stories more relevant to viewers, the BBC does not generally use shots of dealer rooms in the city but tries to report the economy from locations around the country. Increased reporting of the economy, in principle, means that more people are aware of issues such as inflation, and such reporting could be seen to be a way of empowering citizens. Conversely one could argue that this does not mean that people know what inflation is, but simply that they are familiar with the term; this is not real empowerment. Generally, economic monetary union (EMU) is only reported in terms of an adversarial political issue. This approach is exacerbated by the attitude of programme editors and news editors who think economics will bore the audience unless the story can either be made personally relevant, or have an adversarial slant.

In newsrooms, economic stories are perceived as being even more boring than political ones. As Chapter 7 shows, hard economic stories falling into the category of economics and government are relatively rarely broadcast, although BBC2's *Newsnight* has a higher percentage of these stories than BBC1, ITN or Channel 4. BBC1's *Breakfast News*, with its *Business Breakfast* hour, concentrates mainly on industrial stories and avoids any pure economic analysis. BBC1's *Children's Newsround* avoids this category completely. When news programmes cover economic stories they are generally related to government figures such as a drop in the unemployment figures which will often be analysed by ITN from a political perspective by the political correspondent. This type of analysis, where an economic story is angled into a political story, is a typical practice of ITN's *5.40 p.m. News* and *News at Ten*. In contrast, at the BBC, the News and Current Affairs Directorate generally uses the economics correspondent to analyse the story from an economic perspective, but, as shown, the journalists are under pressure to try to find an adversarial political perspective on the story.

It is only when industrial stories, such as strikes or business news, are included in the category that many editors really begin to consider it a story, and cease to try to dilute it by turning it into a marginally less boring political one. This is because stories about strikes or factory closures can be told in a people-oriented way. Stories about strikes consistently revolve around the inconvenience to the public and the damage to industry (Glasgow University Media Group, 1976, 1980). In many cases business or economics stories are illustrated by graphics, or by an attempt to explain such concepts in terms of the effect they will have on the individual; the budget, for example, is often explained in such terms.

Law, order and crime

The coverage of crime by the BBC is carefully considered and their priority is to avoid causing panic or fear in the population by distorting facts, or giving a false impression of the frequency of criminal acts. Many journalists working for the BBC's News and Current Affairs Directorate are aware of the danger of creating moral panics, or of blaming certain groups for the subversion of cultural mores. Therefore, there is a great deal of discussion at the BBC's meetings when they have to consider covering any kind of crime story: 'we're not into straightforward reports on crime events which don't tell you anything about the state of England [*sic*], we want to be analytical, look at the issue and in trend-setting terms, not like ITN which just takes a nasty incident and does it straight' (BBC programme editor).

This attitude to crime reporting is reflected in the BBC's regional centres. For example, when a woman was shot and killed by her partner in a pub garden, the approach by the BBC was to make sure that the story was placed in some kind of context. At the *Look North News* morning meeting it was implicitly understood that the story would not simply be reported straight, but an issue must be linked to it. In this case the issue was 'obsession', and the news story was later supplemented by a BBC Radio Leeds phone-in on the subject, later that evening.

The principle of finding an issue behind an event can prove to be rather difficult for the *Look North News* team. On one occasion they received news of a shooting in Sheffield. At the morning meeting it was decided that the issue behind this lead story would be the increase in armed crime. However, having committed a lot of resources to covering the story it turned out that the gun used in the shooting had been a riveting gun. As one journalist quipped, 'we can't do a piece on the increase in riveting gun crime!', and the analytical angle had to be abandoned for this story.

Both *Calendar News* and *Look North News* cover a high percentage of stories related to violence, law and crime (see Table 14 in Chapter 7). It is not surprising that stories about crime need to be carefully monitored to ensure that coverage of a plethora of crimes in a small regional locality does not become distorted. *Calendar News* has no such censorship, but the nature of the programme itself is more oriented to light and trivial stories. Therefore the majority of stories about violent crime appear in the short newsbelts during the opt-outs. The list of deaths and crime often reads like a shopping list, and could be particularly alarming to people since the news in this part of the programme is much more localised (often relating to just one main city and two or three towns). There is no attempt to analyse or explain the context of the crimes or violent occurrences. After having observed in the *Calendar News* newsroom Hetherington (1989:61) also commented on this phenomenon: 'There are days when *Calendar* seems to depend too much on short news items, with a bias towards crime, misfortune and catastrophe.'

Some regional events such as the disappearance of a child are often reported in more depth from the studio. This is because a human interest angle can be taken from the tragedy. *Calendar News* in particular stays with this kind of story and regularly does updates and appeals for help. Recently both *Calendar News* and *Look North News* used a missing girl's fourteenth birthday to go over the story again.

Human interest

Michael Schudson (1978) argues that there is a connection between the information mode of news and the educated middle classes and between the story model and the less well-educated working classes. *GMTV News*, *Big Breakfast News*, *Calendar News*, ITN's *5.40 p.m. News* and to some extent *News at Ten* are aiming to entertain and tell a story to the audience. The format of these programmes is one of friendly interaction and accessibility between the presenter and the audience, the stories often comprise human interest content, and the audience is entertained, made emotional or cheered up. The majority of human interest stories in the regional news are about ordinary persons doing extraordinary things, such as 'Somalians protesting to the Housing Association about racism' (*Calendar News*), or about ordinary people becoming victims, such as 'Baby who will die if falls asleep is one today' (*Calendar News*) or 'gift of life, two Yorkshire boys who died in a fire last week give their organs to a baby' (*Look North News*).

As noted by Galtung and Ruge (1965), the involvement of an elite person can increase the chance of a story becoming news:

> Human interest stories are very difficult to define, but a sex scandal wouldn't be covered by the early evening news for its own sake unless it had other ingredients in it like a politician! Therefore Chris de Burgh's infidelities were not newsworthy enough last week because he's not big enough, but Michael Barrymore drying out or Michael Jackson's troubles are, because the people are very famous and are household names. (ITN programme editor, *5.40 p.m. News*)

Prince Charles's comments about smacking children being a good idea easily became the lead story for ITN ahead of a story about mass genocide in Rwanda. In contrast, the BBC journalists mused amongst themselves why it was that ITN journalists believed that smacking children in Britain was more important than massacring thousands of them in Rwanda.

ITN's *5.40 p.m. News* obviously has a higher commitment to human interest stories than all the other mainstream news programmes, with the exception of *GMTV News*, *Calendar News* and the two children's programmes, BBC1's *Children's Newsround* and *Big Breakfast News*. For example, in May 1994, ITN's *5.40 p.m. News* ran a story about Richard Gere and Cindy Crawford not getting divorced. This elicited a lot of sarcastic comments in the BBC newsroom, especially as it was a European election day.

ITN's *News at Ten* has a different attitude to the human interest story from the *5.40 p.m. News* and often does not take a lot of the stories for its bulletin. The reinstatement of its light 'and finally' piece attracted criticism from the *Observer* (19 July 1992:10):

> ITN's *News at Ten* is reintroducing its 'And finally' end piece, 'traditionally devoted to animals, children and royalty'. After footage from Sarajevo, we'll be treated, for example, to the sight of some loveable ducks on a surfboard. The ducks are there not just to cheer us up but to reach those subliminal zones of ourselves which long to believe that the horror of Sarajevo is just so much nasty make-believe.

In contrast to the ITN approach, BBC News and Current Affairs, although housing a specialist unit called Social Affairs which covers health, social security, education, urban affairs, the media, the arts, religion, science, sport and home affairs, tends to have a different commitment to human interest stories (although as outlined above these are starting to creep onto the running orders). In spite of this, however, the head of the Social Affairs Unit, Polly Toynbee, complained (in 1994) that she always needed a 'fat peg' in order to beat the heavy competition and get onto the news programmes. In other words, at the BBC in 1994 the harder stories covering politics and the economy or international news tended to push out softer domestic pieces, even if they were well researched by a specialist unit. This seems unlikely to be the case from 1999 onwards, when softer domestic stories will have specific relevance for the *Six O'Clock News* audience.

Health

An editor of ITN's *5.40 p.m. News* will generally try to cover a health story because research has shown that the audience likes them. This shows how audience research may shape or influence news values and agendas in different television newsrooms. There are not always many good health stories available. When stories relating to the so-called flesh-eating 'killer bug' necrotising fasciitis were extensively reported in June 1994, first by the press and then by the broadcasting media, ITN's *5.40 p.m. News* and *News at Ten* covered the gruesome tale at some length. *News at Ten* actually led with it. *Channel 4 News* and BBC2's *Newsnight* took a higher stance than the rest of the broadcast media and attempted to analyse the media's reaction to the scare. BBC1's news programmes took a similar line to ITN on the subject, but omitted the worst pieces of film showing huge scars and amputations on the victims of the disease. The high newsworthy value of the story related to several factors. First of all, the media had seized upon the story and so there was a media frenzy, with the same four or five victims appearing on most news programmes on the same day (see the 'me too tendency': Bell, 1991). Secondly, there were several victims all willing to show the devastating results of the disease by baring amputated limbs and gaping wounds for the cameras, providing good visuals (Tunstall, 1971). Thirdly, the story was of a negative nature (Galtung and Ruge, 1965). Fourthly, it was easy to simplify the story for the audience, although there remained a mystery about the cause of the disease: the matter-of-fact displaying of the results of it could not have been simpler to film and so the audience could be entertained with visual thrills (Postman, 1989).

The so-called killer-bug scare had significance for the audience, and the journalists themselves became interested in the phenomenon, which is often a good indicator that the story will be covered. The different approaches to the story taken by the different news programmes reflect the differences in their conceptions of what is newsworthy, what is in poor taste and what is in the public interest.

Environment, disasters and accidents

The environment is usually poorly covered by television news. BBC1's *Children's Newsround* has the highest commitment to stories about it, but most other news programmes cover few. Often stories about the environment are converted to other content categories, and this tendency is also reflected by the press (Harrison, 1992). Despite the claims by many journalists that news is of an unpredictable or *ad hoc* nature, relatively few accidents and disasters appear in television news on a regular basis. However, major accidents are well covered and become part of the national psyche, as did the Hillsborough disaster, the sinking of the *Herald of Free Enterprise*, the aircrash at Lockerbie, the train crash in West London and so on. When a major accident occurs, the newsroom atmosphere changes. The whole news operation is devoted to ensuring that its particular programme(s) gets the best coverage. The air of excitement and anticipation in the newsroom sometimes contrasts rather sharply with the death and destruction which have just occurred. Journalists are often accused of being unfeeling or parasitic at such times, but there is no doubt that they feel very strongly about what they are witnessing and become involved in the disaster (Deppa, 1993).

Therefore there is a curious contradiction at work which is often expressed through gallows humour. Journalists sometimes seem to hope for a disaster to occur: 'There's a test firing of a Trident missile today from a royal navy sub – it will have to be covered. If it's successful it will be boring, but if it goes wrong, now that's a good story' (BBC1 programme editor). They can also seem to reject the 'ordinary' accident callously in favour of something more interesting: 'Surely the fire at the Scarborough Hostel is only a story if it is arson or abuse of safety regulations? If it's just another unfortunate accident it isn't worth marking' (BBC1 editor, TV News Programmes). It is also clear that 'death has to be different. Four killed in a car crash would not be a story because it happens all the time. But a mother and three young children, or four people on the way to a wedding, or the best man and the groom would be covered' (ITN programme editor).

Sometimes different approaches to a disaster are made by different television news programmes. For example, *Channel 4 News*, in a quest to be distinctive, invested time and resources in the long-term coverage of the aftermath of the sinking of the cargo ship *The Derbyshire*. The ship lost all hands, including several British sailors. The families of the sailors spent months campaigning for an investigation into the cause of the accident. *Channel 4 News* followed the underwater search, which discovered the ship had broken into three main pieces but that the central one looked as if it had exploded. The correspondent and producer concerned prepared a package to be shown the following week.

The regional newsroom journalists are usually the first journalists at a disaster scene if it happens in their area. If the disaster is networked by the London news organisations then the regional journalist may spend much of his or her time feeding the London machine. This can be difficult for the regional editors, who then have to try to tell the same story in a different way. The regions will often continue to cover a story long after the national network news has dropped it. For example, the *Look North News* correspondent who covered the Hillsborough disaster in April 1989 spent two or three years covering the aftermath of the event. Regional correspondents covered such issues as the collection of donations, the myriad of ceremonies for the victims, updates on the condition of victims such as Tony Bland, who was left in a coma, the counselling process and so on. The correspondent believes this fulfilled an important long-term function in the region and, unlike the initial national television news media coverage, supported people and tried to help them to come to terms with the Hillsborough disaster. This highlights one of the valuable and important roles of local television news in providing people with useful and relevant information about their own region, covering issues and events, and providing historical context and continuity, which are often neglected by national television news.

The structure and historical origins of a news organisation, and the particular programme visualisation (Cottle, 1993) of the different news programmes, do exert influence on the types of news story which they broadcast. These factors also shape what is deemed by news programmes to be both newsworthy and in the public interest. As I have shown, different British terrestrial television news programmes have a particular affinity for certain types of story and a distinctive way of telling those stories.

These can be explained in relation to different spheres of newsworthiness (see Figure 7) where tension exists at the boundaries between the areas. Area C represents all the events which occur in the world. Although these may be of interest and importance to some people, they are not newsworthy and therefore will not become television news. Area B contains potential news stories which may or may not be reported by different television news pro-

Figure 7   *Spheres of newsworthiness*

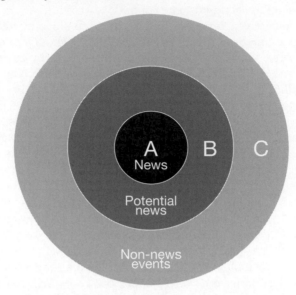

grammes. This area can be conceived of as a pool in which television journalists can fish for the types of mid-ranking news story that make their news
programmes distinctive and ensure some diversity of news coverage. It is
particularly when news programmes have to select middle-ranking stories
that the main differences in their selection priorities are apparent, and it is
here that the BBC and ITN programmes still exhibit their greatest differences.
Area A contains big news stories and media events which are covered in
similar ways by all news programmes (e.g. the ending and aftermath of the
Waco siege; elections; cabinet reshuffles; the death of Diana, Princess of
Wales; and so on). In the case of very big stories, initially similar information is given, the same sources and news agencies are used and journalists
stress the same features of the event. Fortunately not all news stories falling
into Area A are treated in exactly the same way. As I have shown in Chapters 7 and 8, there is some differentiation in the way that the same story area
is covered by different news programmes. We therefore see some differentiation *between* story types which are selected and *within* storylines in different
terrestrial news programmes.

I have shown that there are qualitative and quantitative differences
between the news output of Channel 3's *GMTV News* and *Calendar News* and
that of *Channel 4 News* at seven o'clock and the BBC's news programmes.
The former are much more inclined to stress or search for the interesting
aspects of an event or an interesting event *per se*, whereas the latter are
much more likely to concentrate on matters of importance. Such organisa-

tional visions about what constitutes the public interest and therefore what informs newsworthiness are translated into the news product and affect the information quality of the news itself.

Of concern is the drift away from the BBC's founding remit to provide a diverse range of news for mass audience programmes. This is occurring due to increased commercialisation of the BBC, the redeployment of resources to BBC twenty-four-hour news, and the paradoxical philosophy of reporting serious political and international stories whilst trying to boost audience figures. This is manifest in a greater inclusion of human interest-type stories in the news content and an increasing tendency to concentrate on entertainment and stylistic devices in the news format, particularly in programmes such as *BBC Breakfast News* and the *Six O'Clock News.* The introduction of twenty-four-hour rolling news and on-line news will reduce journalistic input into the news production process other than in a technical sense (a story will only need to be gathered once, but will then be able to be retold in many ways). The editing role will be compromised as journalists will have less time or less opportunity for reflection and interpretation of events, and will need to reprocess and repackage information quickly to suit a divergent range of outlets, as the proliferation of digital, cable and satellite channels results in an increasing range of branded or niche-marketed news products. It will be left to the non-mainstream programmes to offer the kind of diversity and range of news stories which have traditionally been provided on mass audience channels by public service broadcasters.

I have argued that the existence of a shared journalistic culture centres upon agreement on the value of a practical application of objective reporting within a range of logistical, legal and practical constraints. The trend towards further restriction of the informational capacity of television news through the increasing commercialisation and competition of the broadcasting institutions in Britain threatens democracy through reduction in information quality. Clearly, the market-led rush towards the provision of niche news products (as terrestrial and global news providers try to find ways of acquiring a share of the market for news) is resulting in an increase in choice and in news programme diversity. However, television journalism can only be perceived as a restricted source of selected information. In this context the trend towards the adoption of populist news values, through copying successful programme format and content styles, threatens the kind of diversity of representation normally supplied by public service broadcasters and further restricts the quality of information provided. Financial and organisational restraints on public service journalism (through cuts and audience- and management-led visualisation of programme content) signals a move away from the public service remit. This is due to restriction of journalistic space for flair and experimentation in the selection and production of news stories. Diversity of access to the media for broadcasting purposes has always been restricted (although it is now easier in principle to gain access as a content supplier, due to the diminishment of frequency scarcity and the avail-ability of relatively cheap cable channels). But whilst choice of programming is increasing as channels proliferate, viewer access to the diverse range of new channels is becoming increasingly restricted via ability to pay. Clearly, those citizens with the financial and intellectual means to access and use the new range of media products will be the information rich in the new multi-media age. Those who are already socially excluded will have their diversity of access, choice and representation further restricted.

9

Conclusion: terrestrial television news as a democratic issue

Terrestrial television news selection takes place within a shared journalistic culture. This culture centres upon an agreement by journalists of the value of a practical application of objective reporting and the adoption of common normative values and expectations. This leads to similar news values and expectations being adopted by all television journalists in many big news stories. Often there is common agreement on the use of particular spokespersons and similar storylines. Nonetheless, programme differentiation does occur in the range of middle-ranking stories that is selected and sometimes in the way that some big news stories are covered. Often BBC1, BBC2, Channel 3 and Channel 4 news providers produce identifiably different news stories and news angles.

The market-oriented rush towards the provision of niche news products, as terrestrial and global news providers try to find ways of acquiring a share of the market for news, is resulting in a variety of information sources. A positive development for the relationship between news and democratic processes would be for terrestrial television news programmes to diversify their content through a response to market forces, thereby providing diversity of choice for the consumer (this may unfortunately be based on ability to pay), and for them simultaneously to provide diversity of representation of minority interests and uneconomic but important worthy news (which the market will fail to provide) via public service broadcasting. Television journalism does have this potential given that newsworthiness is constructed by the journalist's zone and mode of operation, resulting in different television news programmes adopting different news values, in relation to different programme visualisations (Cottle, 1993). This zone and mode of operation are defined by the dynamic relationship between political, historical and economic macro influences and the organisational, cultural and professional normative assumptions and practices of the particular television newsroom. The journalist's zone of operation, therefore, is a framework within which, through which and by which the journalist participates in the understand-

205

ing and interpretation of an event (as a journalist and not just as a neutral individual). This participation occurs through the adoption of a particular mode of understanding and by way of a certain historical consciousness, which in this case is 'journalistic'. Such an historical consciousness is both grounded and perpetuated in the sharing, by all journalists, of a set of formulas, practices and normative assumptions as well as a journalistic mythology, which are passed down to new generations of journalists. Journalistic practice is adapted to the designated style of each organisation and each news programme and is only one way of doing the job (style is not universal). It is the fragmentation and diversification of the news genre itself which has allowed different television news programmes to be constituted from a variety of different news sub-genres, resulting in further differences in news content, format and newsroom epistemologies.

This has resulted in different branding and niche-marketing of different television news programmes and therefore, it follows, differing definitions by journalists, in different television newsrooms and news organisations, of what is in the public interest and therefore what is newsworthy. The question is not so much whether television can provide a diverse range of information as how well it can do so within the current broadcasting climate. The issue is how far television journalism is skewing its content in response to market forces, at the expense of diversity of representation of minority interests and equitable access to information.

Diversity of information is vital for a healthy democracy. Any democracy relies upon a plurality of views and voices, and, more significantly, any conception of citizenship is related to the idea of a 'polis' or a collection of citizens who hold different views. It is unlikely that the full range of content diversity will be available to audiences in the new information age. It is clear that the market place will provide diversity of choice of outlets, but uneconomic and unpopular areas of representation are likely to be neglected, compromising content diversity. Access to content is being increasingly restricted by ability to pay. A diverse range of information products will probably be available only to the wealthy, exacerbating the distance between the information rich and information poor (Schiller, 1996).

This is of concern in relation to the role of television news as an important institution of the public sphere, with a vital role to play in the enhancement of the citizen's ability to act competently in the public domain. Television news has an important part in a democracy as an institution which embodies citizenship and which enhances ideological, cultural and social plurality. The significance of television news has long been recognised by successive governments, and its role as a business involved with the public interest has been grounded in a commitment to careful regulation of the television medium. A positive version of the notion of public interest is one which aims to capture the essence of what is in the public good or what constitutes good public service. Such aims can be and are reflected to a significant extent in the notion of newsworthiness demonstrated in the programme output of those television organisations which are still adhering to a particular ideal of public service broadcasting. BBC News and Current Affairs still shows some commitment, but a reduced one, to a type of television news production and selection that contains stories which the broadcasting organisation deems to be important and worthy. But because 'worthy' means 'important but possibly not interesting', and may even be irrelevant to the concerns of the viewers, the BBC is reducing its commitment to such stories in fear of losing viewers. The 1998 Programme Strategy Review conducted at the BBC shows that the organisation is minimising the opportunities for worthy stories to be broadcast. For some critics this is too much. Alison Pearson remarked that 'the BBC is the market leader in current affairs yet behaves like a new kid on the block, pathetically eager to give us sweeties if we will be its friend' (*Daily Telegraph*, 10 October 1998). ITN's *Channel 4 News* attempts to set a news agenda which covers those important events which are neglected by other news services, and aims both to cover and analyse events and issues (although the introduction of a much more informal way of presenting the news in 1998 showed that this programme too felt compelled to change its approach to presentational formats and style). Nonetheless this news programme is a good indicator of how a *minority* niche audience programme can provide good-quality, in-depth news.

Problematically, public interest can have elastic and ambiguous meanings (McQuail, 1992) and can be stretched by television news programme makers to include varying degrees of entertainment devices and human interest journalism. The BBC has introduced a variety of entertaining format changes (such as a new studio set, and other devices such as graphics to help tell and sell the story), and will continue to do so; but the content of BBC news (especially the *Nine O'Clock News* and BBC2's *Newsnight*) in the main still avoids an excessive coverage of human interest or people-centred stories, although this may be changing. In contrast, ITN's Channel 3 news programmes, *GMTV News*, Channel 4's *Big Breakfast News* and Yorkshire Tyne-Tees Television's *Calendar News* programmes all show a strong commitment to a high percentage of human interest coverage. A key concern is that over-concentration on making news friendly, accessible and easily understood may be counter-productive if the news contains the wrong type of information, or does not contain enough useful or relevant information to enable citizens to assess or analyse critically the institutions and events which affect their lives. The current trend is towards the maintenance of mainstream mass audiences through introducing a faster tempo to the news programmes and providing interesting and entertaining news stories. The use of entertainment devices to maintain audience interest often results in a reduction in complex content and context in favour of personalisation, simplification, short sound-bites (Gitlin, 1991b) and interesting format devices.

I have argued that television news has reached a critical junction in

Britain in the 2000s. The nature of its predicament is strongly related to developments occurring in technology. The 1980s and 1990s saw an unprecedented growth in the power and diversity of media technology. The growth of satellite, cable, optic fibre technology, computerised newsrooms, digital cameras, the Internet, and the capacity for technologies to merge has led in principle to a much greater access to information and a massive growth in outlets requiring information. There are several problems in relation to the ability of citizens to access a diverse range of information. First, despite optimism about the possibilities of alternative public spheres and counter-cultures arising around new media such as the Internet, there is little sign that such alternative public spheres can gain access to the so-called 'official' public sphere. Non-mainstream voices are still generally denied access to the mainstream media (nothing has changed with the advent of new audiovisual forms). Secondly, access to many of the new media outlets is based on ability to pay and therefore excludes poorer socio-economic groups (this has always been an issue, but as the range of potential access points increase in greater numbers than the free-to-air channels, this disproportionately disadvantages those who do not have the means to access the new media subscription-based outlets). Thirdly, access to a range of information sources does not necessarily result in a more knowledgeable citizenry if it is subjected to information overload (a new problem), since information needs to be interpreted reliably. Such developments are dangerous for the depth and breadth of public knowledge and place limitations on the democratic processes, if only because democracy means a multivocal environment.

Technological convergence and development will not manifest themselves immediately, but will result in anomalies and problems that will have to be addressed by educators of journalists and television organisations for years to come. Such problems will revolve around the maintenance of an increasingly fragmented audience, the difficulties of sustaining a place in the schedules for mainstream prime-time news programmes (ITN's *News at Ten* was not able to survive as a ten o'clock programme), and a reassessment of the role of journalists as helpful interpreters or mere conduits of a blizzard of information. In the last case, journalists and their organisations clearly have an important choice to make. The function of the journalist as a helpful interpreter of the mountains of information which are now available is vital in enabling citizens to attempt to understand some of the complex events and issues occurring in the world. In an era where we are all increasingly becoming specialists with narrow but detailed knowledge of particular areas of life, it becomes even more crucial for the journalist to have an overview of international, national and local events in order to be able to interpret and pass on relevant and useful information to those people who depend on it. The temptation, however, appears to be for some terrestrial television news journalists and news programmes to over-simplify the complex, in the belief that anything too demanding or involved would lose audience interest. The alternative tactic seems to be to opt out of the editing process altogether by prioritising the transmission of raw footage of dramatic live events.

In the United States, for example, those television news shows which have exhibited the tendency to simplify news or to over-emphasise the live and dramatic are said to offer only nuggets of news. Events are chopped up, artificially flavoured and served in bite-sized pieces (Hoggart, 1995) or presented as real-life drama. Both types of news are easy and rather pleasant to watch, but once television news programmes begin to offer news in easily digestible and undemanding form, they start to prioritise the human interest dimensions of every event, or to resort to visual clichés to encapsulate the complexity of a scene. It was far easier for British journalists to cover the events in Waco by showing a burning building, crying relatives and a pontificating president than it was to explain the complicated, behind-the-scenes constructions and negotiations. Media researchers Barnett and Gaber (1993) argue that in order to boost ratings news at ITN is becoming increasingly 'tabloid' (their word), emphasising crime and human interest stories and carrying fewer political and foreign stories than the BBC, although this is denied by ITN management.

Transnational influences are having an increasing impact upon Western democracies (Waters, 1995). Some analysts and commentators are concerned about such developments, as they fear that power and influence are shifting away from elected national governments towards unelected, supranational bodies (Keane, 1991; Marr, 1995). Related to this is an increasing difficulty in identifying key centres of power within nation states. This may present problems for those journalists trying to act in the public interest as thorough and analytic interpreters.

Historically, in Britain information about the nation (national television news)[1] has been emphasised over and above the importance of local communication (regional news) and overseas news (international news). A disturbing trend is the rationalisation which is occurring by both BBC news and ITN in relation to their international news coverage (see Chapter 7). Some of ITN's international bureaux have been closed, and at the BBC the World Service has been redesigned. Regional coverage is being compromised by the ITV system's spate of take-overs and mergers, which are changing the commitment to regional coverage, and by the BBC's closure of local radio outlets and its production of fewer programmes in the regions. Such activity is particularly contradictory when we consider the increasingly important role international news must have in relation to the process of globalisation. Due to the process of globalisation, the nation seems to be less self-sufficient and is more dependent in international terms (Leca, 1992). It becomes more

---

[1] National news providers, with the exception of S4C, have tended to be skewed towards English news.

difficult for the state to explain its political, economic and social position con-vincingly unless it can use the international context as its referent. The changing commitment to local and international news now exhibited by both the BBC and ITV systems represents a very unreflective approach to the selection and production of television news.

Politico-economic changes and the new commercialisation of television news are centred upon the belief that competitive market forces will be driven by consumer demand, ensuring that consumers will get what they want (Gunter, 1993). Such concentration on individual consumer choice as the key right of public life has infiltrated and influenced contemporary gov-ernmental and popular conceptions of citizenship and public interest. Although free-market philosophy has been a theme of British television broadcasting since the creation of the ITV system in the 1950s, the balance of state policy was, until the 1980s and 1990s, weighted against it through regulation and support for the BBC. Currently, the balance is now weighted in favour of the application of a free-market philosophy to the whole broad-casting industry (Harrison, 2000). This change has initiated broad debate about the role of public service broadcasting in Britain, and has highlighted concerns about the relationship of television news to the public sphere and democracy and the interpretation of what constitutes the public interest.

A crisis in television news will probably be precipitated by further deregu-lation of television and relaxation of ownership rules. Great concern is expressed by many about Rupert Murdoch's ability to escape national media legislation, as well as about the implications of cross-media ownership for the regional ITV system in Britain. Murdoch's potential to establish priorities and set successful precedents in all areas of broadcasting may formulate future standards and audience expectations. His expediency in taking the BBC World Service off his northern satellite beam in order to get Star accepted in China is one such precedent, as is his acquisition of major sporting events for subscription television.

It is only possible to analyse British television news in relation to the pro-liferation of different television news programmes in the terrestrial news domain. The generic model of the ideal type television news genre I devel-oped in Chapter 1 (see Figure 1) shows that influences from different genres from the 'not-news' environment can, and do, act upon and affect the con-tent, production and possibly audience reception of television news (although audience research is beyond the remit of this book). In an era of global and converging technology, the distinction and borderline between news and entertainment, news and education, news and fiction are constantly shifting and adapting (Garber *et al.*, 1993). Increasing divergence and diversity in television news may not be a positive development, as the fragmentation of television news into a proliferation of television news programmes consti-tuted from different news sub-genres may eventually result in a two-tier news service. In this scenario, mass audiences choose between a variety of news products which exhibit diversity, primarily through their packaging and presentation. In this case, diversity of choice is increased for the consumer because the number of news programmes increases, or the existing news programmes differentiate themselves from each other to target specific desirable audiences.

A minority of viewers will also have access to a more varied range of television news which would be unlikely to appeal to the majority. We have already seen how it is the minority news programmes such as BBC2's *Newsnight*, *Channel 4 News* and S4C which are producing the most diverse representation of minority issues, languages and events. These programmes provide the kind of variety of coverage which is associated with the type of pluralistic news service that public service broadcasters have traditionally been expected to deliver. It appears that the type of news diversity commonly delivered by public service broadcasters to mass audiences in Britain will be relegated to inconvenient slots or to minority channels or eventually to specific subscription channels. Even the *Nine O'Clock News*, as it competes with terrestrial, cable and satellite entertainment programmes, may lose viewers to lighter programmes if it covers only serious news or international stories.

Of some comfort is that this analysis of the reporting of the routine, ordinary, everyday domestic news stories has shown that differences still exist between mass audience television news programmes shown by BBC1 and Channel 3. To date the BBC's news and current affairs still tends to prioritise different stories from ITN's *Channel 4 News* and ITN's Channel 3 news, and therefore between them they provide a breadth of news coverage. A range of free-to-air television news programmes still exists, each exhibiting a particular rationale, newsroom epistemology, interpretation of public interest, and differing approaches to what constitutes newsworthiness. Whilst it is reassuring that this variety exists, its current form is under threat. In order for television news to retain its position as an important institution of the public sphere and contribute to and receive input from alternative public spheres, those programmes which set the top line in terms of news informational quality must not slip away from their high principles (although this book has shown that this is now likely to occur in practice). The loss of a top line in news programming may result in a gradual shift down-market for all television news programmes, leaving the so-called high ground to minority audience programmes, and a variety of versions of popular news programmes for the masses.

It is only possible to answer the question of what British terrestrial television news contributes to the public sphere and democratic process up to a point. One problem of any such analysis is that it is confined to the present and cannot at this stage do anything other than speculate regarding the changing nature of television news to come. Useful future research could consider the effects of the following over time: increasing reliance on the wire services; use of the same sources; continued technological developments; and the homogenising tendency of the market ethic, coupled with the reduction of the interpretative role of the journalist, to see how in practice the quality of journalistic output is affected. Over time one could assess whether Galtung and Ruge's (1965) unpredictability factor is being increasingly compromised due to more and more planning; whether the showing of raw footage of live events will be prioritised; whether there will be an increase in symbiosis between politicians and the media, resulting in a greater emphasis in the news of Boorstin's (1964) pseudo-events; or whether content will increasingly be subverted to the format requirements of a medium which requires an ever-faster tempo and stresses visual excitement.

News by its very nature changes constantly, but the BBC's overhaul of its news provision in its attempt to attract a younger audience to watch its news programmes has to result in a deliberate change in the news values in order to attract those viewers. The BBC's shift away from the Birtian format of the late 1980s, towards a more populist, audience-centric approach, continues the inexorable relativisation of information quality in news. This is rationalised by the BBC management as a pragmatic adjustment which is required in order to be more accountable to the audience's requirements, and which can therefore be justified as being in accordance with a public service remit.

Currently the BBC does still cover a wider variety of international stories than ITN and has invested more in its political reporting. Although ITN's *Channel 4 News* is commercial news it also provides serious news, choice, analysis and diversity. But the pressures which affected broadcasting institutions in the 1980s and 1990s have had profound implications for the whole rationale and ethos of public service broadcasting in Britain, as both the BBC and ITV systems begin to drift away from their founding remit. The diversification of broadcast products in the name of consumer choice complements and coincides with the emergence of demassified, consumerist and post-Fordist society in the late 1980s and 1990s (Hall and Jacques, 1990).

Clearly the television medium faces problems as an information source, since more information can be contained on the front page of a broadsheet newspaper than can be broadcast in a news bulletin which lasts about twenty-five minutes. Consequently television news is less detailed in content than the newspapers. Television news is, however, perceived to be important by many viewers, who believe that they receive most of their information from television. Although this has been challenged by Robinson and Levy (1986), the key issue is the central part terrestrial television news plays as an information source and the belief and trust which it still evokes from a mass audience. Politicians and other senior figures also recognise the important role terrestrial television news can play in their fortunes (McNair, 1994). *Sky News* is trying extremely hard to become as attractive as the BBC and ITN news programmes to politicians. This has been a difficult task because it reaches far fewer viewers, and yet *Sky News* is now a serious competitor to both the BBC and ITN and is staffed by ex-BBC and ITN journalists. The pressure from competitors is clearly affecting the BBC's understanding of public service broadcasting principles. The BBC has responded to the competitive threat from *Sky News* by introducing *News-24*, by making its programmes 'warmer' and more accessible, and by planning to adopt the rolling news format of fifteen-minute news bulletins into its *Breakfast News* programme. It is ironic that as the BBC seeks to become more warm and friendly, *Sky News* has rebranded itself as more mature and authoritative.

I have argued that the belief in the possible reformation of a public sphere in which citizens can actively engage in public debate and argument is utopian, when related to terrestrial television news in a British public service broadcasting system or to commercial news generally. However, this does not mean that the news organisations and journalists working within them do not have a socially responsible role in providing information which is as useful, enlightening and informative as possible within the constraints of the medium. This means that television journalism should not succumb to the increasing pressures which will further reduce television news as an information source. The BBC and ITN therefore have a responsibility for the future of broadcast journalism.

But good intentions may have to be compromised. If the BBC ceases to invest strongly in its mainstream news product due to its need to reconcile the pressures of commercialism with public service broadcasting (it needed to make a 30 per cent efficiency saving in its News Directorate in the five years from 1998 to help to fund twenty-four-hour news), then it is likely to initiate a change in the standards of all British television news. The pressure to maintain credible viewing figures for the BBC has forced it to change its conception of what constitutes newsworthiness and the public interest, and to reinvent its news values in different news programmes. We will see evidence of change if the BBC begins to include more human interest information in more of its news stories, if it tells its stories from a people perspective, if it reduces investment in overseas and political stories, and if it eventually marginalises those stories which are too complicated, worthy or demanding from mainstream, peak-time news programmes. As Simon Hoggart (1995:20) notes, the rot may have set in as early as 1995 for BBC2's *Newsnight*. 'Even *Newsnight* precedes its interviews with a pert, wrapped-up-with-string-and-a-ribbon style package.' As digital terrestrial and satellite news channels begin to draw viewers away from the established terrestrial television news programmes, then it is likely that a news format based upon entertaining and interesting the audience will gain a competitive edge in the battle for ratings. The BBC's attempt to reconcile market pressures with public service broadcasting may turn it into a hybrid institution which delivers a two-tier news service.

ITN made many of its adaptations to the new commercialisation of television news in the late 1980s and early 1990s by rationalising its news operation and making staff cuts. ITN's *News at Ten* in particular has been accused of becoming more tabloid in content, and the organisation has already shown itself to be quite capable of adapting and changing to meet any contractor's requirements. It can produce popularist mainstream news programmes and more serious minority news programming, a technique the BBC appears to be copying.

If the more popularist format becomes the norm for the mainstream news programmes, John Keane's (1991:192–3) prophecy may come to pass, and citizens, instead of seeking to engage actively in politics and contribute in the public sphere, 'will amuse themselves to death, spending their spare time "grazing" the new abundance of pre-censored, commercialised radio, television, newspapers and magazines. Perhaps they will be persuaded to privatise themselves, to regard politics as a nuisance, to transform themselves silently and unprotestingly from citizens to mobile and private consumers.'

To avoid such apathy television news should take an active part in enabling the public to participate in and judge the events and issues which affect it. Television journalistic practice charges journalists with the role of working with public concern by analysing and interpreting the data which exists 'out there' on behalf of the public. Institutions such as academia in general and journalism should be an important part of the public sphere and have a role to play in interpreting and presenting information to the public. A critical difference, however, is the time-scale to which such agencies work. Journalism has to work to a short time-scale and therefore is restricted in the depth of analysis, in the rigour of research methodology, and by the format constraints of the programme structure.

Relatively slow take-up of satellite and cable television indicates that terrestrial television news is perceived as a vital and primary source of news about the world for a mass audience (Curran, 1998) and is likely to remain so for some time (Barnett, 1998). If British terrestrial television is freed from its public service responsibilities it is unlikely that the gaps will be filled by the market through the proliferation of satellite, cable, digital or on-line services. Whilst the market has the potential to generate dedicated news or information channels, according to Curran (1998) they tend to attract elite audiences and increase the knowledge gap between the general public and elites. Terrestrial broadcasters are also particularly significant in an era of information overload and specialisation, when mass interest programmes and expert journalistic interpretation are needed to clarify events and retain a sense of social cohesion.

Television news has a number of useful roles it could play in the empowerment of citizens in a liberal democracy. The excavation and analysis of the unaccountable areas of public life at sub-national, national and European level would enable citizens to understand and perhaps even control events which affect them. By exposing injustice and corruption, television news does enable the public to make a judgement about the validity and authority of political institutions, but, as Fallows (1996) points out, there is a danger that a public which is continuously exposed to information about politicians who are shown to be scheming endlessly will cease to take an interest in the political news coverage or even in the political process itself. A balance obviously has to be struck between the presentation of important issues to the public and the temptation to politicise or personalise them.

The diversification of the television news genre reflects the fragmentary nature of the audience. But this does not mean that it adequately and accurately represents the diverse range of views which currently exist in British society. Fortunately television news does sometimes exhibit some of these properties and will take up a minority issue, expose scandals in public life, and bring our attention to atrocities and injustice. In recent years it has addressed such issues as the unaccountability of quangos, the greed of the chairs of the public utilities, corruption in government, human rights abuses in China, genocide in Rwanda and famine in Ethiopia.

Some of the trends potentially leading to further diminishment of information quality identified in this book are disturbing and raise concerns about the value and role of British terrestrial television news in a democratic state now. Such concerns are valid. Above all, terrestrial television news is about our relationship to political and democratic processes, our sense of identity, our feelings of safety, our understanding and tolerance of other members of our society. Although British terrestrial television news is a public service and carefully regulated, it still serves some interests partially and some not at all. Nonetheless television news also has strengths. These lie in the evolution of the public service broadcasting idea, which according to Scannell and Cardiff (1991) arose to guarantee (informally) rights of access (via universal service obligation) and rights of representation of a diverse range of voices.

It is this pluralistic approach in particular which is being challenged through competition and pressure to increase ratings. If terrestrial television news exists only as an alternative source of information about the world, alongside satellite, cable and on-line news, it must remain a distinctive news form, constituted from different and distinctive news programmes. It is essential that a diversity of terrestrial television news provision remains free at source via the operation of universal service obligation. This means that investment in public service broadcasting must continue, with the BBC protected from market forces (via financial investment) and the ITV system continuing to invest heavily in a quality news provider.

Appendix I:
Television News Code Book

Domestic television news content categories

Code	Content category	Categories used in other studies and notes
01–07	**Parliamentary Politics**	The generic category of politics was used by Hartley (1989).
01	*General conflicts and disagreements between government and other parties or inter-party conflict. Everyday Parliamentary conflict and activity in the Houses of Parliament, or campaigning for elections.*	Gans (1980) used the category 'Government conflicts and disagreements'. I have widened this to include 'all parties'. The Glasgow University Media Group (1976) listed each party separately. I further widen this category to include 'crime, scandals and investigations' (Wallis and Baran, 1990). However, this does not include personal scandals, which will be coded under category 05. Examples are the Matrix Churchill arms to Iraq investigation once it had focused on the government, Parliamentary scrutiny of Bills, government proposals, Calcutt Reports I and II, Clive Soley's Private Member's Bill on press freedom, disagreements in Parliament about the Maastricht Bill, discussion of White and Green Papers and so on, and campaigning for elections, i.e. the 'democratic' parliamentary process.
02	*Government policies which are actually enacted and announced as* faits accomplis *by government and the media.*	Examples are the Broadcasting Bill 1990, government allowing private companies to invest in the NHS, etc.

Code	Content category	Categories used in other studies and notes
03	*Government reports of official information*	See Wallis and Baran (1990). Examples are papers released containing government facts and figures, such as statistics on crime or single parents, and so on. If the reports or figures specifically refer to education, health, the economy, crime or the environment then they are coded under those headings in the appropriate content category.
04	*Personnel changes in Parliament*	Gans (1980) used the category 'Government personnel changes'. I have widened this category to include Parliamentary changes, e.g. John Smith being replaced by Tony Blair, and so on.
05	*Politicians' personal lives*	See the Glasgow University Media Group (1976). Examples are David Mellor and Antonia de Sanchez; Norman Lamont and his credit card debt; politicians on holiday or retiring; and the death of John Smith, Labour leader, when it focused specifically on him as a person – once the story was devoted to the implications for the Labour Party and the leadership contest, it would be coded as 01. Other multifarious examples are: Peter Lilley forgetting his job title, Anne Widdecombe becoming a Catholic, and more recent stories such as the Tory Party and the allegations of sleaze and corruption. These are not classed as social affairs or law and order because the actions of politicians often have implications for politics.
06	*Politicians on official business abroad*	When the focus is on the British politician and not on the host country; where British interests are being represented abroad. Examples are John Major visiting Saudi Arabia and India, the British ambassador visiting China, British political statements on Bosnia or the Waco siege.

Code	Content category	Categories used in other studies and notes
07	*Everyday local government activities and conflicts*	When the focus is purely on the local government and not on central government's actions relating to local government. An example is a story specifically about financial crisis in the Western Isles Council.
08–10	**Economics**	The generic category of economics was used by Hartley (1989), Carroll (1989), and Stempel (1989).
08	*Economics and government*	The enactment or the direct impact of government policies or government action, such as tax increases, adjustments to the Public Sector Borrowing Requirement (PSBR), or direct arrangements with other countries such as USA/UK Open Sky talks, or membership and withdrawal of British membership of the Exchange Rate Mechanism (ERM), and its effects on the economy and Opposition statements regarding government action.
09	*Economics, City and currency news*	This category is an amalgamation of the Glasgow University Media Group's (1976) two separate categories, 'Economy, City' and 'Economy, Currency'. In my study category 09 refers to the specific spot in the news programme which is devoted to 'City' news, when the exchange rates and FTSE Index are given, usually accompanied by graphics.
10	*Industrial/public sector and business news*	An amalgamation of two categories, 'Business' and 'Industry', identified by the Glasgow University Media Group (1976). Examples are CBI business forecasts, industrial and public sector redundancies, industrial reports, industrial disputes, general recession and recovery stories, announcements of profits and losses, high street spending, retail figures, and so on.

Code	Content category	Categories used in other studies and notes
		In order to separate variable 08 from variable 10, the story will be classified as 08 *only* if it is totally slanted towards the Chancellor and government policy.

11–13 Education

11	*Education and government*	The enactment or the direct impact of government policies on education, where the direct focus is on the Minister for Education, i.e. questions in the House of Commons or Opposition statements.
12	*Education and schools, colleges and universities*	General education stories about educational institutions and teachers or school children putting government policies into action, or boycotting them. Examples are stories about school teachers boycotting testing in schools.
13	*Official reports and statistics*	Non-governmental reports on education.

14–15 Law, order and crime stories

Ericson *et al.*, (1991) studied aspects of crime and deviance, legal control and justice in television news. They selected eleven categories under the heading of 'Law and order'. My categories below take these into account.

| 14 | *Acts of violence and control of violence* | Examples are 'terrorist' attacks, violent demonstrations, mass random killing (the Dunblane massacre), riots, control by armed forces or police in a violent confrontation (Brixton riots), the British Army in Northern Ireland, police control during the miners' strike in 1983, the British role in the rest of the world if it is violent (Falklands War) or has a remit to control violence (peace-keeping forces, or British UN forces under attack in Bosnia). Other examples are violent crime, hit and run, murder, armed robbery, shooting, stabbing incidents, rape or other reports of violent action. |

Code	Content category	Categories used in other studies and notes
15	*Criminal proceedings, inquests and reports of non-violent crime*	Stempel (1989) included this category and Gans (1980) included 'Scandals and investigations'. This category therefore includes all court cases (regardless of whether the crime was violent or non-violent). Examples are extradition orders, investigation into Robert Maxwell's pension fund and subsequent court cases, the trial of nurse Beverley Allitt, police statements of a general and routine nature, inquests into all deaths including suicides, and reports of non-violent crime such as theft (without the use of firearms).
16–21	*Social affairs*	Used by Harrison (1991a), in a previous content analysis which examined geographic bias in television news, as a 'Human interest/other' category.
16	*Human interest (light)*	Langer (1987) concentrated on the 'Other or soft' news on television and provides a good analysis of this category. Gerdes (1980) included a category 'Arts, entertainment, humorous, light and unusual', while Grundy (1980) used the categories 'Nostalgia and history' and 'Animals, celebrities and personalities' – 'ordinary' people doing unusual things, or triumphing over adversity. See Brunsdon and Morley (1978). Examples therefore include light and humorous stories, unusual reversals such as 'man bites dog', stories about celebrities such as the wedding of Raquel Welch's son, cat rescues, cute animal stories, historic occasions, nostalgia, centenaries and ceremonies.
17	*Human interest (serious)*	This category reflects the more serious side to human interest stories, which tend, as illustrated above, to be portrayed as always being light-hearted and humorous. However, some stories about 'ordinary' people are told for their tragic content, and often the

Code	Content category	Categories used in other studies and notes

'ordinary' person is simply a victim of circumstance.

Examples are stories about the British survivors of the Waco Siege, who were pursued for macabre reasons, and to try to glean more information about the 'insane' cult leader David Koresh; and about victims of disasters and accidents such as the Hillsborough survivor, Tony Bland, who was on a life support machine until his parents agreed, in the face of much publicity and opposition, to cut off his food supply and allow him to die. Other examples are stories about victims of crime, which have been criticised for making it appear that such crime is on the increase; for instance, the death of Jamie Bulger was extensively reported, and became part of the national psyche, increasing the fear of such crime and searching for spurious connections such as using video violence as a way of explaining a phenomenon which has neither increased nor decreased over the last hundred years. In all these cases as well as in many more, the 'ordinary' person is pursued not for having done something extraordinary, but often for just surviving a catastrophe. This is an important distinction from category 16, which quite often deals with trivia. Sometimes the serious side of human interest can be very intrusive indeed, which has led to a wide debate about the notion of public interest versus the right to privacy.

| 18 | *Individual or community action* | Stories about members of the community or individuals campaigning for their rights. |

Examples are Somali women campaigning for housing rights, petitions to parliament, lobbying, and so on.

Code	Content category	Categories used in other studies and notes
19	*Sport*	Sport at home, fixtures and results, or British sport such as British cricket abroad. Examples are stories about British sporting personalities at home and abroad.
20	*Royalty*	Langer (1987) listed the category 'Vice-royalty and monarchy' as 'other' or 'soft' news. Examples are the break-up of the marriage of the Prince and Princess of Wales, the visit of Prince Charles to Egypt, 'Camillagate', 'Squidgygate' and British royal family stories at home and abroad.
21	*British Forces*	Informational stories specifically about 'our lads' at home and abroad.
22–25	**Health**	
22	*Health and government*	Stempel (1989) included the category of 'Health and welfare'. Examples are the enactment or the direct impact of government policies on the NHS and Opposition statements, speeches by the Health Secretary, launch of government schemes, etc.
23	*Scientific medical discoveries*	Stempel (1989) included the category of 'Science and invention'. Examples are stories about breakthroughs in health and medical care or glamorous medical feats such as lung and liver transplants.
24	*Official reports and statistics or general health stories*	Non-government reports on health. An example is the report that midwives give extra care to pregnant women in the South Yorkshire region.
25	*Private health organisations and charities/help lines*	Examples are stories about the opening of national help lines for cancer, or the Action Asthma survey.
26–28	**Environment**	
26	*Environmental pollution and disasters*	An example is the *Braer* tanker oil spill, where the primary concern is about

Code	Content category	Categories used in other studies and notes

pollution. Using foreign examples, the distinction I am making is between a concern for pollution (e.g. Chernobyl, where, in spite of deaths, the main concern was about the environmental consequences) compared with a concern for injury and for loss of life, (e.g. Bhopal). The latter would therefore have been classified under 'International accidents and disasters' (46) and Chernobyl under 'International environment' (44). If similar incidents occurred in the UK, the same distinction would be made between concern by the media for environmental consequences (26) and concern for loss of life (30).

27   *Official reports, meetings and forums*

An example is the coverage of British political activity and representation at the Rio Summit in June 1992. In fact, much of the latter reporting was actually political in content (Harrison, 1992), and would be coded under the category 06 where the focus was on the politician and not on the environment; other aspects of the reporting were environmental, however, and would be coded as 27 when they related particularly to British environmental issues.

28   *Conservation and animal rights*

Examples are the activities of Greenpeace, debates on deer hunting and fox hunting, and general stories about the state of the environment which are instigated not by a report or official forum, but by the news media itself.

29   **Scientific discoveries and research**

Examples are inventions, or new technological breakthroughs.

30   **Disasters and accidents**

This category was used by Wallis and Baran (1990), Gerdes (1980) and Langer (1987), and in various forms by others. The Glasgow University Media Group, (1976) had the category 'Disasters', which coded all accidental deaths even if there was only one fatality. The category also includes aircraft

Code	*Content category*	*Categories used in other studies and notes*
		near misses. Gans (1980) had the category of 'Disasters, actual and averted' while Stempel (1989) had the category, 'Accidents and disasters'. Examples are any stories relating to natural disasters, human-made disasters, car/rail crashes, motorway pile-ups (not joy-riding), air crashes, fires, gas leaks and explosions, floods, storms, and so on.
31	**Religion**	Stories which are particularly about religion, church or church services, but not when the service is part of a larger story. For example, the funeral of Jamie Bulger would not be coded as a church service, even though much of the news story was filmed in church. Similarly the story about Anne Widdecombe converting to Catholicism focused mainly on her as a personality and would be coded as 05. However, other more general stories about the ordination of women priests and its repercussions would be coded as 'Religion'.
32	**Weather**	This is not the weather forecast, which has been excluded from this analysis, even when it appears in the news programme. It also does not include stories about violent and damaging weather such as floods or storms, which are coded as accidents and disasters. Examples are stories such as 'this is the hottest summer for two hundred years', or 'this is the mildest December on record', etc.
33	**Other**	Langer (1987) and Grundy (1980) both used this category for items which do not fit into any of the existing categories, but are not sufficiently represented to warrant the creation of a separate category. This category was included to avoid having missing content category data.

International television news content categories

Code	Content category	Categories used in other studies and notes
34	**European/EEC politics**	This category relates to the Annan Report (*Report of the Committee on the Future of Broadcasting, 1977*), which argued that television news should include more EEC news. Examples are Denmark's rejection of the Maastricht Treaty, the debate and referenda on entry to the European Union, European Parliamentary affairs and meetings, and other European political stories such as the Italian referendum.
35	**Politics in the rest of the world**	Examples are the United States elections and coverage of President Clinton's policies, Russian politics, elections in India and South Africa, and so on. Other examples are the political implications of actions; for instance, following the fire at Waco, Texas, the FBI's tactics were debated in the political arena, and some news programmes such as *Channel 4 News* chose to reflect that, whereas other programmes tended to ignore the development, preferring simply to cover Waco as a violent and exciting event.
36	**International economy**	Examples are stories about Russian inflation, international trade talks when the focus is not on the British economy or Chancellor, and stories about the EC economy in general.
37	**International business affairs**	Examples are the German rail strike, a three-day air strike in Spain, etc.
38	**International law, crime and criminal proceedings**	Coverage of all non-violent crimes and subsequent proceedings. Examples are reports about the managing director of Fiat on a corruption charge. Violent crime, such as shootings, riots and so on, would be coded as 'International violence' (40).

Code	Content category	Categories used in other studies and notes
39	**International disputes**	Stories about the negotiations which take place between different countries in the world, such as talks between the United States and Russia. This category does not include Britain (which would be coded as domestic news). The category covers the non-violent aspects of peace keeping or reconciliation and may occur at the beginning, at the end or in the middle of conflicts. An example is the peace talks on Bosnia, where the reporting emphasises the peace and reconciliation process and does not report the violence which has occurred or is occurring.
40	**International violence**	Examples are 'terrorism', war or deaths due to human intervention (the war in Bosnia), law and order enforcement. (US troops in Somalia, the FBI and the ending of the Waco Siege in Texas), the funerals of people killed violently (such as Chris Hani) and the filming of demonstrations and anger which occur at such funerals.
41	**International human interest (light)**	All light human interest stories. Examples are stories about international pop celebrities, a story about a German actress, and so on. (See category 16 for a finer distinction.)
42	**International human interest (serious)**	All serious human interest stories (see category 17 for a finer distinction). Examples are the story about the blinded Bosnian boy who was flown to the United States for eye surgery, and became a 'celebrity' by being the victim of war; and stories about issues such as Ethiopian Jews being denied entrance to join their families in Israel; i.e. stories about 'ordinary' people being the victims of circumstance or crime.
43	**International health**	Examples are stories about AIDS in Africa, kidney transplants and donations in India, etc.

Code	Content category	Categories used in other studies and notes
44	**International environment**	Stories about pollution, such as Chernobyl, the rain forest, or the Rio Summit when the focus was on the international environment and not on the political delegates. See the distinction made in category 26 between environmental disasters and general disasters and accidents, where the former concentrates on the environmental consequences at Chernobyl and the latter on loss of life at Bhopal, which would be classified under 'International accidents and disasters' (46).
45	**International science**	International scientific breakthroughs. Examples are improvements on the Stealth Bomber or Nasa technology, etc.
46	**International accidents and disasters**	Examples are earthquakes, floods, typhoons, cyclones (Bangladesh 1992), or any violent deaths or damage caused by accident, whether human-made catastrophe such as Bhopal or 'Acts of God' causing famine and drought. Famine caused by war in Sudan would be coded as 35, as the violence to another human being began from malevolent or intentional action by another, and therefore cannot be classed as an accident. Where the cause of the famine is not spelt out it has been coded as an 'Act of God' under 46.
47	**International education**	Examples are stories about the education system in America, but not stories which cover education from a political perspective, such as government reforms, which would be classed as either 34 or 35.
48	**International sport**	An example is a story which covers a cricket match between Australia and South Africa played in Sydney.
49	**International religion**	Examples are stories about the pope's visit to Bangladesh or any other country but Britain, about a convent in France, etc.

Code	*Content category*	*Categories used in other studies and notes*
50	**Other**	Items which do not fit into any of the above categories but are not sufficiently represented to warrant the creation of a separate category.

Appendix II:
Television News Coding Frame

The Coding Frame is divided into two parts. The first part was completed for every news programme and obtained general information about the programme itself. The information collected concentrated on such criteria as the channel on which the news programme appeared, its transmission date, its start time, and the overall programme length in minutes and seconds. The analysis excluded all advertisements, weather forecasts, newspaper assessments, handovers, chatty exchanges between presenters, technical problems, musical introductions and end titles. Headline and summary content categories were drawn from the code book and the total length in seconds devoted to the headlines and summaries was recorded. Finally the total length of national news and total length of international news in the programme were calculated in minutes and seconds. When added together, these last two equalled the overall news output time.

The second part of the Coding Frame contains information about each television news story (see Chapter 1). In order to ensure that stories were correctly allocated in relation to their appropriate content category, some stories are ostensibly about the same thing, e.g. the story about the ending of the Waco siege in Texas, might have been coded under three different categories. For example, on BBC1's *Nine O'Clock News* on 20 April 1993 the lead story was about the ending of the Waco siege. Three separate reporters, each framed by an introduction by the presenter, presented three pieces of film. The first was about President Clinton's announcement that he took full responsibility for the decision made by the FBI to attack the compound. This 'story' included an introduction by the presenter, John Humphrys, which lasted for forty-seven seconds, plus a further twenty-eight seconds of graphics describing the 'cult's' compound. The reporter's film then lasted a further two minutes and forty-four seconds. This 'story' was coded as 'International politics', number 35 in the TV News Code Book (Appendix I). The second Waco 'story' followed immediately. John Humphrys again introduced the reporter, this time with a short twelve-second piece accompanied by a still photograph of the compound in flames. The second reporter then presented a piece relating the aftermath of the fire, filmed at the Waco compound; the pictures showed the FBI tanks attacking the compound and the fire starting and quickly taking hold until the building was completely engulfed. This piece lasted two minutes and twenty-two seconds and was coded as 'International violence', number 40 in the TV News Code Book. The third 'story' devoted to the Waco siege followed immediately after the second 'story'. Again John Humphrys gave a short introduction, lasting for nineteen seconds, again accompanied by a still photograph at his side. The third reporter then presented a piece about the British families of the 'cult' members living in Britain, and their distress at the violent end to the siege. This was coded as a domestic story, 'Human interest (serious)', number 17 in the TV News Code Book.

Each news story identified was given a story number, and general information relating to the television news programme was included in order to locate each individual news story within the appropriate channel and news programme. Information was also obtained as to whether the particular news story described was a headline or summary story, in order to gauge the importance and prominence the news programme accorded particular story categories. Each story length was also recorded, again to act as an indicator of the importance of the story in relation to other news stories and its position in the news programme.

On the Coding Frame, under 'Story information', Item 3.5 (Story identifier) was included in order to allow the identification of particular story categories quickly using a Statistics Package for Social Scientists (SPSS). All local news bulletin stories which occurred within national news programmes (e.g. *Look North* during *BBC Breakfast News* and *Calendar News* during *GMTV News*) were indicated by placing 700 in the boxes. All stories relating to the end and the aftermath of the Waco siege which occurred on the national news were recorded using the number 800. On the occasion where a Waco victim was identified by *Look North* as living within its region, the story was identified by the number 870.

Coding Frame

A Programme information

1.1	Programme number	☐☐	(1–2)
1.2	Channel: BBC1 ☐ BBC2 ☐ ITV3 ☐ C4 ☐		(3)
1.3	Transmission date	☐☐☐☐	(4–7)
1.4	Time start	☐☐☐☐	(8–11)
1.5	Programme length – *news stories only* (i.e. excluding all adverts/weather/ papers/chat/handovers/fillers etc.)	☐☐☐ ☐☐ mins secs	(12–16)
1.6	Headlines (content category) 1	☐☐	(17–18)
	2	☐☐	(19–20)
	3	☐☐	(21–2)
	4	☐☐	(23–4)
	5	☐☐	(25–6)
1.7	Total length of headlines (secs)	☐☐☐	(27–9)

1.8   Summary   (content category)   1   ☐☐   (30–1)

                                     2   ☐☐   (32–3)

                                     3   ☐☐   (34–5)

                                     4   ☐☐   (36–7)

                                     5   ☐☐   (38–9)

1.9   Total length of summary (secs)   ☐☐☐   (40–2)

1.10 Total length of national news   ☐☐☐ ☐☐   (43–7)
                                               mins   secs

1.11 Total length of international news   ☐☐☐ ☐☐   (48–52)
                                               mins   secs

B Story information

2.1   Story number   ☐☐☐☐   (1–4)

2.2   Programme number   ☐☐   (5–6)

2.3   Channel: BBC 1 ☐   BBC2 ☐   ITV3 ☐   C4 ☐   (7)

2.4   Transmission date   ☐☐☐☐   (8–11)

2.5   Time start   ☐☐☐☐   (12–15)

2.6   Programme length – (mins and secs)   ☐☐☐ ☐☐   (16–20)
                                             mins   secs

2.7   Was this story a headline?   Yes ☐   No ☐   (21)

2.8   Was this story a summary?   Yes ☐   No ☐   (22)

Story content (time in secs)

2.9   Story categories   ☐☐   (23–4)

3.0   Total story length   ☐☐☐☐   (25–8)

Story format (time in secs)

3.1   Presenter   ☐☐   (29–30)

3.2   Presenter and spokesperson(s)   ☐☐☐   (31–3)

3.3   Presenter and reporter (two-way)   ☐☐☐   (34–6)

3.4   Presenter and film (oov [out of vision] or underlay) ☐☐☐   (37-9)

3.5   **Story identifier**   ☐☐☐   (40–2)
      (local news bulletins in national news programmes = 700, Waco stories = 800,
      local news bulletin stories about Waco victims = 870)

3.6   Computer graphics   ☐☐   (43–4)

3.7   Reporter and film   ☐☐☐   (45–7)

3.8   Library film   ☐☐☐   (48–50)

Bibliography

Abercrombie, N. (1996), *Television and Society*, Cambridge, Polity Press.

Alali, A. O. and K. K. Eke (1991) (eds), *Media Coverage of Terrorism*, Newbury Park, Sage.

Allen, R. and N. Miller (1993), *Broadcasting Enters the Marketplace*, London, John Libbey.

Alter, P. (1985), *Nationalism*, London, Arnold.

Altheide, D. L. (1976), *Creating Reality: How the News Distorts Events*, Thousand Oaks, CA, Sage.

Altheide, D. L. (1985), *Media Power*, Beverley Hills, Sage.

Altheide, D. L. and R. P. Snow (1979), *Media Logic*, Thousand Oaks, CA, Sage.

Anderson, B. (1983), *Imagined Communities*, London, Verso.

Ang, I. (1985), *Watching Dallas*, London, Routledge.

Ang, I. (1991), *Desperately Seeking the Audience*, London, Routledge.

Asp, K. (1983), 'The Struggle for the Agenda: Party Agenda, Media Agenda, and Voter Agenda in the 1979 Swedish Election Campaign', *Communication Research*, 10:3, 333–55.

Badii, N. and W. J. Ward (1980), 'The Nature of News in Four Dimensions', *Journalism Quarterly*, 57, 243–8.

Bailey, G. A. and L. W. Lichty (1972), 'Rough Justice on a Saigon Street: A Gatekeeper Study of NBC's Tet Execution Film', *Journalism Quarterly*, 49, 221–38.

Bakhtin, M. (1929), *Marxism and the Philosophy of Language*, New York, Seminar Press, trans. by V. N. Volosinov, 1973.

Ball, G. and P. Routledge (1996), 'A Nation of Snoopers', *Independent on Sunday*, 29 December.

Bantz, C. R. (1985), 'News Organizations: Conflict as a Crafted Cultural Norm', *Communication*, 8, 225–44.

Barendt, E. (1993), *Broadcasting Law*, Oxford, Oxford University Press.

Barker, C. (1997), *Global Television*, Oxford, Blackwell.

Barkun, M. (1994), 'Reflections after Waco: Millennialists and the State', in J. R. Lewis (ed.), *From the Ashes: Making Sense of Waco*, Lanham MD, Rowman and Littlefield.

Barnett, S. (1993) (ed.), *Funding the BBC's Future*, BBC Charter Review Series,

London, BFI.

Barnett, S. (1997), 'New Media, Old Problems: New Technology and the Political Process', *European Journal of Communication*, 12(2), 193–218.

Barnett, S. (1998), 'Raining on Sky's Parade', *Media Guardian*, 28 September.

Barnett, S. and A. Curry (1994), *The Battle for the BBC*, London, Aurum.

Barnett, S. and I. Gaber (1993), *Changing Patterns in Broadcast News*, London, Voice of the Listener and Viewer.

Bass, A. Z. (1969), 'Refining the "Gatekeeper" Concept: A UN Radio Case Study', *Journalism Quarterly*, 46, 69–72.

Baudrillard, J. (1976), *Symbolic Exchange and Death*, trans. by I. H. Grant, London, Sage, 1993.

Baudrillard, J. (1983), *In the Shadow of the Silent Majorities, or, The End of the Social and Other Essays*, trans. by P. Foss, J. Johnson and P. Patton, New York, Semiotext(e).

BBC (1992), *Report and Accounts 1991–92*, London, BBC.

BBC (1993a), *Producers' Choice*, London, BBC.

BBC (1993b), *Extending Choice*, London, BBC.

BBC (1993c), *Producers' Guidelines*, London, BBC.

BBC (1993d), 'BBC Style Guide for News and Current Affairs', internal document.

BBC (1993e), *Report and Accounts 1992–93*, London, BBC.

BBC (1994a), *Report and Accounts 1993–94*, London, BBC.

BBC (1994b), 'Guide to Newsgathering', March, internal document.

BBC (1995), *Report and Accounts 1994–95*, London, BBC.

BBC (1996a), *Extending choice in the Digital Age*, London, BBC.

BBC (1996b), *Producers' Guidelines*, London, BBC.

BBC (1996c) *Report and Accounts 1995–96*, London, BBC.

BBC (1996d), 'BBC News and Current Affairs Report 95–96', internal document.

BBC (1997a), *The BBC's Digital Service Proposition: A Consultation Document*, London, BBC.

BBC (1997b), *The BBC's Digital Service Proposition: A Response to Public Consultation*, London, BBC.

BBC On-Line (1998), 'BBC News: The Future – Research and Challenges', <*http://www.bbc.co.uk/info/news/newsfuture/foreword.html*>.

Beardsworth, A. (1986), 'Analysing Press Content: Some Technical and Methodological Issues', *Sociological Review Monograph*, 29, 371–96.

Behr, R. L. and S. Iyengar (1985), 'Television News, Real World Cues, and Changes in the Public Agenda', *Public Opinion Quarterly*, 49, 38–57.

Bell, A. (1991), *The Language of News Media*, Oxford, Blackwell.

Bell, D. (1973), *The Coming of Post-Industrial Society*, London, Heinemann.

Bell, E. (1997) 'Cartlong to Fade out Central TV Name', *Observer*, 5 January.

Bell, P., K. Boehringer and S. Crofts (1982), *Programmed Politics: A Study of Australian Television*, Sydney, Sable.

Benton, M. and P. J. Frazier (1976), 'The Agenda Setting Function of the Mass Media at Three Levels of "Information Holding"', *Communication Research*, 3:3, 261–74.

Berelson, B. (1971), *Content Analysis in Communication Research*, New York, Hafner.

Berger, A. A. (1991), *Media Analysis Techniques*, London, Sage.

Berkowitz, D. (ed.) (1997), *Social Meanings of News*, Thousand Oaks, CA, Sage.

Billington, R., S. Strawbridge, L. Greensides and A. Fitzsimons (1991), *Culture and*

Society, London, Macmillan Education.

Biocca, F. (1991), *Television and Political Advertising: Signs, Codes and Images*, Hillsdale NJ, Lawrence Erlbaum.

Birt, J. (1995), 'Why our Interviewers Should Stop Sneering and Start to Listen', *The Times*, 4 February.

Birt, J. and P. Jay (1975a), 'Television Journalism: The Child of an Unhappy Marriage between Newspapers and Film', *The Times*, 30 September.

Birt, J. and P. Jay (1975b), 'The Radical Changes Needed to Remedy TV's Bias Against Understanding', *The Times*, 1 October.

Birt, J. and P. Jay (1976a), 'How Television News Can Hold the Mass Audience', *The Times*, 2 September.

Birt, J. and P. Jay (1976b), 'Why Television News is in Danger of Becoming an Anti-Social Force', *The Times*, 3 September.

Blackhurst, C. (1996), 'The Conflict of Interests', *Media Guardian*, 30 September.

Blankenberg, W. (1970), 'News Accuracy: Some Findings on the Meaning of the Term', *Journalism Quarterly*, 47, 375–86.

Blumenthal, S. (1993), 'The Syndicated Presidency', *New Yorker*, 5 April.

Blumler, J. G. (1969), 'Producers' Attitudes towards TV Coverage of an Election Campaign: A Case Study', in P. Halmos (ed.), *Sociological Review Monograph*, 13, 85–116.

Blumler, J. G. (1992), *Television and the Public Interest*, London, Sage.

Blumler, J. G. (1993), 'The Increasing Self-Commercialisation of the BBC: Profit or Peril?', in S. Barnett (ed.), *Funding the BBC's Future*, London, BFI.

Bolton, R. (1995), 'Agenda Benders', *New Statesman and Society*, 24 March.

Bolton, R. (1996), 'Don't Take the Vision out of Telly', *Observer*, 14 January.

Bonney, B. and H. Wilson (1983), *Australia's Commercial Media*, London, Macmillan.

Boorstin, D. (1964), *The Image: A Guide to Pseudo Events in America*, New York, Harper and Row.

Bowers, D. R. (1967), 'A Report on the Activity of Publishers in Directing Newsroom Decisions', *Journalism Quarterly*, 44, 43–52.

Boyd-Barrett, O. (1980), 'The Politics of Socialisation: Recruitment and Training for Journalism', *Sociological Review Monograph*, 29, 307–40.

Boyd-Barrett, O. and C. Newbold, (1995) (eds), *Approaches to Media*, London, Arnold.

Boyer, J. H. (1981), 'How Editors View Objectivity', *Journalism Quarterly*, 58, 24–8.

Bradford, R. W. (1994), 'Who Started the Fires? Mass Murder, American Style', in J. R. Lewis (ed.), *From the Ashes: Making Sense of Waco*, Lanham MD, Rowman and Littlefield.

Breed, W. (1955), 'Social Control in the Newsroom: A Functional Analysis', *Social Forces*, 33, 326–35.

Briggs, A. (1961), *The Birth of Broadcasting: The History of Broadcasting in the United Kingdom. Vol. II: The Golden Age of Wireless, 1927–1939*, Oxford, Oxford University Press.

Briggs, A. (1995), *The Birth of Broadcasting: The History of Broadcasting in the United Kingdom. Vol. V: Competition 1955–1974*, Oxford, Oxford University Press.

Broadcasting Act (1990), London, HMSO.

Broadcasting Act (1996), London, HMSO.

Broadcasting Research Unit (1985), *The Public Service Idea in British Broadcasting*, London, BRN.

Broadcasting Research Unit (1989), *Quality in Television*, London, John Libbey.

Broadcasting White Paper (1988), *Broadcasting in the 1990s: Competition, Choice and Quality*, Cm 517, London, HMSO.

Brookes, R. (1996), 'Bland and Birt: Old Pals Act Too Cosy for BBC's Comfort', *Observer*, 14 January.

Bruhn-Jensen, K. (1986), *Making Sense of the News*, Aarhus, Denmark University Press.

Brunsdon, C. (1990), 'Quality in Television', *Screen*, 31:1.

Brunsdon, C. and D. Morley (1978), *Everyday Television: "Nationwide"* London, BFI.

Buckalew, J. K. (1969), 'A Q-Analysis of Television News Editors' Decisions', *Journalism Quarterly*, 46, 135–7.

Burns, T. (1969), 'Public Service and Private World', in P. Halmos (ed.), *Sociological Review Monograph*, 13, 53–73.

Burns, T. (1972), 'Commitment and Career in the BBC', in D. McQuail (ed.), *Sociology of Mass Communications*, Harmondsworth, Penguin.

Burns, T. (1977), *The BBC: Public Institution: Private World*, London, Macmillan.

Burton, G. (1990), *More than Meets the Eye*, London, Routledge.

Calhoun, C. (1992) (ed.), *Habermas and the Public Sphere*, Cambridge MA, MIT Press.

Calhoun, C. (1994) (ed.), *Social Theory and the Politics of Identity*, Oxford, Blackwell.

Canino, G. J. and A. C. Huston (1986), 'A Content Analysis of Prime-Time TV and Radio News in Puerto Rico', *Journalism Quarterly*, 63, 150–4.

Cardiff, D. P. and P. Scannell (1987), 'Broadcasting and National Unity', in J. Curran, A. Smith and P. Wingate (eds), *Impacts and Influences: Essays on Media and Power in the Twentieth Century*, London, Methuen.

Carey, J. W. (1988), *Media, Myths and Narrative*, Newbury Park, Sage.

Carey, J. W. (1989), *Communication as Culture*, Boston MA, Unwin Hyman.

Carroll, R. L. (1989), 'Content Values in TV News Programmes in Small and Large Markets', *Journalism Quarterly*, 62, 877–82.

Cashmore, E. (1994), *... And There Was Television*, London, Routledge.

Castells, M. (1996), *The Rise of the Network Society*, Cambridge MA, Blackwell.

Catlow, L. (1997), 'Television News', unpublished MA Thesis, University of Sheffield.

Cawelti, J. G. (1977), *Adventure, Mystery and Romance*, Chicago, University of Chicago Press.

Channel 4 (1994), *J'Accuse the News*, 1 November.

Chase, L. and S. J. Baran (1973), 'An Assessment of Quantitative Research in Mass Communications', *Journalism Quarterly*, 53, 308–11.

Chibnall, S. (1977), *Law and Order News*, London, Tavistock.

Chibnall, S. (1980), 'Chronicles of the Gallows: The Social History of Crime Reporting', *Sociological Review Monograph*, 29, 179–218.

Chippendale, P. and C. Horrie (1990), *Stick It Up Your Punter*, London, Heinemann.

Chomsky, N. (1989), *"Necessary Illusions": Thought Control in Democratic Societies*, London, Pluto Press.

Chomsky, N. (1992), *Deterring Democracy*, London, Vintage.

Clyde, R. W. and J. K. Buckalew (1969), 'Inter-Media Standardisation: A Q-Analysis of News Editors', *Journalism Quarterly*, 46, 349–51.

Cohen, A. A., H. Adoni and C. R. Bantz (1990), *Social Conflict and Television News*, London, Sage.

Cohen, A. A., M. R. Levy, I. Roeh and M. Gurevitch (1995), *Global Newsrooms: Local*

Audiences, London, John Libbey.

Cohen, B. C. (1963), *The Press and Foreign Policy*, Princeton NJ, Princeton University Press.

Cohen, E. D. (1992) (ed.), *Philosophical Issues in Journalism*, Oxford, Oxford University Press.

Cohen, S. and J. Young (1973) (eds), *The Manufacture of the News*, London, Constable.

Collins, R. (1990), *Television: Policy and Culture*, London, Unwin Hyman.

Collins, R., J. Curran, N. Garnham, P. Scannell, P. Schlesinger and C. Sparks (1986) (eds), *Media, Culture and Society*, London, Sage.

Collins, R., N. Garnham and G. Locksley (1988), *The Economics of Television: The UK Case*, London, Sage.

Commission of the European Communities (1984), *Television without Frontiers*, Green Paper on the Establishment of the Common Market for Broadcasting (COM, 84,300 final), Brussels, CEC.

Commission of the European Communities (1992), *European Community Audiovisual Policy*, European file 6/1992, Luxembourg, Office for Official Publications of the European Commission.

Commission of the European Communities (1994), *Growth, Competitiveness, Employment: The Challenges and Ways Forward into the 21st Century*, White Paper, Luxembourg, Office for Official Publications of the European Commission.

Corner, J. (1995), *Television Form and Public Address*, London, Arnold.

Cottle, S. (1993), *TV News, Urban Conflict and the Inner City*, Leicester, Leicester University Press.

Cottle, S. (1994), 'Participant Observation: Researching News Production', unpublished paper.

Cox, G. (1995), *Pioneering Television News*, London, John Libbey.

Crick, B. (1991) (ed.), *National Identities*, Oxford, Blackwell.

Culf, A. (1995), 'Seeing Red at White City', *Media Guardian*, 19 June.

Curran, J. (1991a), 'Rethinking the Media as a Public Sphere', in P. Dahlgren and C. Sparks (eds), *Communication and Citizenship*, London, Routledge.

Curran, J. (1991b), 'Mass Media and Democracy: A Reappraisal', in J. Curran and M. Gurevitch (eds), *Mass Media and Society*, London, Arnold.

Curran, J. (1996), 'Mass Media and Democracy Revisited', in J. Curran and M. Gurevitch (eds), *Mass Media and Society* (2nd edition), London, Arnold.

Curran, J. (1998), 'Crisis of Public Communication: A Reappraisal', in T. Liebes and J. Curran (eds), *Media, Ritual and Identity*, London, Routledge.

Curran, J. and M. Gurevitch (1991) (eds), *Mass Media and Society*, London, Arnold.

Curran, J. and M. Gurevitch (1996) (eds), *Mass Media and Society* (2nd edition), London, Arnold.

Curran, J. and J. Seaton (1997), *Power without Responsibility*, London, Routledge.

Curran, J., M. Gurevitch and J. Woollacott (1984) (eds), *Mass Communication and Society*, London, Arnold.

Dahlgren, P. (1992), 'What's the Meaning of This? Viewers' Plural Sense-Making of TV News', in P. Scannell, P. Schlesinger and C. Sparks (eds), *Culture and Power*, London, Sage.

Dahlgren, P. (1995), *Television and the Public Sphere*, London, Sage.

Dahlgren, P. and C. Sparks (1991) (eds), *Communication and Citizenship*, London,

Routledge.
Dahlgren, P. and C. Sparks (1992) (eds), *Journalism and Popular Culture*, London, Sage.
Davidson, A. (1992), *Under the Hammer*, London, Mandarin.
Davie, G. (1961), *The Democratic Intellect*, Edinburgh, University of Edinburgh Press.
Davis, D. K. (1990), 'News and Politics', in D. L. Swanson and D. Nimmo (eds), *New Directions in Political Communication*, London, Sage.
Dayan, D. and E. Katz (1992), *Media Events*, Cambridge MA, Harvard University Press.
Deans, J. and S. Armstrong (1996), 'ITN Faces Squeeze Over New ITV Deal', *Broadcast*, 13 September.
Dearing, J. W. and E. M. Rogers (1996), *Agenda Setting*, Thousand Oaks CA, Sage.
Dennis, E. E. (1989), *Reshaping the Media*, London, Sage.
Deppa, J. (1993), *The Media and Disaster: Pan Am 103*, London, David Fulton.
Diamond, L. and M. F. Plattner (1994) (eds), *Nationalism, Ethnic Conflict, and Democracy*, Baltimore and London, Johns Hopkins University Press.
Dominick, J. R. (1977), 'Geographic Bias in National TV News', *Journal of Communication*, 27, 94–9.
Dominick, J. R., A. Wurtzel and G. Lometti (1975), 'TV Journalism vs. Show Business: A Content Analysis of Eyewitness News', *Journalism Quarterly*, 52, 213–18.
Donahew, L. (1967), 'Newspaper Gatekeepers and Forces in the News Channel', *Public Opinion Quarterly*, 31, 61–8.
Downs, A. (1962), 'The Public Interest: Its Meaning in a Democracy', *Social Research*, 29:1, 1–36.
Dubrow, H. (1982), *Genre*, London, Methuen.
During, S. (1993) (ed.), *The Cultural Studies Reader*, London, Routledge.
Durkheim, E. (1952), *Suicide: A Study in Sociology*, London, Routledge and Kegan Paul.
EBU (1998), 'The Public Service Broadcasting Remit: Today and Tomorrow', European Broadcasting Union Press Release, 29 April.
Edgar, P. (1980) (ed.), *News in Focus*, Melbourne, Macmillan.
Eldridge, J. (1993) (ed.), *Getting the Message*, London, Routledge.
Eldridge, J. and L. Eldridge (1994), *Raymond Williams: Making Connections*, London, Routledge.
Elliott, P. (1972), *The Making of a TV Series*, London, Constable.
Elliott, P. (1982), 'Intellectuals, the "Information Society" and the Disappearance of the Public Sphere', *Media, Culture and Society*, 4, 243–53.
Epstein, E. J. (1973), *News from Nowhere*, New York, Random House.
Ericson, R. V., P. M. Baranek and K. B. L. Chan (1991), *Representing Order: Crime, Law and Justice in the News Media*, Milton Keynes, Open University Press.
Etzioni, A. (1985), 'The Functioning of Organisations', in D. S. Pugh, D. J. Hickson and C. R. Hinings (eds), *Writers on Organisations*, Harmondsworth, Penguin.
Etzioni, A. (1993), *The Spirit of Community*, London, Fontana Press.
Evans, H. (1983), *Good Times, Bad Times*, London, Weidenfeld and Nicolson.
Ewing, K. D. and C. A. Gearty (1993), *Freedom Under Thatcher*, Oxford, Oxford University Press.
Fallows, J. (1996), *Breaking the News*, New York, Pantheon.
Farnham, D. and S. Horton (1993) (eds), *Managing the New Public Services*, London, Macmillan.

Fathi, A. (1973), 'Problems in Developing Indices of News Value', *Journalism Quarterly*, 50, 497–501.

Ferguson, M. (1990) (ed.), *The New Imperatives*, London, Sage.

Fishman, M. (1980), *Manufacturing the News*, Austin TX, University of Texas Press.

Fiske, J. (1981), *Reading the Popular*, London, Unwin Hyman.

Fiske, J. (1982), *Introduction to Communication Studies*, London, Routledge.

Fiske, J. (1987), *Television Culture*, London, Routledge.

Fiske, J. (1991), *Understanding Popular Culture*, London, Routledge.

Fiske, J. and J. Hartley (1990), *Reading Television*, London, Routledge.

Flegel, R. C. and S. H. Chaffee (1971), 'Influences of Editors, Readers and Personal Opinions on Reporters', *Journalism Quarterly*, 48, 645–51.

Fletcher, M. and B. Macintyre (1993), 'Clinton Backs FBI Over Decision to Storm Waco', *The Times*, 21 April.

Foote, J. S. and M. E. Steele (1986), 'Degree of Conformity in Lead Stories in Early Evening Network TV Newscasts', *Journalism Quarterly*, 63, 19–23.

Foster, R. (1992), *Public Broadcasters*, Edinburgh, Edinburgh University Press.

Fowler, R. (1991), *Language in the News*, London, Routledge.

Frampton, K. (1985), 'Towards a Critical Regionalism: Six Points for an Architecture of Resistance', in H. Foster (ed.), *Postmodern Culture*, London, Pluto Press.

Franklin, B. (1992) (ed.), *Televising Democracies*, London, Routledge.

Franklin, B. and D. Murphy (1991), *What News? The Market, Politics and the Local Press*, London, Routledge.

Fraser, N. (1992), 'Rethinking the Public Sphere: A Contribution to the Critique of Actually Existing Democracy', in C. Calhoun (ed.), *Habermas and the Public Sphere*, Cambridge MA, MIT Press.

Frean, A. (1995), 'Birt Attacks "Sneering Confrontation" Interviewers', *The Times*, 4 February.

Fry, A. (1996), 'TV in the Digital Age', *Marketing Focus*, 28 November.

Galtung, J. (1974), 'A Rejoinder', *Journal of Peace Research*, 11, 157–60.

Galtung, J. and M. Ruge (1965), 'The Structure of Foreign News', *Journal of Peace Research*, 2, 64–91.

Gans, H. J. (1980), *Deciding What's News*, London, Constable.

Garber, M., J. Matlock and R. L. Walkowitz (1993) (eds), *Media Spectacles*, London, Routledge.

Garnham, N. (1973), *Structures of Television*, BFI TV Monograph 1, London, BFI.

Garnham, N. (1986), 'Contribution to a Political Economy of Mass-Communication', in R. Collins, J. Curran, N. Garnham, P. Scannell, P. Schlesinger and C. Sparks (eds), *Media, Culture and Society*, London, Sage.

Garnham, N. (1990), *Capitalism and Communication: Global Culture and the Economics of Information*, London and Newbury Park, Sage.

Garnham, N. (1992), 'The Media and the Public Sphere', in C. Calhoun (ed.), *Habermas and the Public Sphere*, Cambridge MA, MIT Press.

Gaunt, P. (1990), *Choosing the News: The Profit Factor in News Selection*, Westport CT, Greenwood Press.

Geertz, C. (1993), *The Interpretation of Cultures*, London, Fontana Press.

Gellner, E. (1994), *Encounters with Nationalism*, Oxford, Blackwell.

Gerdes, P. R. (1980), *TV News in Brief: A Research Report*, Kensington, University of New South Wales.

Gilder, G. (1994), *Life after TV*, New York, W.W. Norton (revised edition).

Gitlin, T. (1980), *The Whole World is Watching: Mass Media in the Making and Unmaking of the New Left*, Berkeley CA, University of California Press.

Gitlin, T. (1991a), 'The Politics of Communication and the Communication of Politics', in J. Curran and M. Gurevitch (eds), *Mass Media and Society*, London, Routledge.

Gitlin, T. (1991b), 'Bites and Blips: Chunk News, Savvy Talk and the Bifurcation of American Politics', in P. Dahlgren and C. Sparks (eds), *Communication and Citizenship*, London, Routledge.

Gitlin, T. (1998), 'Public Sphere or Public Sphericules?', in T. Liebes and J. Curran (eds), *Media, Ritual and Identity*, London, Routledge.

Glaser, B. G. and A. L. Strauss (1967), *The Discovery of Grounded Theory Strategies for Qualitative Research*, Chicago, Aldine.

Glasgow University Media Group (1976), *Bad News*, London, Routledge.

Glasgow University Media Group (1980), *More Bad News*, London, Routledge.

Glasgow University Media Group (1982), *Really Bad News*, London, Writers and Readers.

Glasser, T. L. (1984), 'Competition and Diversity among Radio Formats: Legal and Structural Issues', *Journal of Broadcasting*, 28:2, 127–42.

Glasser, T. L. (1992), 'Objectivity and News Bias', in E. D. Cohen (ed.), *Philosophical Issues in Journalism*, Oxford, Oxford University Press.

Glover, D. (1990), *The Sociology of Mass Media*, Lancashire, Ormskirk, Causeway Press.

Gold, D. and J. L. Simmons (1965), 'News Selection Patterns among Iowa Dailies', *Public Opinion Quarterly*, 29, 425–30.

Goldberg, P. (1994), 'FBI uses "Cults" as Bait', in J. R. Lewis (ed.), *From the Ashes: Making Sense of Waco*, Lanham MD, Rowman and Littlefield.

Golding, P. (1981), 'The Missing Dimension: News Media and the Management of Social Change', in E. Katz and T. Szescko (eds), *Mass Media and Social Change*, London, Sage.

Golding, P. (1990), 'Political Communication and Citizenship: The Media and Democracy in an Inegalitarian Social Order', in M. Ferguson (ed.), *Public Communication: The New Imperatives*, London, Sage.

Golding, P. and Elliott, P. (1979), *Making the News*, Harlow, Longman.

Golding, P. and G. Murdock (1991), 'Culture, Communications, and Political Economy', in J. Curran and M. Gurevitch (eds), *Mass Media and Society*, London, Arnold.

Gonzenbach, W. J., M. D. Arant and R. L. Stevenson (1992), 'The World of US Network Television News: Eighteen Years of International and Foreign News Coverage', *Gazette*, 50, 53–72.

Goodwin, A. and G. Whannel (1990) (eds), *Understanding Television*, London, Routledge.

Goodwin, P. and W. Stevenson (1993) (eds), *Responses to the Green Paper*, London, BFI.

Gowing, N. (1994), 'Real-Time Television Coverage of Armed Conflicts and Diplomatic Crises: Does it Pressure or Distort Foreign Policy Decisions?', working paper, unpublished.

Grade, M. (1991), 'Does Television Really Matter?', inaugural lecture of the Institute for Modern Cultural Studies at the University of Nottingham, *Occasional Papers in*

Modern Cultural Studies, 1.

Greenslade, R. (1994), 'Is News at Ten Really Tabloid TV?', *The Times*, 8 June.

Greenwood, W. and T. Welsh (1994), *McNae's Essential Law for Journalists*, London, Butterworth.

Grey, D. L. (1966), 'Decision-Making by a Reporter under Deadline Pressure', *Journalism Quarterly*, 43, 419–28.

Grundy, B. (1980), 'Where is the News?: A Content Analysis of a Week's Television News in Australia', in P. Edgar (ed.), *News in Focus*, Melbourne, Macmillan.

Gunter, B. (1987), *Poor Reception*, Hillsdale NJ, Lawrence Erlbaum.

Gunter, B. (1993), 'The Audience and Quality in Television Broadcasting', *Media Information Australia*, 70, 53–60.

Gunter, B. and J. McAleer (1990), *Children and Television: The One Eyed Monster*, London, Routledge.

Gunter, B. and M. Svennevig (1988), *Attitudes to Broadcasting over the Years*, London, John Libbey.

Gunter, B. and P. Winstone (1992), *TV: The Public's View*, London, John Libbey.

Gunter, B. and P. Winstone (1993), *Television: The Public's View 1992*, London, John Libbey.

Gunter, B. and J. Sancho-Aldridge and P. Winstone (1994), *Television: The Public's View 1993*, London, John Libbey.

Gurevitch, M. (1991), 'The Globalization of Electronic Journalism', in J. Curran and M. Gurevitch (eds), *Mass Media and Society*, London, Arnold.

Gurevitch, M., T. Bennett, J. Curran and J. Woollacott (1982) (eds), *Culture, Society and the Media*, London, Methuen.

Habermas, J. (1984), *The Theory of Communicative Action*, Cambridge, Polity Press.

Habermas, J. (1987), *The Theory of Communicative Action, Volume Two: The Critique of Functionalist Reason*, Cambridge, Polity Press.

Habermas, J. (1989), *Structural Transformation of the Public Sphere*, Cambridge, Polity Press.

Halberstam, J. (1992), 'A Prolegomenon for a Theory of News', in E. D. Cohen (ed.), *Philosophical Issues in Journalism*, Oxford, Oxford University Press.

Hall, A. (1993a), 'Hellfire', *Daily Mirror*, 20 April.

Hall, A. (1993b), 'Chain Gang from Hell', *Daily Mirror*, 21 April.

Hall, S. (1973), 'The Determinations of News Photographs', in S. Cohen and J. Young (eds), *The Manufacture of the News*, London, Constable.

Hall, S. (1977), 'Culture, the Media and the "Ideological Effect"', in J. Curran, M. Gurevitch and J. Woollacott (eds), *Mass Communication and Society*, London, Arnold.

Hall, S. (1980a), 'Cultural Studies: Two Paradigms', *Media and Society*, 2, 57–72.

Hall, S. (1980b), 'Encoding/Decoding', in S. During (ed.), *The Cultural Studies Reader*, London, Routledge, 1993.

Hall, S. and M. Jacques (1990) (eds), *New Times*, London, Lawrence and Wishart.

Hall, S., C. Critcher, T. Jefferson, J. Clarke and B. Roberts (1978), *Policing the Crisis: Mugging, the State and Law and Order*, London, Macmillan.

Hall, T. (1996), Speech for Oslo Media Seminar, BBC, 24 October.

Halloran, J., P. Elliott and G. Murdock (1970), *Demonstrations and Communication*, Harmondsworth, Penguin.

Handy, C. B. (1993), *Understanding Organisations*, Harmondsworth, Penguin.

Hargreaves, I. (1996), 'Interview with John Birt', *New Statesman*, 21 June.

Harris, R. (1990), *Good and Faithful Servant: The Unauthorized Biography of Bernard Ingham*, London, Faber and Faber.

Harrison, J. L. (1991a), 'News Evaluation Survey: International/National News', unpublished report for Yorkshire Television.

Harrison, J. L. (1991b), 'News Evaluation Survey: Regional News Coverage', unpublished report for Yorkshire Television.

Harrison, J. L. (1992), 'What the Papers Said: An Analysis of Press Coverage of UNCED by Four Quality British Newspapers', *Integrated Environmental Management*, Oxford, Blackwell Scientific.

Harrison, J. L. (1995), 'British Television News in the 1990s: Newsworthiness in a Multi-Organisational and Multi-Programme Environment', PhD thesis, University of Sheffield.

Harrison, J. L. (1997), 'Rescheduling the News: An Analysis of ITN's *News at Ten*', *PERC Policy Paper 10*, University of Sheffield, Political Economy Research Centre.

Harrison, J. L. (2000), *The Changing Face of TV*, Reading, Garnet Publishing.

Harrison, J. L. and K. B. Sanders (1997), 'The Press, Privacy and the People, *British Editor*, 1, 2–7.

Harrison, J. L. and L. M. Woods (1999), 'European Citizenship. Can European Audiovisual Policy Make a Difference?', unpublished paper.

Harrison, M. (1985), *TV News: Whose Bias?*, Hermitage, Policy Journals.

Hart, A. (1991), *Understanding the Media: A Practical Guide*, London, Routledge.

Hart, J. (1966), 'Foreign News in US and English Daily Newspapers: A Comparison', *Journalism Quarterly*, 43, 443–8.

Hart, R. P. (1996), 'Easy Citizenship: Television's Curious Legacy', in K. Jamieson (ed.), *The Annals of the American Academy of Political and Social Science: The Media and Politics*, Thousand Oaks CA, Sage.

Hartley, J. (1989), *Understanding News*, London, Routledge.

Hartley, J. (1992), *Tele-ology: Studies in Television*, London, Routledge.

Hartman, P. and C. Husband (1973), 'The Mass Media and Racial Conflicts', in S. Cohen and J. Young (eds), *The Manufacture of News*, London, Constable.

Harvey, D. (1990), *The Condition of Postmodernity*, Oxford MA, Blackwell.

Harvey, S. and K. Robins (eds) (1993), *The Regions, the Nations and the BBC*, BBC Charter Review Series, London, BFI.

Held, D. (1989), *Political Theory and the Modern State*, London, Sage.

Held, V. (1970), *The Public Interest and Individual Interests*, New York, Basic Books.

Heller, H. and P. Edwards (1992), *Policy and Power in Education: The Rise and Fall of the LEA*, London, Routledge.

Herman, E. S. and R. W. McChesney (1997), *The Global Media*, Washington DC, Cassell.

Hetherington, A. (1989), *News in the Regions*, London, Macmillan.

Hetherington, A. and K. Weaver (1992), 'Business as Usual: The Impact of Television Coverage on Press Reporting of the Commons', in B. Franklin (ed.), *Televising Democracies*, London, Routledge.

Hicks, R. G. and A. Gordon (1974), 'Foreign News Content in Israeli and US Newspapers', *Journalism Quarterly*, 51, 639–44.

Hill, D. B. (1985), 'Viewer Characteristics and Agenda Setting by Television News', *Public Opinion Quarterly*, 49, 340–50.

Hodgson, F. W. (1989), *Modern Newspaper Practice*, London, Heinemann.

Hoffmann-Reim, W. (1987), 'National Identity and Cultural Values: Broadcasting Safeguards', *Journal of Broadcasting*, 31:1, 57–72.

Hoggart, R. (1995), *The Way We Live Now*, London, Chatto and Windus.

Hoggart, S. (1995), 'Filleted Fish: Whose News? Democracy and the Media', *New Statesman and Society*, 24 March.

Hogwood, B. (1995), 'The "Growth" of Quangos: Evidence and Explanations', *Parliamentary Affairs*, 48, 207–25.

Holsti, O. R. (1969), *Content Analysis for the Social Sciences and Humanities*, Reading MA, Addison-Wesley.

Hood, S. (1980), *Hood on Television*, London, Routledge.

Horrie, C. and S. Clarke (1994), *Fuzzy Monsters: Fear and Loathing at the BBC*, London, Heinemann.

Horsman, M. (1997), *Sky High*, London, Orion Business Books.

Hughes, R. (1991), *Nothing If Not Critical*, London, Harvill.

Hume, E. (1996), 'The New Paradigm for News', in K. Jamieson (ed.), *The Anna of the American Academy of Political and Social Science: The Media and Politics*, Th u-sand Oaks CA, Sage.

Hvitfelt, H. (1994), 'The Commercialization of the Evening News: Changes in Narrative Techniques in Swedish Television News', *Nordicom Review*, 2, 33–41.

IBA (1974), *ITV: Guide to Independent Television*, London, IBA.

IBA (1985), *TV and Radio*, London, IBA.

Inglis, F. (1990), *Media Theory: An Introduction*, Oxford, Blackwell.

ITC (1991a), *Advertising and Sponsorship on Independent Television*, London, ITC.

ITC (1991b), *Introducing the ITC*, London, ITC.

ITC (1991c), *Cable, Satellite and Local Delivery in the UK*, London, ITC.

ITC (1991d), *Listening to the Viewer*, London, ITC.

ITC (1991e), *Report and Accounts*, London, ITC.

ITC (1992), *Report and Accounts*, London, ITC.

ITC (1993a), *Report and Accounts*, London, ITC.

ITC (1993b), *Memorandum on the Future of the BBC*, London, ITC.

ITC (1994), *Report and Accounts*, London, ITC.

ITC (1995), 'The ITC Performance Review of ITN', unpublished notes.

ITC Press Releases (1993), London, ITC.

Iyengar, S., M. D. Peters and D. R. Kinder (1982), 'Experimental Demonstrations of the "Not-So-Minimal" Consequences of Television News Programmes', *American Political Science Review*, 76:4, 848–58.

Jameson, F. (1991), *Postmodernism: Or, the Cultural Logic of Late Capitalism*, London, Verso.

Johnson, J. M. (1975), *Doing Field Research*, New York, Free Press.

Johnstone, J. W. C., E. J. Slawski and W. D. Bowman (1972), 'The Professional Values of American Newsmen', *Public Opinion Quarterly*, 73, 522–40.

Jones, C. A. and G. Baker (1994), 'Television and Metaphysics at Waco', in J. R. Lewis (ed.), *From the Ashes: Making Sense of Waco*, Lanham MD, Rowman and Littlefield.

Jones, N. (1995), *Soundbites and Spin Doctors*, London, Cassell.

Jones, R. L. and R. E. Carter (1959), 'Some Procedures for Estimating "News Hole" in Content Analysis', *Public Opinion Quarterly*, 23:3, 399–403.

Katz, E. (1996), 'And Deliver Us from Segmentation', in K. Jamieson (ed.), *The Annals* of the American Academy of Political and Social Science: The Media and Politics, Thousand Oaks CA, Sage.

Katz, E. and P. Lazarsfeld (1955), *Personal Influence*, NewYork, Free Press.

Katz, E. and T. Szescko (1981) (eds), *Mass Media and Social Change*, London, Sage.

Keane, J. (1991), *The Media and Democracy*, Cambridge, Polity Press.

Kearney, H. (1991), 'Four Nations or One?', in B. Crick (ed.) *National Identities*, Oxford, Blackwell.

Kent, A. (1996), *Risk and Redemption: Surviving the Network News Wars*, New York, Viking Press.

Kent, R. (1994) (ed.), *Measuring Media Audiences*, London, Routledge.

Kimball, P. (1994), *Down-Sizing the News: Network Cutbacks in the Nation's Capital*, Washington DC, Woodrow Wilson Centre Press.

Kingdom, J. (1991), *Government and Politics in Britain*, Cambridge, Polity Press.

Koch, J. (1990), *The News as Myth*, New York, Greenwood Press.

Krippendorf, K. (1980), *Content Analysis: An Introduction to its Methodology*, London, Sage.

Lang, K. and G. E. Lang (1968), *Politics and Television*, Chicago, Quadrangle Books.

Langer, J. (1987), 'Celebrities to Catastrophes: The "Other News" on TV', unpublished PhD Thesis, La Trobe University, Melbourne, Australia.

Langer, J. (1992), 'Truly Awful News on Television', in P. Dahlgren and C. Sparks (eds), *Communication and Citizenship*, London, Routledge.

Leca, J. (1992), 'Questions on Citizenship', in C. Mouffe (ed.), *Dimensions of Radical Democracy: Pluralism, Citizenship, Community*, London, Verso.

Leff, D. R., D. L. Protess and S. C. Brooks (1986), 'Crusading Journalism: Changing Public Attitudes and Policy-Making Agendas', *Public Opinion Quarterly*, 50, 300–15.

Lemert, J. B. (1974), 'Content Duplication by the Networks in Competing Evening Newscasts', *Journalism Quarterly*, 51, 238–44.

Lewin, J. (1947), 'Frontiers in Group Dynamics. II. Channels of Group Life: Social Planning and Action Research', *Human Relations*, 1:2, 143–53.

Lewin, K. (1943), 'Forces behind Food Habits and Methods Of Change', *The Problem of Changing Food Habits*, National Research Council Bulletin 108, 35–65.

Lewis, J. (1991), *The Ideological Octopus*, London, Routledge.

Lewis, J. R. (1994) (ed.), *From the Ashes: Making Sense of Waco*, Lanham MD, Rowman and Littlefield.

Lichtenburg, J. (1991), 'In Defence of Objectivity', in J. Curran and M. Gurevitch (eds), *Mass Media and Society*, London, Arnold.

Liebes, T. and J. Curran (1998) (eds), *Media, Ritual and Identity*, London, Routledge.

Lippmann, W. (1922), *Public Opinion*, London, Macmillan.

Livingstone, S. and P. Lunt (1994), *Talk on Television*, London, Routledge.

Lorimer, R. (1994), *Mass Communications*, Manchester, Manchester University Press.

Lule, J. (1991), 'The Myth of My Widow: A Dramatic Analysis of News Portrayals of a Terrorist Victim', in A. O. Alali and K. K. Eke (eds), *Media Coverage of Terrorism*, Newbury Park, Sage.

McClure, K. (1992), 'On the Subject of Rights: Pluralism, Plurality and Political Identity', in C. Mouffe (ed.), *Dimensions of Radical Democracy: Pluralism, Citizenship, Community*, London, Verso.

McCombs, M. E. (1981), 'The Agenda-Setting Approach', in D. D. Nimmo and K. R.

Sanders (eds), *Handbook of Political Communication*, Thousand Oaks CA, Sage.

McCombs, M. (1995), *Building through Communication*, Austin TX, University of Texas.

McCombs, M. E. and D. L. Shaw (1972), 'The Agenda-Setting Function of Mass Media', *Public Opinion Quarterly*, 36:2, 176–87.

McCombs, M. E. and D. L. Shaw (1993), 'The Evolution of Agenda-Setting Research: Twenty-Five Years in the Marketplace of Ideas', *Journal of Communication*, 43:2, 58–67.

McDaniel, D. O. (1973), 'Film's Presumed Advantages in Presenting Television News', *Journalism Quarterly*, 50, 146–9.

McDonnell, J. (1991), *Public Service Broadcasting: A Reader*, London, Routledge.

MacGregor, B. (1997), *Live, Direct and Biased?*, London, Arnold.

McGuigan, J. (1992), *Cultural Populism*, London, Routledge.

McIntyre, I. (1993), *The Expense of Glory: A Life of John Reith*, London, HarperCollins.

McLaughlin, L. (1993), 'Feminism, the Public Sphere, Media and Democracy', *Media, Culture and Society*, 15, 599–620.

McLeod, J., C. J. Glynn and D. G. McDonald (1983), 'Issues and Images: The Influence of Media Reliance in Voting Decisions', *Communication Research*, 10:1, 37–58.

McLuhan, M. (1964), *Understanding Media*, London, Routledge.

McManus, J. H. (1994), *Market-Driven Journalism: Let the Citizen Beware*, Thousand Oaks CA, Sage.

McNair, B. (1994), *News and Journalism in the UK*, London, Routledge.

McQuail, D. (1972) (ed.), *Sociology of Mass Communications*, Harmondsworth, Penguin.

McQuail, D. (1990), 'Western Europe: "Mixed Model" Under Threat?', in J. Dowing, A. Mohammadi and A. Sreberny-Mohammadi (eds), *Questioning the Media*, London, Sage.

McQuail, D. (1992), *Media Performance: Mass Communication and the Public Interest*, London, Sage.

McQuail, D. (1994), *Mass Communication Theory*, London, Sage.

Madge, T. (1989), *Beyond the BBC*, London, Macmillan.

Malcolm, J. (1991), *The Journalist and the Murderer*, London, Bloomsbury.

Mannheim, K. (1936), *Ideology and Utopia*, London, Routledge and Kegan Paul.

Marquand, D. (1991) 'Nations, Regions and Europe', in B. Crick (ed.), *National Identities*, Oxford, Blackwell.

Marr, A. (1995), *Ruling Britannia*, London, Michael Joseph.

Marsh, D. and R. W. W. Rhodes (1992) (eds), *Policy Networks in British Government*, London, Clarendon Press.

Masterman, L. and P. Kiddey (1983), *Understanding Breakfast TV*, Milton Keynes, Media Press.

Mather, G. (1993), *Regulation of the BBC*, London, BFI.

Media Guides (1995–9), London, Fourth Estate.

Melody, W. H. (1990), 'Communication Policy in the Global Information Economy: Whither the Public Interest?', in M. Ferguson (ed.), *Public Communication: The New Imperatives*, London, Sage.

Merrill, J. C., J. Lee and E. J. Friedlander (1994), *Modern Mass Media*, London, HarperCollins.

Michael, J. (1990), 'Regulating Communications Media: From the Discretion of Sound Chaps to the Arguments of Lawyers', in M. Ferguson (ed.), *Public Communication: The New Imperatives*, London, Sage.

Miller, N. and R. Allen (1994) (eds), *Broadcasting Enters the Marketplace*, London, John Libbey.

Miller, N. and C. Norris (1989) (eds), *Life After the Broadcasting Bill*, Manchester, Manchester Monographs.

Miller, W. (1991), *Media and Voters*, London, Clarendon Press.

Milliband, R. and J. Saville (1973) (eds), *Socialist Register*, London, Merlin.

Mills, K. (1990), *A Place in the News*, New York, Columbia University Press.

Molina, G. (1987), 'Mexican Television News: The Imperatives of Corporate Rationale', *Media Culture and Society*, 9, 2.

Molotch, H. and M. Lester (1974), 'News as Purposive Behaviour: On the Strategic Use of Ritual Events, Accidents and Scandals', *American Sociological Review*, 39, 101–12.

Moorman, O. (1994), 'Killed by Semantics: Or Was it a Keystone Kop Kaleidoscope Kaper?', in J. R. Lewis (ed.), *From the Ashes: Making Sense of Waco*, Lanham MD, Rowman and Littlefield.

Morley, D. (1980), *The "Nationwide" Audience*, London, BFI.

Morley, D. (1988), *Family Television: Cultural Power and Domestic Leisure*, London, Routledge.

Morley, D. (1992), *TV, Audiences and Cultural Studies*, London, Routledge.

Morley, D. and Robins, K. (1995) *Spaces of Identity*, London, Routledge.

Mouffe, C. (1992) (ed.), *Dimensions of Radical Democracy: Pluralism, Citizenship, Community*, London, Verso.

Mowlana, H. (1997), *Global Information and World Communication*, London, Sage.

Mukerji, C. and M. Schudson (1991), *Rethinking Popular Culture*, Berkeley CA, University California Press.

Mulgan, G. (1990), *The Question of Quality: The Broadcasting Debate 6*, London, BFI.

Mulgan, G. and R. Paterson (1993) (eds), *Reinventing the Organisation*, BBC Charter Review Series, London, BFI.

Mumby, D. and C. Spitzack (1985), 'Ideology and Television News: A Metaphorical Analysis of Political Stories', *Central States Speech Journal*, 34:3, 162–71.

Murdock, G. (1973), 'Political Deviance: The Press Presentation of a Militant Mass Demonstration', in S. Cohen and J. Young (eds), *The Manufacture of News*, London, Constable.

Murdock, G. (1980), 'Class, Power and the Press: Problems of Conceptualisation and Evidence', *Sociological Review Monograph*, 29, 37–70.

Murdock, G. (1982), 'Large Corporations and the Control of the Communications Industries', in M. Gurevitch, T. Bennett, J. Curran and J. Woollacott (eds), *Culture, Society and the Media*, London, Methuen.

Murdock, G. and P. Golding (1973), 'For a Political Economy of Mass Communications', in R. Milliband and J. Saville (eds), *Socialist Register*, London, Merlin.

Murdock, G. and P. Golding (1977), 'Capitalism, Communication and Class Relations', in J. Curran, M. Gurevitch, and J. Woollacott (eds), *Mass Communication and Society*, London, Arnold.

Murroni, C., R. Collins and A. Coote (1996), *Converging Communications: Policies for the 21st Century*, London, Institute for Public Policy Research.

Neale, S. (1980), *Ex Genre*, London, BFI.

Negrine, R. (1989), *Politics and the Mass Media in Britain*, London, Routledge.

Negrine, R. (1996), *The Communication of Politics*, London, Sage.

Neuman, W. R. (1991), *The Future of the Mass Audience*, Cambridge, Cambridge University Press.

Newcombe, H. (1974), *TV: The Most Popular Art*, New York, Anchor.

Nimmo, D. D. and K. R. Sanders (1981) (eds), *Handbook of Political Communication*, London, Thousand Oaks CA, New Delhi, Sage.

Nowell-Smith, G. and T. Wollen (1991) (eds), *After the Wall*, London, BFI.

O'Keefe, G. J. and L. E. Atwood (1981), 'Communication and Election Campaigns', in D. D. Nimmo and K. R. Sanders (eds), *Handbook of Political Communication*, London, Thousand Oaks CA, New Delhi, Sage.

O'Malley, T. (1994), *Closedown*, London, Pluto Press.

Oakeshott, M. (1975), *On Human Conduct*, Oxford, Oxford University Press.

Oskamp, S. (1988) (ed.), *Television as a Social Issue*, Thousand Oaks CA, Sage.

Ostgaard, E. (1965), 'Factors Influencing the Flow of News', *Journal of Peace Research*, 2, 39–63.

Palmer, S. (1994), 'Excavating Waco', in J. R. Lewis (ed.), *From the Ashes: Making Sense of Waco*, Lanham MD, Rowman and Littlefield.

Parenti, M. (1993), *Inventing Reality*, New York, St Martin's Press.

Parsigian, E. K. (1987), 'News Reporting: Method in the Midst of Chaos', *Journalism Quarterly*, 64, 721–30.

Patterson, T. E. (1994), *Out of Order*, New York, Vintage Books.

Patterson, T. E. and R. D. McClure (1976), *The Unseeing Eye: The Myth of Television Power in National Elections*, New York, Putnam.

Paxman, J. (1991), *Friends in High Places*, Harmondsworth, Penguin.

Peak, S. and P. Fisher (1996) (eds), *The Media Guide*, London, Fourth Estate.

Perkins, V. (1972), *Film as Film*, Harmondsworth, Penguin.

Peterson, S. (1979), 'Foreign Gatekeepers and Criteria of Newsworthiness', *Journalism Quarterly*, 56, 116–25.

Peterson, S. (1981), 'International News Selection by the Elite Press: A Case Study', *Public Opinion Quarterly*, 45, 143–63.

Philo, G. (1990), *Seeing and Believing: The Influence of Television*, London, Routledge.

Porter, V. (1993), 'The Consumer and Transfrontier Television', *Consumer Policy Review*, 3, 3.

Postman, N. (1989), *Amusing Ourselves to Death*, London, Methuen.

Pugh, D. S., D. J. Hickson and C. R. Hinings (1985), *Writers on Organisations*, Harmondsworth, Penguin.

Purvis, S. (1994), 'The Myth of Tabloid Television', *Media Guardian*, 13 June.

Ranson, S. (1992), *The Role of Local Government in Education*, London, Longman.

Read, D. (1992), *The Power of News: The History of Reuters*, Oxford, Oxford University Press.

Reeves, P. (1993), 'Koresh Denied Cult Children Safe Refuge', *Independent*, 21 April.

Reeves, P. and R. Cornwell (1993) 'Waco Siege Fall-Out Hits Washington', *Independent*, 21 April.

Report of the Broadcasting Committee (1926), Crawford Report, Cmnd 2599, London, HMSO.

Report of the Broadcasting Committee (1936), Ullswater Report, Cmnd 5091, London, HMSO.

Report of the Broadcasting Committee (1962), Pilkington Report, Cmnd 1753, London, HMSO.

Report of the Committee on the Financing of the BBC (1986), Peacock Report, Cmnd 9824, London, HMSO.

Report of the Committee on the Future of Broadcasting (1977), Annan Report, Cmnd 6753, London, HMSO.

Report of the Secretary of State for National Heritage (1992), *The Future of the BBC: A Consultation Document*, Green Paper, Cmnd 2098, London, HMSO.

Report of the Secretary of State for National Heritage (1994), *The Future of the BBC: Serving the Nation, Competing World-Wide*, Cmnd 2621, London, HMSO.

Reville, N. (1991), *Broadcasting: The New Law*, London, Dublin and Edinburgh, Butterworth.

Reynolds, G. (1997), 'It's Not Over Yet for BBC News', *Daily Telegraph*, 23 September.

Rheingold, D. (1994a), *The Internet and the Public Sphere: Virtual Community: Homestead on the Electronic Frontier*, New York, Harper Perennial.

Rheingold, D. (1994b), *The Virtual Community: Surfing the Internet*, London, Martin Secker and Warburg.

Robertson, G. and A. Nicol (1990), *Media Law*, London, Longman.

Robinson, G. J. (1970), 'Foreign News Selection is Non-Linear in Yugoslavia's Tanjug Agency', *Journalism Quarterly*, 47, 340–51.

Robinson, J. P. and M. R. Levy (1986) *The Main Source*, London, Sage.

Roche, M. (1987), 'Citizenship, Social Theory, and Social Change', *Theory and Society*, 16, 363–99.

Roche, M. (1992), *Rethinking Citzenship*, Cambridge, Polity Press.

Rock, P. (1973), 'News as Eternal Recurrence', in S.. Cohen and J. Young (eds), *The Manufacture of the News*, London, Constable.

Rosengren, K. E. (1970), 'International News: Intra and Extra Media Data', *Acta Sociologica*, 13, 96–103.

Rosengren, K. E. (1974), 'International News: Methods, Data and Theory', *Journal of Peace Research*, 11, 145–56.

Rosengren, K. E. (1977), 'Four Types of Tables', *Journal of Communication*, 27:1, 67–75.

Sande, O. (1971), 'The Perception of Foreign News', *Journal of Peace Research*, 8, 221–37.

Sasser, E. L. and J. T. Russell (1972), 'The Fallacy of News Judgement', *Journalism Quarterly*, 49, 280–4.

Scannell, P. (1986), 'The Stuff of Radio', in J. Corner (ed.), *Documentary and the Mass Media*, London, Arnold.

Scannell, P. (1989), 'Public Service Broadcasting and Modern Public Life', *Media, Culture and Society*, 11:2, 135–66.

Scannell, P. (1991) (ed.), *Broadcast Talk*, London, Sage.

Scannell, P. (1993), 'The Origins of BBC Regional Policy', in S. Harvey and K. Robins (eds), *The Regions, the Nations and the BBC*, London, BFI.

Scannell, P. and D. Cardiff (1991), *A Social History of British Broadcasting. Volume 1: 1922–1939*, Oxford, Blackwell.

Scannel, P., P. Schlesinger and C. Sparks (1992) (eds), *Culture and Power*, London, Sage.

Schiller, H. (1996), *Information Inequality*, London, Routledge.

Schiltz, T., L. Sigelman and R. Neal (1970), 'Perspective of Managing Editors on Coverage of Foreign Policy News', *Journalism Quarterly*, 47, 716–21.

Schlesinger, P. (1987), *Putting Reality Together*, London, Methuen.

Schlesinger, P. (1991), *Media, State and Nation*, London, Sage.

Schlesinger, P. (1995), 'Europeanisation and the Media: National Identity and the Public Sphere', working paper.

Schlesinger, P. and H. Tumber (1994), *Reporting Crime*, Oxford, Oxford University Press.

Schlesinger, P., G. Murdock and P. Elliott (1983), *Televising Terrorism: Political Violence in Popular Culture*, London, Constable.

Schleuder, J., M. McCombs and W. Wanta (1991), 'Inside the Agenda-Setting Process: How Political Advertising and TV News Prime Viewers to Think about Issues and Candidates', in F. Biocca (ed.), *Television and Political Advertising*, Hillsdale NJ, Lawrence Erlbaum.

Schudson, M. (1978), *Discovering the News: A Social History of American Newspapers*, New York, Basic Books.

Schudson, M. (1991), 'The Sociology of News Production Revisited', in J. Curran and M. Gurevitch (eds), *Mass Media and Society*, London, Arnold.

Scramm, W. (1949), 'The Nature of News', *Journalism Quarterly*, 26, 259–69.

Semetko, H. A., J. G. Blumler, M. Gurevitch and D. H. Weaver (1991), *The Formation of Campaign Agendas*, Hillsdale NJ, Lawrence Erlbaum.

Seymour-Ure, C. (1968), *The Press, Politics and the Public*, London, Methuen.

Seymour-Ure, C. (1974), *The Political Impact of Mass Media*, London, Constable.

Seymour-Ure, C. (1991), *The British Press and Broadcasting since 1945*, Oxford, Blackwell.

Shaw, C. (1993) (ed.), *Rethinking Governance and Accountability*, BBC Charter Review Series, London, BFI.

Shoemaker, P. J. (1984), 'Political Group Viability as Predictor of Media Attitudes', *Journalism Quarterly*, 61, 889–92.

Shoemaker, P. J. (1991), *Gatekeeping*, London, Sage.

Shoemaker, P. J. and E. K. Mayfield (1987), 'Building a Theory of News Content: A Synthesis of Current Approaches', *Journalism Monographs*, 103.

Shoemaker, P. J. and S. D. Reese (1996), *Mediating the Message*, New York, Longman.

Sigal, L. V. (1973), *Reporters and Officials: The Organisation and Politics of Newsmaking*, Lexington, D. C. Heath.

Silverstone, R. (1985), *Framing Science: The Making of a BBC Documentary*, London, BFI.

Silverstone, R. (1994), *Television and Everyday Life*, London, Routledge.

Simpson, J. (1994), *Furthering International Understanding*, London, English Speaking Union Lecture, Foreign and Commonwealth Office.

Skovmand, M. and K. C. Schroder (1992) (eds), *Media Cultures*, London, Routledge.

Smith, A. D. (1986) *The Ethnic Origins of Nations*, Oxford, Blackwell.

Smith, A. D. (1991), *The Age of the Behemoths: The Globalisation of Mass Media Firms*, London, Twentieth Century Fund.

Smith, R. F. (1971), 'US News and Sino-Indian Relations: An Extra Media Study', *Journalism Quarterly*, 48, 447–58.

Smith R. F. (1979), 'On the Structure of Foreign News: A Comparison of the New York Times and the Indian White Papers', *Journal of Peace Research*, 6, 23–6.

Smith, R. R. (1979), 'Mythic Elements in Television News', *Journal of Communication*, 29, 75–82.

Snider, P. B. (1967), 'Mr Gates Revisited: A 1966 Version of the 1949 Case Study', *Journalism Quarterly*, 44, 419–27.

Soloski, J. (1989), 'News Reporting and Professionalism: Some Constraints on the Reporting of the News', *Media, Culture and Society*, 11, 207–28.

Soothill, K. and S. Walby (1991), *Sex Crime in the News*, London, Routledge.

Sorlin, P. (1994), *Mass Media*, London, Routledge.

Sparks, C. (1991), 'Goodbye Hildy Johnson: The Vanishing Serious Press', in P. Dahlgren and C. Sparks (eds), *Communication and Citizenship*, London, Routledge.

Sparkes, V. M. and J. P. Winter (1980), 'Public Interest in Foreign News', *Gazette*, 20, 149–70.

Staab, J. F. (1990), 'The Role of News Factors in News Selection: A Theoretical Reconsideration', *European Journal of Communication*, 5:4, 423–43.

Stempel, G. H. (1989), 'Topic and Story Choice of Five Network Newscasts', *Journalism Quarterly*, 65, 750–2.

Stevenson, N. (1995), *Understanding Media Cultures*, London, Sage.

Stevenson, W. (1993) (ed.), *All Our Futures: The Changing Role and Purpose of the BBC*, BBC Charter Review Series, London, BFI.

Stevenson, W. (1994) (ed.), *Responses to the Green Paper*, BBC Charter Review Series, London, BFI.

Strauss, A., L. Schatzman, R. Bucker, D. Ehrlich and M. Sabshin (1981), *Psychiatric Ideologies and Institutions*, New Brunswick NJ, Transaction.

Tabor, J. D. (1994), 'The Waco Tragedy: An Autobiographical Account of One Attempt to Avert Disaster', in J. R. Lewis (ed.), *From the Ashes: Making Sense of Waco*, Lanham MD, Rowman and Littlefield.

Tabor, J. D. and E. V. Gallagher (1995), *Why Waco: Cults and the Battle for Religious Freedom in America*, Berkeley CA, University of California Press.

Tannenbaum, P. H. and M. D. Lynch (1962), 'Sensationalism: Some Objective Message Correlates', *Journalism Quarterly*, 39, 317–23.

Thompson, J. B. (1990), *Ideology and Modern Culture*, Cambridge, Polity Press.

Thompson, J. B. (1994), 'Social Theory and the Media', in D. Crowley and D. Mitchell (eds), *Communication Theory Today*, Cambridge, Polity Press.

Thompson, K. and J. Tunstall (1971) (eds), *Sociological Perspectives*, Harmondsworth, Penguin.

Tipton, L., R. D. Haney and J. R. Basehart (1975), 'Media Agenda-Setting in City and State Election Campaigns', *Journalism Quarterly*, 52, 15–23.

Toffler, A. (1970), *Future Shock*, New York, Pan-Collins.

Toffler, A. (1980), *The Third Wave*, New York, Pan-Collins.

Tracey, M. (1977), *The Production of Political Television*, London, Routledge and Kegan Paul.

Tuchman, G. (1978), *Making News*, New York, Free Press.

Tunstall, J. (1970), *Media Sociology*, London, Constable.

Tunstall, J. (1971), *Journalists at Work*, London, Constable.

Tunstall, J. (1977), *The Media are American*, London, Constable.

Tunstall, J. (1980), 'The British Press in the Age of Television', *Sociological Review Monograph*, 29, 9–36.

Tunstall, J. (1983), *The Media in Britain*, London, Constable.

Tunstall, J. (1993), *Television Producers*, London, Routledge.

Tunstall, J. and M. Palmer (1991), *Media Moguls*, London, Routledge.

Turner, G. (1990), *British Cultural Studies: An Introduction*, London, Unwin Hyman.

Tusa, J. (1994), 'Programme or Products: The Management Ethos and Creative Values', James Cameron Memorial Lecture, 14 June, City University.

Victor, P. (1994), '*News at Ten* Takes a Turn Towards the Tabloids', *Independent on Sunday*, 22 May.

Wallis, R. and S. Baran (1990), *The Known World of Broadcast News*, London, Routledge.

Walzer, M. (1992), 'The Civil Society Argument', in C. Mouffe (ed.), *Dimensions of Radical Democracy: Pluralism, Citizenship, Community*, London, Verso.

Waters, M. (1995), *Globalization*, London, Routledge.

Waugh, E. (1938), *Scoop*, Harmondsworth, Penguin.

Weaver, P. H. (1994), *News and the Culture of Lying: How Journalism Really Works*, New York, Free Press.

Webster, F. (1995), *Theories of the Information Society*, London, Routledge.

Weir, S. and W. Hall (1994) (eds), *Ego-Trip: The Democratic Audit of the UK*, Colchester, Human Rights Centre, University of Essex.

Wenham, B. (1997) 'The lessons *Tonight* can Still Teach Today', *Evening Standard*, 19 February.

White, D. M. (1950), 'The Gatekeeper: A Case Study in the Selection of News', *Journalism Quarterly*, 27, 383–90.

Whittaker, B. (1981), *News Limited*, London, Minority Press Group.

Williams, G. (1996), *Britain's Media: How They Are Related, Media Ownership and Democracy*, London, Campaign for Press and Broadcasting Freedom.

Williams, R. (1962), *Communications*, Harmondsworth, Penguin.

Williams, R. (1974), *Television: Technology and Cultural Form*, London, Fontana/Collins.

Williams, R. (1985), *Towards 2000*, London, Penguin.

Williamson, J. (1991), *Decoding Advertisements: Ideology and Meaning in Advertising*, London, Marion Boyars.

Willis, J. (1990), *Journalism: State of the Art*, New York, Praeger.

Wimmer, R. D. and J. R. Dominick (1991), *Mass Media Research: An Introduction*, Belmont CA, Wadsworth.

Woods, P. (1986), *Inside Schools: Ethnography in Educational Research*, London, Routledge.

Woollacott, J. (1982), 'Messages and Meanings', in M. Gurevitch, T. Bennett, J. Curran and J. Woollacott (eds), *Culture, Society and the Media*, London, Methuen.

Yelland, D. (1993), 'Hell Fire', *Sun*, 20 April.

Zhao, X. and S. H. Chaffee (1991), 'Campaign Advertisements Versus Television News as Sources of Political Issue Information', *Public Opinion Quarterly*, 59:1, 41–65.

Index

251